St. Louis Community College

Library

5801 Wilson Avenue
St. Louis, Missouri 63110

FIGURES IN BLACK

FIGURES IN BLACK

Words, Signs, and the "Racial" Self

Henry Louis Gates, Jr.

New York   Oxford
OXFORD UNIVERSITY PRESS
1987

Oxford University Press

Oxford   New York   Toronto
Delhi   Bombay   Calcutta   Madras   Karachi
Petaling Jaya   Singapore   Hong Kong   Tokyo
Nairobi   Dar es Salaam   Cape Town
Melbourne   Auckland

and associated companies in

Beirut   Berlin   Ibadan   Nicosia

Published by Oxford University Press, Inc.,
200 Madison Avenue, New York, New York 10016

Library of Congress Cataloging-in-Publication Data

Gates, Henry Louis.
Figures in Black.

Includes index.
Contents: Theory and the Black tradition—Phillis
Wheatley and the African muse—Rhetorical strategies
in Frederick Douglass's Narrative—[etc.]
1. American literature—Afro-American authors—
History and criticism.   2. Afro-Americans in literature.
3. Slavery and slaves in literature.   4. Race in
literature.   I. Title.
PS153.N5G27   1987   810′.9′896073   86–21782
ISBN 0–19–503564–X

2 4 6 8 9 7 5 3 1

Printed in the United States of America
on acid-free paper

'Tis said that words and signs have power
O'er sprites in planetary hour;
But scarce I praise their venturous part,
Who tamper with such dangerous art.
Sir Walter Scott, *Lay of the Last Minstrel*

White people leave money to their children, but Black people teach theirs signs, which is far better.
Julia Peterkin, *Black April*

Anywhere they go, my people know the signs.
Henry Allen

For
Houston A. Baker, Jr.,
Kimberly W. Benston,
and Robert G. O'Mealley—
friends indeed

Acknowledgments

During the ten years when the contents of this book were taking shape, several friends and colleagues gave me the benefit of their support—and the benefit of the doubt. *Figures in Black* would never have been written without the encouragement of many people who seemed to believe in my work long before I was confident enough to do so. I would like to thank the following people for their kindness and generosity: Anthony Appiah, Kimberly W. Benston, John W. Blassingame Sr., Malcolm Brachman, Kit Luce, Dexter Fisher, William Forbath, Bruce Hawley, Leon Forrest, Dominic Gambardella, Ishmael Reed, Paul Johnson, Mel Watkins and Harvey Shapiro, Robert O'Meally, Robert Silvers, Erroll McDonald, Allida Davison, Wole Soyinka, Carl Brandt, David Brion Davis, Susan Rabiner, Sheldon Meyer, Curtis Church, John Wright, Robert Farris Thompson, Paul Edward Gates, Jonathan and Marianne Fineberg, John and Delgra Childs, Sander Gilman, Richard Popkin, John Holloway, James Olney, Fredric Jameson and Susan Willis, Robert and Michele Stepto, Nancy Stepan, Barbara Johnson, W. J. T. Mitchell, James A. Snead, J. Hillis Miller, Geoffrey H. Hartman, Kitty Mrosovsky, Frank Poueymirou, and Duke Anthony Whitmore. I would like to thank Sharon Adams for her patience and sustenance, and Maggie and Liza Gates for their good will. But it was the late Charles T. Davis who taught me to work to my capacities, to love the literature that I was interpreting, and to hold it in the same regard as any Western critic holds Western literature. It was Mr. Davis, I learned so poignantly upon his death, for whom I wrote as my "ideal Reader." I continue to do so.

Some of the chapters in this book were presented as lectures at various universities and professional gatherings. While the pressures to "perform" on these occasions may at times seem burdensome, the opportunity to share my "ideas in progress" in the presence of my colleagues has been crucial to my development both as a scholar and as a member of the profession of literary critics. I am delighted to acknowledge my debt to Robert Stepto and Dexter Fisher, Robert Hemenway, Jerry W. Ward (each of whom invited me to speak at annual MLA conventions), Richard Popkin and the Clark Memorial Library at UCLA, Thomas Whitaker and the Yale Faculty English Colloquia, Claudia Mitchell-Kernan and Richard Yarborough at the Afro-American Studies program at UCLA, Valerie Smith and Lee Mitchell at Princeton, Paul Lauter and Mary Helen Washington and their 1982 conference on Reconstructing American Literature, and Peter Brooks and the Fellows of the Yale Whitney Humanities Center.

Earlier versions of some of the essays I have expanded into the chapters of this book were published by the following organizations and journals, to which I express my appreciation: *Black American Literature Forum, Critical Inquiry,* the Modern Language Association, *Harvard Educational Review, Times Literary Supplement, New York Times Book Review, The Yale Review,* and the *A.D.E. Bulletin.* The essays have all been revised to some degree for this book.

Completion of the manuscript was made possible by a generous Prize Fellowship from the MacArthur Foundation, a Rockefeller Fellowship, and grants from the National Endowment for the Humanities and the Menil Foundation.

Gwendolyn Williams and Candace Ruck typed the manuscript through its several drafts with great patience and speed.

My debt to each of these individuals and institutions is of an enormity difficult to acknowledge or to repay.

Several of the essays collected in this book appeared in print in different forms, under the following titles and in the following places: "Preface to Blackness: Text and Pretext," "Dis and Dat: Dialect and the Descent," and "Binary Oppositions in Chapter

One of *The Narrative of the Life of Frederick Douglass,"* in *Afro-American Literature: The Reconstruction of Instruction,* Dexter Fisher and Robert B. Stepto, eds. (New York: Modern Language Association, 1979); "Introduction," *Our Nig,* by Harriet E. Wilson (New York: Random House, 1983); "Criticism in the Jungle," in *Black Literature and Literary Theory* (New York: Methuen, 1984); "Songs of a Racial Self," *New York Times Book Review,* January 11, 1981; "Frederick Douglass and the Language of the Self," *The Yale Review* (Summer 1981); "On the Blackness of Blackness: A Critique of the Sign and the Signifying Monkey," *Critical Inquiry* (June 1983); "Phillis Wheatley and the African Muse," in *Critical Essays on Phillis Wheatley,* ed. William H. Robinson (Boston: G. K. Hall, 1982). The author is grateful for permission to reprint all or parts of these essays.

Contents

Introduction

Samuel Johnson wrote that much that appears foolish in human behavior can be traced to one cause: the failure to imitate those we least resemble. During the past decade, I have tried to draw upon the extraordinarily rich and diverse body of contemporary literary theory to analyze the writings of African and Afro-American authors published in English between the eighteenth century and the present. I have not done this to proclaim my devotion to one theory of criticism as opposed to another, as if I were a convert to some new religion. Nor have I undertaken this task in apish imitation of the theorists of literary criticism whose efforts in this century have emerged as seminal influences upon all of us who seek to confront the possibilities—and pitfalls—of either theorizing about our endeavor as an institution or drawing upon highly refined tools of close reading which, if utilized subtly enough, help readers to understand even more fully how remarkably complex an act of literary language can be. To imitate these theories of criticism drawn from the Western literary tradition, or to attempt to apply them as if they were universal procedures similar, say, to surgical techniques, would be both naive and self-subversive, because theories of criticism arise from a remarkably small group of specific texts. These groups of texts have tended to elicit from critics generalized rules or modes of practical analysis, as well as larger theories of the nature and function of both literature and its criticism. To attempt to lift

literary theory from its concrete textual grounds and then to apply
it to another body of texts is an enterprise not without grave risks
for the critic.

This realization came only by degrees. I began a project with
Afro-American literature and contemporary literary theory in
graduate school exactly ten years ago. In tutorials on the theory
of criticism at the University of Cambridge, John Holloway decided to allow me to experiment by letting contemporary theories (Russian Formalism, French Structuralism, Anglo-American
Practical Criticism, among others) inform my close readings of
black texts. I realize now that so very much of my subsequent
work was shaped by those experimental exercises with Professor
Holloway. Although he did not say so at the time, I believe he
encouraged my experiments so that I could achieve a certain
critical distance or stance as a reader of a literature I was too
close to experientially to be able to see its rhetorical strategies.
Especially in my painful beginning supervisions, I could only
approach black literature by analyzing its content, by analyzing
what I thought it was saying to me about the nature of my experiences as a black person living in a historically racist Western
culture. I encountered no similar difficulties when explicating
canonical Western texts. The difference, I see clearly now, was
a difference of significance. Explicating white texts was a delight-
ful if arduous academic exercise, which I soon began to approach
as intellectual play. Analyzing black texts, on the contrary, was
both extraordinarily personal and political for me as a black
person reading literature in one of the most esteemed and traditional departments of English in the Western academy. Not only
was I the only black graduate student in English at Cambridge,
but I was also the first—or at least the first in anyone's recollection. While this may not seem so important in retrospect, at the
time it seemed all-important to me, fed as I had allowed myself
to be on fantasies of meeting a certain challenge for "the race"
in literature just as W. E. B. Du Bois had done in sociology at
Heidelburg, or as Alain Locke had done in philosophy at Oxford. It is somewhat embarrassing to admit this today, but I felt
as if I were embarked upon a mission for all black people, especially for that group of scholars whom our people have traditionally called "race men" or "race women," the intellectuals who

collect, preserve, and analyze the most sublime artifacts of the black imagination. To compound the difficulties of my project, I elected to abandon my undergraduate training in History and began anew at Cambridge in literary studies. I had not even known before that a text *could* be analyzed formally, and I most certainly did not know how to go about doing it. The problem of distance that I was experiencing in analyzing black texts only made an already difficult task more difficult.

Time and diligence helped to assuage one problem, but contemporary literary theory enabled me to assuage the more serious problem of reading black literature. No doubt in part because of an enforced marginality that I, as a black person, felt acutely at Cambridge, it never occurred to me that I *could* be part of one school of criticism or another. My interests in black literature seemed to have no welcome place in these schools, be they formal or structural, thematic or historical. Instead, literary theory functioned in my education as a prism, which I could *turn* to refract different spectral patterns of language use in a text, as one does with daylight. Turn the prism this way, and one pattern of color emerges; turn it that way, and another pattern configures. Early on, it was the play of the spectra of language in a text that motivated me to study the history of criticism.

In this way, I learned fairly systematically about the history and theory of criticism and somewhat haphazardly about the range of related rhetorical strategies that comprise the Afro-American literary tradition. Oddly enough, however, and perhaps fortunately for a young and tentative graduate student eager to excel, I never felt less than marginal vis-à-vis the theories that I studied, and it was this sense of marginality that saved me from what I think of as the embarrassment of conversion (full baptismal immersion, new language and all), an ironic devotee of one school of criticism over all others. No, critical theory was not a way of life, it seemed to me; rather, it was a device that enabled me to communicate with my professors in a more or less common language, even if I was attempting to speak in a critical dialect of Afro-American literature. Just as any student of the history of criticism soon sees the folly of embracing one theory as divine revelation, so too has my sense of "textual marginality" kept me from becoming an advocate for any particular theory of criticism.

The ironic—and sometimes even problematic—relationship be-tween the academic study of so-called canonical and noncanonical literatures, it seems to me, serves to create a healthy distance between the critic who writes about black literature, for example, and his colleagues who write about the Western tradition. For the black critic, the languages of contemporary criticism are imagina-tive constructs or white fictions to be analyzed and explicated just as any other literary text. Never does the relation of margin-ality that the black tradition bears to the Western tradition allow the critic to see beyond the textual nature even of the most seem-ingly transparent literary theory. Never can the black critic em-brace these theories like one can embrace a religious belief or a thing.

Figures in Black is a book of hypothesis and experimentation. Most of the chapters consist of a close reading of a black text through the prism of one of the many contemporary critical meth-ods of analyzing literature. I practice a sort of critical bricolage. While one result of this book's organization is to demonstrate the relationship of literary theory to Afro-American literature, another result is to address, in different ways, a question of fun-damental importance to those of us whose professional activity is devoted to explicating noncanonical literatures. Let me put the question in the baldest manner: How "white" is literary theory? How "black" can a criticism be which is related to one of the several modes of analysis commonly grouped under a rubric of structural or post-structural criticism? Just as critics of Afro-American literature have often categorized the pre-1900 imitative poetry of black authors as that of the Mockingbird School, can we as critics escape a mockingbird relation to theory, one des-tined to be derivative, often to the point of parody? Or, to shift the ground of the question somewhat, can we escape the supposed racism of so many theorists of criticism, from David Hume and Immanuel Kant through the Southern Agrarians? Can it be a legitimate exercise to translate theories drawn from a literary tradition that has often been perpetuated by white males who represent blacks in their fictions as barely human, if they deem it necessary to figure blacks at all? Aren't we justified in being suspicious of a discourse in which blacks are signs of absence? Shouldn't we resist the lure even of that tradition's critical discourse and define our critical endeavor against it? Let us consider these questions, made more than valid by the history of the slave and the ex-slave in Western culture.

There are complex historical reasons for the resistance to theory among critics of black literature, reasons that stem in part from healthy reactions against the marriage of logocentrism and ethnocentrism in much of Western aesthetic discourse. Although there have been a few notable exceptions, theory as a subject of inquiry on its own has only recently begun to sneak its way into the discourse of Afro-American literature. The implicit racism of some of the Southern Agrarians who became the "New Critics" did not serve to speed this process much. Sterling Brown has summed up the relation of the black tradition to the Western critical tradition. In response to Robert Penn Warren's line from "Pondy Woods":

"Nigger, your breed ain't metaphysical."

Brown replies:

"Cracker, your breed ain't exegetical."*

No tradition is "naturally" metaphysical or exegetical, of course. Only recently have some scholars attempted to convince critics of black literature that the racism of the Western critical tradition was not a sufficient reason for us to fail to theorize about our own endeavor or even to make use of contemporary theoretical innovations when this seemed either useful or appropriate. Perhaps predictably, a number of these attempts share a concern with that which, in the received tradition of Afro-American criticism, has been most repressed: close readings of the text itself. This return of the repressed—the very language of the black text— has generated a renewed interest among our critics in theory. My charged advocacy of the relevance of contemporary theory to reading Afro-American and African literature closely has been designed as the prelude to the definition of principles of literary criticism peculiar to the black literary traditions themselves, related to and compatible with contemporary critical theory generally, yet "indelibly black," as Robert Farris Thompson puts it. All theory is text-specific, and ours must be as well. Lest I be

* I discuss Brown's parody at some length in Chapter 3 of *The Signifying Monkey.*

misunderstood, I have tried to work through contemporary theories of literature not to apply them to black texts, but to transform these by translating them into a new rhetorical realm. These attempts have been more or less successful; nevertheless, I have tried to make them at all times interesting episodes in one critic's reflection on the black tradition, which I mean when I write "the tradition" and from which I extract a canon of texts to which I return again and again to read in different ways.

It is only through this critical activity that the profession, in a world of dramatically fluid relations of knowledge and power, at a time of the reemerging presence in the academy of the tongues of Babel, can redefine itself away from a Eurocentric notion of a hierarchical canon of texts—mostly white, Western, and male—and encourage and sustain a truly comparative and pluralistic notion of the institution of literature. What all students of literature share in common is the practice of interpretation, even where we do not share in common the same texts. The hegemony implicit in the phrase "the Western tradition" reflects material relationships primarily and not so-called universal, transcendent normative values. Value is specific, both culturally and temporally. The sometimes vulgar nationalism implicit in would-be literary categories such as (white) "American Literature" or the not-so-latent imperialism implied by the vulgar phrase "Commonwealth Literature" are extraliterary designations of control, symbolic of material and concomitant political relations, rather than literary ones. We, the scholars of our profession, must eschew these categories of domination and ideology and insist upon the fundamental redefinition of what it is to speak of "the canon."

Whether we realize it or not, each of us brings to a text an implicit theory of literature, or even an unwitting hybrid of theories, a gumbo as it were. To become aware of contemporary theory is ideally to become aware of one's own presuppositions, those ideological and aesthetic assumptions that we bring to a text unwittingly. It is incumbent upon those of us who respect the integrity of the black tradition to turn to this very tradition to define self-generated theories about the black literary endeavor. But we must, above all, respect the integrity, the tradition, of the black work of art by bringing to bear upon the explication of its meanings all of the attention to language that we may learn from several developments in contemporary theory. By the very process of application, we re-create, through revision, the critical theory at hand. As our familiarity with the black tradition and with literary theory expands, we shall invent our own theories, as some have begun to do—black, text-specific theories.

I have tried to utilize contemporary theory to defamiliarize the texts of the black tradition, to create a distance between this black reader and our black texts, so that I may more readily see the formal workings of those texts. Wilhelm von Humboldt describes this phenomenon in the following way:

> Man lives with things mainly, even, exclusively—since sentiment and action in him depend upon his mental representations—as they are conveyed to him by language. Through the same act by which he spins language out of himself he weaves himself into it, and every language draws a circle around the people to which it belongs, a circle that can only be transcended insofar as one at the same time enters another one.

I have turned to literary theory as a second circle. I have done this to preserve the integrity of black texts, by trying to avoid confusing my experiences as an Afro-American with the black act of language that defines a text. On the other hand, by learning to read a black text within a black formal cultural matrix and explicating it with the principles of criticism at work in both the Euro-American and the African-American traditions, I believe that we critics can identify and produce richer structures of meaning than are possible otherwise.

This is the challenge of the critic of Afro-American literature: not to shy away from literary theory, but rather to translate it into the black idiom, renaming principles of criticism where appropriate, but especially naming indigenous black principles of criticism and applying these to explicate our own texts. It is incumbent upon us to protect the integrity of our tradition by bringing to bear upon its criticism any tool of sensitivity to language that is appropriate. And what do I mean by appropriate? Simply this: *any* tool that enables the critic to explain the complex workings of the language of a text is an appropriate tool. For it is language, the black language of black texts, that expresses the distinctive quality of our literary tradition. A literary tradition, it seems apparent, is to a large extent defined by its past, its received structures. We have the special privilege of explicating the black tradition in ever closer detail. We shall not meet this challenge by remaining afraid of, or naive about, literary theory; we will only inflict upon our literary tradition the violation of the uninformed reading. We are the keepers of the black literary tradition. No matter what theories we seem to embrace, we have more in common with each other than we do with any other critic of any other literature. We write for each other and for our own contemporary writers. This relation is one of trust, if I may. How can any aid to close reading of the texts of the black tradition be inimical to our modes of criticism?

Aware that every theory arises from a specific body of texts and that a method of reading is text-specific, I have attempted over the past decade to analyze black literature using my own variants of "formalism," "structuralism," and "post-structuralism," catch-all words broad enough to encompass most theoretical developments in literary criticism since, on one hand, I. A. Richards published *Practical Criticism* in 1925 and, on the other, the Russian Formalist movement, roughly between 1914 and 1930.

I found it advantageous to embark upon this admittedly curious method of explicating the Afro-American literary tradition because black criticism, since the early nineteenth century, seems in retrospect to have thought of itself as essentially just one more front of the race's war against racism. Texts, it seems to me, were generally analyzed almost exclusively in terms of their content, as if a literary form were a vacant enclosure that would be filled with this or that matter. This matter, moreover, was "the Black Experience," and an author tended to be judged on his or her fidelity to "the Black Experience." This, it seemed to me, was a dead end for black literary studies.

Gradually, I began to see that both modes of mimesis, of the literary representation of reality, as well as modes of reading, or interpretation, were complex responses to concrete social situations and to received modes of discourse. Ways of seeing and of representing, for writer and critic alike, were conventions complexly related to material and textual factors. I have come to this realization only slowly but began to understand it while preparing an essay for a graduate school supervision on period formation in literary history. In the manner of completing assignments that I have outlined above, I decided to write about the Harlem Renaissance as much to see if Afro-American literature could be analyzed like English literature as for any other purpose. I had been struck, while an undergraduate History major at Yale, by an idea that I encountered first in a letter James Weldon Johnson sent to Carl Van Vechten in 1926. Encountering it again as a graduate student, entirely by accident, led to that sort of epiphany through which younger scholars sometimes begin to understand how to use criticism and theory rather than merely to mimic it. "I am coming to believe," Johnson had written to Van Vechten, "that nothing can go farther to destroy race prejudice than the recognition of the Negro as a creator [of] and contributor to American civilization." The arbitrariness of this purported relation between race prejudice and the creation of art as a sign of civilization struck me forcefully. That this arbitrary association did not apparently trouble either Johnson and his peers or Van Vechten and his seemed to be of such import to the history of the black tradition that I decided to attempt to trace this simultaneously aesthetic and political notion. I learned that this particular theory of the function of art not only was shared by most writers and critics of the New Negro Renaissance but also gave to that literary movement its peculiar and paradoxical stance of postulating on one hand a direct social and political relationship between art and life, between black political progress and the creation of formal literature, but on the other hand debunking the propaganda function of black art and advocating ideas of literary excellence derived often from late Victorian poetic standards. As for the origins of this relationship between racial progress and art, between discrete demonstrations of Western civilization and the obliteration of race prejudice, I learned only that this was a received idea.

Charting in some detail this received idea became the object of my doctoral thesis, which attempted to locate the origins of this use of black literature as evidence of the "humanity" of blacks in the Enlightenment of Europe, although it was prefigured in the seventeenth century. I have been fascinated with this idea and have referred to it in various ways in my critical essays. It remains difficult for me to believe that any human being would be demanded to write himself or herself into the human community. Much of my work in black criticism arises from my analysis of the racist uses to which the absence of black writing has been put since the eighteenth century. More relevant in the context of this book, however, I realized that the black tradition's own concern with winning the war against racism had led it not only to accept this arbitrary relationship but to embrace it, judging its own literature by a curious standard that derived from the social applications of the metaphors of the great chain of being, the idea of progress and the perfectibility of man, as well as the metaphor of capacity derived initially from eighteenth-century comparative studies of the anatomy of simian and human brains and then translated into a metaphor for intelligence and the artistic potential of a "race."

Simultaneously, I realized that, because of these arbitrary presuppositions, the belief that Afro-American literature existed primarily to "contain the Black Experience" meant that a myth of familiarity obtained when the black critic read a black text. I wanted to draw upon theories of interpretation that would enable me to defamiliarize the black text—in the words of the Russian Formalists, "to make the text strange." As Frederick Douglass figured the matter, I wanted to step outside the circle so that I could trace its contours:

> I did not, when a slave, understand the deep meaning of those rude and apparently incoherent songs. I was myself within the circle; so that I neither saw nor heard as those without might see and hear.

I felt it necessary to do this so that I could see the text as a structure of literature and not as a one-to-one reflection of (my) life. I have tried to use contemporary theory to explicate the modes of representation that, taken together, define the Afro-American literary tradition and to analyze the unspoken assumptions and presuppositions by which this literature has been judged since its most conscious beginnings in the eighteenth century.

If my experiences are in any way typical, the relationship between the development of Afro-American criticism and contemporary literary theory can be divided into four moments: the

Black Aesthetic, Repetition and Imitation, Repetition and Difference, and Synthesis. Let us consider each of these moments in order.

By Repetition and Imitation, I mean the often unreflective mimicry of theories borrowed from European and American literary critics. *Black Aesthetic* theorists were diametrically opposed to this position. As a number of commentators have noted, the "energy" of Afro-American scholarship seems to be especially present in black literary criticism published in the last decade or so. The impetus of the Black Arts movement of the sixties, the literary and aesthetic wing of the Black Power movement, served two functions to which the academic critics of the seventies and eighties are heir: the resurrection of "lost" black primary texts, certainly, and the concomitant need to define the principles of criticism upon which a "genuinely black" aesthetic could be posited. The work collected by Larry Neal and Amiri Baraka in their important anthology, *Black Fire* (1968), and the criticism collected by Addison Gayle, Jr., in *Black Expression* (1969) and *The Black Aesthetic* (1971) codified Black Aesthetic theory. The veritable quest for a Black Aesthetic, the signal contribution of the Black Arts movement, generated a remarkable amount of literary criticism and theory about Afro-American literature. Neither students nor professors of literature nor creative writers were immune to the strident calls for sophisticated definitions of a *black* aesthetic theory. Whether we defined our work with or against the Black Aesthetic proponents, who often identified themselves politically as Black Nationalists, this highly organized and infectious movement of letters affected virtually everyone writing about black literature between 1965 and the early seventies. Poets such as Don L. Lee and Sonia Sanchez, in addition to Neal and Baraka, publishing regularly in journals such as *The Journal of Black Poetry* and *Negro Digest* (later renamed *Black World* and then *First World,* edited by the late Hoyt Fuller), served to define both the issues to be debated and the very terms of these debates.

What were these issues and the terms in which they were debated? One repeated concern of the Black Aesthetic movement was the nature and function of black literature vis-à-vis the larger political struggle for Black Power. How useful was our literature

to be in this centuries-old political struggle, and exactly how was
our literature to be useful? A full explication of this debate is
demanded but would be out of place here. Suffice it to say that
two especially interesting positions seem to have emerged in
retrospect, which have shaped directly the directions that Afro-
American criticism has subsequently assumed. The first is that
black criticism, most properly, should valorize (and demonstrate
in what ways literature can contribute to) a larger political and
economic analysis of the position of the black person living in
the United States. Second, and just as important, the Black Aesthetic should repudiate the received terms of academic, or white,
literary critical methods and theories.

All sorts of colorful and impassioned corollaries stem from
these two premises, most notably that the history of black literature in this country splits along a great divide: those artists who
represent "the Black Experience" most realistically or mimeti-
cally, and those who represent it metaphorically or allegorically.
One way to figure this great divide symbolically is to imagine at
the paramount position of influence and emulation in the traditions of Richard Wright on one side and Ralph Ellison on the
other. Their black textual antecedents and heirs, then, fall on
either side of the divide, with a few canonical writers straddling
the precipice more or less precariously. Still another corollary is
that the experience represented by an author in a text is so unique
in Western culture that only black critics are able to make
normative judgments because only they can gauge how "true" or
"real to our lives" any particular text might be. Finally, a third
corollary is that the racism of the Western tradition makes most,
if not all, non-black theories of criticism and literature at least
suspect, if not invalid for the black critic to utilize.

I do not intend by this summary to argue that this was all
the Black Aesthetic was about, for that movement was large and
sprawling, even if it was so energetic and compelling. No one,
moreover, could argue against the notion that the Black Arts
movement virtually single-handedly created a broad community
of black readers, from the streets of Harlem to the hallowed halls
of Harvard, whose purchasing power led all sorts of traditional
commercial publishing houses and fly-by-night, short-lived publishers to reprint and market widely (often sensationally) the

past and present works of the Afro-American tradition. What's more, even conservative black academic critics and professors of literature (such as Charles T. Davis, George Kent, J. Saunders Redding, Darwin T. Turner, and many others) not only reacted to the Black Aesthetic movement in one way or another but also were called upon by major English and American Studies departments to integrate their academic faculty and curricula. Most of us writing today about black literature in the academy owe our undergraduate scholarships, our graduate fellowships, and even our positions and promotions at least indirectly to the Black Arts and Black Power movements.

The academic response to the popular Black Arts movement is directly relevant here. Older critics and scholars, as I have suggested earlier, reacted to the Black Aesthetic movement either positively or negatively. Nowhere is the complexity of these re-actions analyzed more clearly than in Charles T. Davis's collection of essays, *Black Is the Color of the Cosmos* (1982). Davis, whose training and work on E. A. Robinson and Walt Whitman did not suggest an affinity for the Black Arts Movement, told a crowded MLA audience in 1969 that, while he found Black Power an objectionable and problematical political position, he thought that the Black Arts movement, while essentially a black and romantic version of the American Marxist movement of the thirties, held every promise of generating a validly black theory of criticism which would arise from black texts themselves, after the limited choices demanded by its political urgencies and ex-cesses were again expanded. Shortly thereafter, he developed black literature courses in the English department curricula at the Pennsylvania State University, then at the University of Iowa, and finally at Yale. Davis, however, did not seem to be a pro-ponent of *one* theory of black literature and encouraged instead a pluralistic criticism that was informed by his previous academic training and yet attempted to explicate what I think of as the "black difference" in discrete black texts. Davis is merely one example of the academic response to the Black Arts movement.

Still another example is to be found in the works of academic critics who attempted to give to the Black Aesthetic the order demanded of traditional approaches to literature. The work of three critics seemed to emerge as the most important and interesting of a larger group. I am thinking here of Houston A. Baker Jr., Addison Gayle Jr., and Stephen Henderson. These three critics, I would argue, brought to bear upon the passionate chaos of the Black Aesthetic movement a remarkable degree of discipline, training, insight, and control, informed as their early work was (1969 to 1975) by a broad experience with literature as an institution. I have analyzed their work elsewhere and do so again below. Suffice it to state here, however, that it was the academic criticism of these three scholars of Afro-American literature that led in my own work to experimentation with theories "lifted" from various twentieth-century schools of criticism. If my analysis of the tautological dead end of their theories of black literature was accurate, then I felt that I could use non-black theories to detour, or step around, a position about black criticism that held no promise for my work.

Despite my critique of their positions, however, the work of Baker, Henderson, and Gayle determined the nature and shape of my critical response as surely (if not as profoundly) as Richard Wright's naturalism shaped Ralph Ellison's modernism. It seemed to me at the time that the most radical shift I could make as a critic of black literature would be to stress that which I have identified as the most repressed element of Afro-American criticism: the language of the text. Accordingly, I argued for a formalism that even then seemed somewhat excessive and too polemical to be a productive theory of criticism. Rather, I meant for it to be *corrective* and polemical, to raise as much heat as light.

Essays such as "Preface to Blackness: Text and Pretext," "Binary Oppositions in Frederick Douglass's *Narrative*," and "Dis and Dat: Dialect and the Descent" (all published in 1979) were polemics for formalism or structuralism as useful methods for explicating Afro-American literature. These essays most properly fall into the second category of criticism listed above, that of *Repetition and Imitation*. Virtually heady with what it seemed possible to say about the rhetorical strategies of black texts, I did not at first think that anything problematical might be entailed in the repetition and imitation of Western theories of criticism in a black milieu. On the contrary, the language of these essays, from here, rings with the tones of the reformer, meant to clear a space in which related work could be achieved.

Perhaps ironically, it was the seriousness with which this polemical critique was argued, criticized, or praised that led to the realization that even this was neither sufficient grounds upon which to theorize about Afro-American literature nor substantial enough to bear an integral relation to the texts I was analyzing. I discovered, with some surprise, that the echoing of other traditions' theories was as fraught with problems as was Black Aesthetic criticism. A third approach, some sort of critique, was called for.

This third approach was *Repetition and Difference.* By this I mean the use of contemporary criticism to read black texts, but a use designed to critique the theory implicitly. Essays such as "Frederick Douglass and the Language of the Self," "The Same Difference: Reading Jean Toomer," and "The Language of Slavery" fall into this category. In these essays, the ironies of the relation of post-structural criticism to Afro-American texts is as much the subject of concern as is the text analyzed. This phase, at least in my work, owed much to the dialogue I was privileged to have with critics of African and Afro-American literature, such as Houston Baker, Kimberly Benston, Michael Cooke, Charles Davis, Robert O'Meally, Wole Soyinka, Robert Stepto, Mary Helen Washington, and Jerry Ward, and with several contemporary theorists at Yale and elsewhere who, while supportive and encouraging, always were critical and demanding that I use my own tradition more fully and, frankly, more boldly. Harold Bloom, Fredric Jameson, Barbara Johnson, Geoffrey Hartman, J. Hillis Miller, and Thomas Whitaker, especially, proffered thorny responses to my work, responses that were both honest and supportive if not always flattering.

These criticisms, along with the important recent work of Appiah, Baker, Benston, Johnson, Snead, and Cornell West, led me to emphasize a sustained interest in the black vernacular tradition as a source field in which to ground a theory of Afro-American criticism, a theory at once self-contained and related by analogy to other contemporary theories. Accordingly, *Figures in Black* concludes with an essay on "The Signifying Monkey," which I hope will be taken as an example of the fourth of the phases I identified above, that of *Synthesis*. The methodological diversity and the critical bricolage of the essays collected here are not meant to argue for a program or a platform but rather to contribute to the study of both Afro-American literature and contemporary criticism the assembled examples of one critic's attempts to address a "two-toned" audience: those whose concern is black literature and those whose concern is the study of the institution of literature today.

Figures in Black chronicles my efforts to do this, as chapters in a tale. Some essays, upon rereading, strike me as more successful attempts to use theory than do others. It took many attempts for me to understand fully the text-specific nature of theory and the concomitant need to discover in the black discursive idiom the sources of a theory of interpretation. This, in the concepts of Signifyin(g) and Masking, I have tried to do. *Figures in Black,* then, is a record or an account of one critic's confrontation with the role of theory in the study of a noncanonical literature. Since what I have attempted to do with literary theory is modeled on what blues and jazz musicians do with received musical conventions, perhaps it is fitting to quote the great blues musician Skip James to state explicitly that level of influence and autonomy to which I aspire in my work:

> After I got that much from those [other guitar players], then I just used my own self: Skip. I don't pattern after anyone or either copycat. I may hear something, but if it's nice enough for me to get an idea about, I think I like a phrase or something, I may get it and put it in where it will be befitting in some of my pieces. But other than that, I don't. It's just Skip's music. . . . I don't sing other people's songs, I don't sing other people's voices. I can't.

Learning to sing one's own songs, to trust the particular cadences of one's own voice, is also the goal of any writer. If I have failed here, my failure does not stem from a lack of knowledge of the desired end to be reached.

Perhaps it will be useful if I try to place the relationship of *Figures in Black* to two other books, also being published by

Oxford University Press. The present volume is the first of three books that treat the nature and function of both Afro-American literature and its criticism. *Figures in Black* considers the several ways in which a discrete black text interacts with and against its critical context. I use the word *context* throughout this book to refer to the textual world that a black text echoes, mirrors, repeats, revises, or responds to in various formal ways. This process of intertextual relation I call Signifyin(g), the trope of revision, of repetition and difference, which I take from the Afro-American idiom.

Implicitly, the analysis of the relationship between a black text and its critical field constitutes a theory of the origins and nature of Afro-American literature. Indeed, what I once thought was merely an anomaly of the New Negro Renaissance's theory about its own endeavor has turned out to be a central repeated *topos* of the tradition itself. As I have argued, this *topos* consists of a dialectical relationship between (white) critical assertions that the person of African descent has not produced, or cannot produce, written art and that, because of this absence or lack, the black person has demonstrated, prima facie, evidence of his or her innate mental inequality with the European. This argument persists from its origins in the seventeenth century at least through the New Negro Renaissance of the 1920s and even surfaces in recent writings by blacks. Wilson Harris, for instance, writing in *History, Fable and Myth in the Caribbean and Guianas* (1970), echoes this idea when he writes:

> The apparent void of history which haunts the black man may never be compensated until an act of imagination opens gateways between civilizations, between technological and spiritual apprehension, between racial possessions and dispossessions in the way the *Aeneid* may stand symbolically as one of the first epics of migration and re-settlement beyond the pale of an ancient world.

In sustained literacy, in the literacy of sublime literature, Harris argues consistent with the tradition's *topos,* shall be found the black's retort to Hegel's strictures on the absence of the memory of written history among black "primitives."

The *topos* of freedom and literacy, which Robert Stepto has traced in *From Behind the Veil* in such marvelous detail in the

Afro-American narrative tradition from the nineteenth century to *Invisible Man* (1952), turns out to be the black tradition's second-generation revision of another trope, the trope of the "Talking Book," or the "voice in the text." Whereas the primal scene of instruction in the slave narratives is the mastery of "letters" (literally, the English alphabet) and its literal and metaphorical relation to a freedom of the body and of the mind, the eighteenth-century black primal *topos* is the refusal of a written text (often the Bible) to speak to its black interlocutor. This Ur-trope, as it were, recurs with key revisions in five of the tradition's earliest slave narratives published between 1770 and 1815. This curious trope, moreover, can be seen to be the black mythic response to demands made in European critical discourse that the black master "the arts and sciences" if he or she is to be truly "free." Anglo-African writing, it seems clear, derived its impulse to claim origins from within this critical discourse of the "Other," and black texts have been locked in a textual dialogue with this critical tradition of absence at least from 1573, when *"el negro,"* Juan Latino, published his first of three books of neo-Latin verse, down through the Harlem Renaissance in this century.

Figures in Black traces my readings of this signifying relationship between black text and white critical context in essays written over the past ten years. In this book, I attempt to outline the chronological shape of this text–context dialectic from Phillis Wheatley to Ishmael Reed. In the second book related to this study, I trace the nature and function of Signifyin(g), the Afro-American tradition's "trope of tropes," a figure for black intertextual revision as well as an intrablack rhetorical strategy. *The Signifying Monkey: A Theory of Afro-American Criticism* charts the tradition's self-contained terms for order, its internal and overriding principles of criticism. *Black Letters in the Enlightenment* consists of my detailed close readings of the first hundred years of the history and theory of European criticism of black creative writing. These three works, while addressing different aspects of a central question, are fundamentally related to each other as three parts of what I hope is a larger whole.

FIGURES IN BLACK

· 1 ·

Literary Theory and the Black Tradition

We have dreamed a dream, and there is no interpreter of it.

Genesis 40:8

Criticism is the *habitus* of the contemplative intellect, whereby we try to recognize with probability the genuine quality of a literary work by using appropriate aids and rules.

. . . The interpreter must know the writer's idiom well, aim at truth without partiality and inquire into the true and false reading.

Note. A painter is known by his painting, a writer by his writing.

The art of interpretation or hermeneutics is the *habitus* of the contemplative intellect of probing into the sense of a somewhat special text by using logical rules and suitable means.

Note. Hermeneutics differs from criticism as the species does from the genus and the part does from the whole.

. . . In every interpretation there occur the author, the literary work, and the interpreter.

Antonius Guillelmus Amo, an African from Guinea. "On Criticism, Hermeneutics, Method," *Treatise on the Art of Philosophising Soberly and Accurately* (1738)

I

The idea of a determining formal relationship between literature and social institutions does not in itself explain the sense of urgency that has, at least since the publication in 1760 of *A Narrative of the Uncommon Sufferings and Surprising Deliverance of Briton Hammon, a Negro Man,* characterized nearly the whole of Afro-American writing. This idea has often encouraged a posture that belabors the social and documentary status of black art.

Indeed, the earliest discrete examples of written discourse by the slave and ex-slave came under a scrutiny not primarily literary. Black formal writing, beginning with the five autobiographical slave narratives published in English between 1760 and 1789, was taken to be collective as well as functional. Because these narratives documented the black's potential for "culture"—that is, for manners and morals—the command of written English virtually separated the African from the Afro-American, the slave from the ex-slave, titled property from fledgling human being. Well-meaning abolitionists cited these texts as proof of the common humanity of bondsman and lord, yet these same texts also demonstrated the contrary for slavery's proponents: the African imagination was merely derivative.

The command of a written language, then, could be no mean thing in the life of the slave. Learning to read, the slave narratives repeat again and again, was a decisive political act; learning to write, as measured against an eighteenth-century scale of culture and society, was an irreversible step away from the cotton field toward a freedom larger even than physical manumission. What the use of language entiled for personal social mobility and what it implied about the public Negro mind made for the onerous burden of literacy, a burden having very little to do with the use of language as such, a burden so pervasive that the nineteenth-century quest for literacy and the twentieth-century quest for form became the central, indeed controlling, metaphors (if not mythical matrices) in Afro-American narrative. Once the private dream fused with a public and therefore political imperative, the Negro arts were committed; the pervasive sense of urgency and fundamental unity of the black arts became a millennial, if not precisely apocalyptic, force.

I do not mean to suggest that these ideas were peculiar to eighteenth-century criticism of black texts. For example, William K. Wimsatt argues that we learn from Herder's Prize Essay of 1773 on the *Causes of the Decline of Taste in Different Nations* that in Germany "the appreciation of various folk and Gothic literatures and the comparative study of ancient, eastern, and modern foreign literatures (the criticism of literature by age and race) were strongly established, and these interests profoundly affected theories about the nature of literature as the expression of, or the power that shaped, human cultures or human nature in general." Wimsatt also reminds us that Friedrick Schlegel "only accented an already pervasive view when he called poetry the most specifically human energy, the central document of any culture."[1] It should not surprise us, then, that *Poems on Various Subjects, Religious and Moral, by Phillis Wheatley, Negro Servant to Mr. Wheatley of Boston,* the first book of poems published by an African in English, became almost immediately after its publication in London in 1773 the international antislavery movement's most salient argument for the African's innate mental equality. That the book went to five printings before 1800 testified far more to its acceptance as a "legitimate" product of "the African muse," as Henri Grégoire wrote in 1808, than to the merit of its sometimes vapid elegiac verse.[2] The eighteen signatures, or "certificates of authenticity," that preface the book, including one by John Hancock and another by the governor of Massachusetts, Thomas Hutchinson, meant to "leave no doubt, that [Phillis Wheatley] is its author."[3] Literally scores of public figures—from Voltaire to George Washington, from Benjamin Rush to Benjamin Franklin—reviewed Wheatley's book, yet virtually no one discussed the book as poetry. It was an unequal contest: the documentary status of black art assumed priority over mere literary judgment; criticism rehearsed content to justify one notion of origins or another. Of these discussions, Thomas Jefferson's proved most central to the shaping of the Afro-American critical activity.

Asserted primarily to debunk the exaggerated claims of the abolitionists, Thomas Jefferson's remarks on Phillis Wheatley's poetry, as well as on Ignatius Sancho's posthumously published *Letters* (1782), exerted a prescriptive influence over the criticism of the writing of blacks for the next 150 years. "Never yet," Jefferson prefaces his discussion of Wheatley, "could I find a Black that had uttered a thought above the level of plain narration; never seen even an elementary trait of painting or sculpture." As a specimen of the human mind, Jefferson continues, Wheatley's poems, as poetry, did not merit discussion. "Religion," he writes, "indeed has produced a Phillis Whately [sic] but it could not produce a poet." "The compositions published under her name," Jefferson concludes, "are below the dignity of criticism. The heroes of the *Dunciad* are to her, as Hercules to the author of the poem." As for Sancho's *Letters,* Jefferson says:

> His imagination is wild and extravagant, escapes incessantly from every restraint of reason and taste, and, in the course of its vagaries, leave a tract of thought as incoherent and eccentric, as is the course of a meteor through the sky. His subjects should have led him to a process of sober reasoning: yet we find him always substituting sentiment for demonstration.[4]

The substitution of sentiment for demonstration is the key opposition in this passage, pitting unreflective emotion against reason. Writing, as I shall argue, was a principle sign of reason, especially since the *spoken* language of black people had become an object of parody at least since 1769 when *The Padlock* appeared on the American stage, including among its cast of characters a West Indian slave called Mungo. We know Mungo's essence by his language, a language represented by a caricature that signifies the difference that separated white from black:

> Me supper ready, and now me go to the
> cellar—But I
> say, Massa, ax de old man now,
> what good him watching do, him
> bolts, and him bars, him walls,
> and him padlocks.[5]

No, blacks could not achieve any true presence by speaking, since their "African"-informed English seems to have only underscored their status as *sui generis,* as distinct in spoken language use as in their peculiarly "black" color. If blacks were to signify as full members of the Western human community, they would have to do so in their writings.

Even before Jefferson allowed himself the outrageous remark that "the improvement of the blacks in body and mind, in the first instance of their mixture with the whites, has been observed by every one, and proves that their inferiority is not the effect merely of their condition of life," advocates of the unity of the human species had forged a union of literary tradition, individual talent, and innate racial capacity. Phillis Wheatley's "authenticators," for instance, announced:

> We whose Names are under-written, do assure the world, that
> the POEMS specified in the following Page, were (as we verily
> believe) written by *Phillis,* a young Negro Girl, who was but a
> few years since, brought an uncultured Barbarian from Africa,
> and has ever since been and now is, under the Disadvantage of
> serving as a Slave of a Family in this Town. She has been ex-
> amined by some of the best judges, and is thought qualified to
> write them.[6]

Further, Wheatley herself asks indulgence of the critic, considering the occasion of her verse. "As her Attempts in Poetry
are now sent into the World, it is hoped the critic will not severely censure their Defects; and we presume they have too much
Merit to be cast aside with contempt, as worthless and trifling
effusions." Wheatley clearly could not imagine a critic as harsh
as Jefferson. "With all their Imperfections," she concludes, "the
poems are now humbly submitted to the Perusal of the Public."
Other than the tone of the author's preface, there was little here
that was "humbly submitted" to Wheatley's public. Her volume
generated much speculation about the nature of the "African
imagination." So compelling did evidence of the African's artistic
abilities prove to be to Enlightenment speculation on the idea
of progress and the precise shape of the *scala naturae* that just
nine years after Wheatley's *Poems* appeared, more than one thousand British lords and ladies subscribed to have Ignatius Sancho's
collected letters published. Even more pertinent in our context,
Joseph Jekyll, M.P., prefaced the volume with a full biographical
account of the colorful Sancho's life, structured curiously around
the received relation between "genius" and "species."

British readers were fascinated by the "African mind" presented in the collected letters to Ignatius Sancho. Sancho was
named "from a fancied resemblance to the Squire of Don Qui-
xote" and had his portrait painted by Gainsborough and engraved
by Bartolozzi. He was a correspondent with Garrick and Sterne
and, apparently, something of a poet as well. "A commerce with
the Muses was supported amid the trivial and momentary inter-
ruptions of a shop," Jekyll writes. Indeed, not only were "the
Poets studied, and even imitated with some success," but "two
pieces were constructed for the stage." Moreover, Sancho composed and published musical compositions. In addition to his

creative endeavors, Sancho was a critic—perhaps the first African critic of the arts to write in English. His "theory of Music was discussed, published and dedicated to the Princess Royal, and Painting was so much within the circle of Ignatius Sancho's judgment and criticism," Jekyll observes, "that several artists paid great *deference* to his opinion."[7]

Jekyll's rather involved biography is a pretext to display the artifacts of the "sable mind," as was the very publication of the *Letters* themselves. *"Her* motives for laying them before the publick," the publisher admits, "were the desire of showing that an untutored African may possess abilities equal to an European." Sancho was an "extraordinary Negro," his biographer relates, although he was a bit better for being a bit bad. "Freedom, riches, and leisure, naturally led to a disposition of African tendencies into indulgences; and that which dissipated the mind of Ignatius completely drained the purse," Jekyll puns. "In his attachment to women, he displayed a profuseness which not unusually characterizes the excess of the passion." "Cards had formerly seduced him," we are told, "but an unsuccessful contest at cribbage with a jew, who won his cloaths, had determined to abjure the propensity which appears to be innate among his countrymen." Here again we see drawn the thread between phylogeny and ontogeny. "A French writer relates," Jekyll explains, "that in the kingdoms of Ardrah, Whydah, and Benin, a Negro will stake at play his fortune, his children, and his liberty." Thus driven to distraction, Sancho was "induced to consider the stage" since "his complexion suggested an offer to the manager of attempting Othello and Oroonoko; but a defective and incorrigible *articulation* rendered it abortive" (emphasis added).

Colorful though Jekyll's anecdotes are, they are a mere pretext for the crux of his argument: a disquisition on cranial capacity, regional variation, skin color, and intelligence. The example of Sancho, made particularly human by the citation of his foibles, is meant to put to rest any suspicion about the native abilities of the Negro:

> Such was the man whose species philosophers and anatomists
> have endeavored to degrade as a deterioration of the human; and
> such was the man whom [Thomas] Fuller, with a benevolence
> and quaintness of phrase peculiarly his own, accounted "God's

Image, though cut in Ebony." To the harsh definition of the naturalist, oppressions political and legislative have added; and such are hourly aggravated towards this unhappy race of men by vulgar prejudice and popular insult. To combat these on commercial principles, has been the labour of [others]—such an effort here [he concludes ironically] would be an impertinent digression.[8]

That Sancho's attainments are not merely isolated exceptions to the general morass is indicated by the state of civilization on the African "slave-coast." Jekyll continues:

Of those who have speculatively visited and described the slave-coast, there are not wanting some who extol the mental abilities of the natives. [Some] speak highly of their mechanical powers and indefatigable industry. [Another] does not scruple to affirm, that their ingenuity rivals the Chinese.

What is more, these marks of culture and capacity signify an even more telling body of data, since the logical extensions of mechanical powers and industry are sublime arts and stable polity:

He who could penetrate the interior of Africa, might not improbably discover negro arts and polity, which could bear little analogy to the ignorance and grossness of slaves in the sugar-islands, expatriated in infamy; and brutalized under the whip and the task-master.

"And he," Jekyll summarizes, "who surveys the extent of intellect to which Ignatius Sancho had attained self-education, will perhaps conclude, that the perfection of the reasoning faculties does not depend on the colour of a common integument."

Jekyll's preface became a touchstone for the literary anthropologists who saw in black art a categorical repository for the African's potential to *deserve* inclusion in the human community. Echoes of Jekyll's language resound throughout the prefaces to slave testimony. Gustavus Vassa's own claim in 1789 that the African's contacts with "liberal sentiments" and "the Christian religion" have "exalted human nature" is vouched for by more than one hundred Irish subscribers. Charles Ball's editor asserts in 1836 that Ball is "embued by nature with a tolerable portion of intellectual capacity."[9] Both Garrison's and Phillips's prefaces to *The Narrative of the Life of Frederick Douglass* (1845) and

James McCune Smith's introduction to Douglass's *My Bondage and My Freedom* (1855) attest to Douglass's African heritage, former bestial status, and intellectual abilities. McCune Smith, a black physician, proffers the additional claims for literary excellence demanded by the intensity of doubt toward the black African's mental abilities:

> The Negro, for the first time in the world's history brought in full contact with high civilization, must prove his title first to all that is demanded for him; in the teeth of unequal chances, he must prove himself equal to the mass of those who oppress him— therefore, absolutely superior to his apparent fate, and to their relative ability. And it is most cheering to the friends of freedom, to-day, that evidence of this equality is rapidly accumulating, not from the ranks of the half-breed colored people of the free states, but from the very depths of slavery itself; the indestructible equality of man to man is demonstrated by the ease with which black men, scarce one remove from barbarism—if slavery can be honored with such a distinction—vault into the high places of the most advanced and painfully acquired civilization.[10]

An 1845 review of Douglass's *Narrative* emphasizes the relevance of each "product" of the African mind almost as another primary argument in the abolitionist's brief against slavery:

> Considered merely as a narrative, we have never read one more simple, true, coherent, and warm with genuine feeling. It is an excellent piece of writing, and on that score to be prized as a specimen of the powers of the black race, which prejudice persists in disputing. We prize highly all evidence of this kind, and it is becoming more abundant.[11]

If an abolitionist reviewer in 1845 would admit that "we prize highly all evidence of this kind," he was only summarizing an antislavery emphasis that was at least a century and a half old. Wheatley and Sancho, and much later even the articulate ex-slave Frederick Douglass, commenced their public careers as the result of experiments to ascertain just how much "natural capacity" lay dormant in the "sable mind." Several enlightened aristocrats in the first half of the eighteenth century abstracted individual black children from the daily routine of slavery and educated them with their own children in experiments to ascertain if the "perfectibility of man" applied equally to blacks and to whites. What was at stake in these experiments was nothing less than the determination of the place of the African on the Great Chain of Being, a place that hovered rather precariously well beneath the European (and every other) "race of man," yet just above—or parallel to—that place reserved for the "orang-outang." As Edward Long put the matter in *The History of Jamaica* (1774), there was a *natural* relation between the ape and the African, and

> If such has been the intention of the Almighty, we are then perhaps to regard the orang-outang as,
> —the lag of human kind,
> Nearest to brutes, by God design'd.

For Long, the ape and the African were missing links, sharing "the most intimate connexion and consanguinity," including even "amorous intercourse." While it might sound hyperbolic to state this today, enlightened antislavery advocates turned to writing to determine and to demonstrate in the most public way just how far removed from the ape the African was in fact. Let us examine briefly four instances of blacks whose literacy would serve as an argument against the bestial status of all black people.

Literacy—the literacy of formal writing—was both a technology and a commodity. It was a commodity with which the African's right to be considered a human being could be traded. The slave narratives repeat figures of the complex relationship between freedom and literacy. But well before the first slave narrative was published, the freedom of literacy became inscribed in the curious education of Wilhelm Amo. In 1707, Amo, at the age of four an African slave, was given to the reigning Duke of Brunswick-Wolfenbuttel as a gift. The duke, in turn, gave the slave as a present to his son, Augustus Wilhelm. Augustus Wilhelm ascended the throne in 1714 and became the influential protector and benefactor of the young slave. Amo was christened Anton Wilhelm in 1708 and was educated in the same manner as were the other children of the royal family. Amo matriculated at the Prussian University of Halle on June 9, 1727. In 1732, he defended his thesis, entitled "De jure Maurorum in Europa," and was promoted to the academic degree of a Candidate of the Laws. In 1730, he received the degree of Magister of Philosophy and

Liberal Arts at the University of Wittenberg, a degree to be re-named Doctor of Philosophy within a few years. In 1734, Amo published a dissertation entitled *Inaugural philosophical disserta-tion on the APATHY of the human mind, or the absence of feel-ing and the faculty of feeling in the human mind and the presence of them in our organic living body,* a thesis on a subject that borders upon psychology and the medical sciences. In 1738, Amo published his treatise on logic, from which the second epigraph of this book is taken, while a university lecturer at Halle. In 1739, Amo assumed a position in the Faculty of Philosophy of Jena. Not much else is known of Amo's life. Fredrick Blumenbach in 1787 wrote that he had been appointed Councillor at the court of the Prussian king some time between 1740 and 1750. We do know, however, that in 1753 Amo was living back in Africa, near his birthplace on the Gold Coast, known today as Ghana, where he lived as a hermit and was widely known as a magician and a doctor. We also know that Amo returned to Africa willingly.[12]

What is remarkable about Amo's life and writings is that dur-ing his lifetime and throughout the Enlightenment they were seized upon by philosophers and critics as proof that the African was innately equal to the European, because this one African had demonstrated mastery of the arts and sciences. His thesis supervisor, for example, wrote that just as Terence, Tertullian, St. Cyprian, and St. Augustine had done for North Africa, Amo proved that those parts of sub-Saharan Africa, populated by beings whose humanity was in doubt, could produce superior intellects. Amo, moreover, demonstrated that from among other "uncivilized" nations outstanding individuals could emerge with the proper formal training.

Let us examine another instance of this curious phenomenon, one that occurred well beyond the confines and luxuries of the palace and the academy. One early eighteenth-century slave's experiences represent the relationship between freedom and liter-acy dramatically and more directly, indeed, than would seem possible. Job, the son of Solomon (Suleiman), a priest of the Fulani, apparently was a person of some distinction in West Africa, until he was captured by the Mandingos and sold into slavery in 1731. From a plantation in Maryland, Job wrote a letter in Arabic to his father. Mail services between early eightteenth-century Maryland and Senegal, of course, were not quite as direct as they are today. Job, now a slave, had absolutely no chance of seeing a letter written in Arabic reach his African father. This letter, nevertheless, by a remarkable set of accidents eventually came into the possession of James Oglethorpe, one of the founders of the colony of Georgia and then the deputy governor of the Royal African Company. Oglethorpe sent the Arabic text up to Oxford, where the Huguenot John Gagnier held the Laudian Chair of Arabic. Gagnier's translation so moved Oglethorpe—about whom Pope wrote, "One, driv'n by strong Benevolence of Soul/Shall fly, like Oglethorpe, from Pole to Pole"—and so impressed him with the strength of Job's character that in June 1732 he gave his bond for the payment of this slave at the price of forty-five pounds. Job, I should add, came to London, was the toast of the Duke of Montague (who would soon thereafter repeat the Duke of Brunswick's experiment with Wilhelm Amo and become patron to Francis Williams and Ignatius Sancho) and of the British royal family, and fourteen months later in 1734 returned, as did Amo, to his father's land. Job Ben Solomon literally wrote his way out of slavery; his literacy, translated into forty-five pounds, was the commodity with which he earned his escape price.[13]

Lest we think that Job's was an isolated incident, there were dozens of instances of this use of literacy as a commodity. As late as 1829, in this country, George Moses Horton's master at North Carolina collected his slave's poems, published them as a book, and then falsely advertised widely in Northern black and antislavery newspapers that all proceeds from the book's sales would be used to purchase Horton's freedom! However, royalties of the 1879 edition of Francisco Calcagno's *Poetas de Color,* published at Habana, were used to purchase the freedom of the slave poet, José de Carme Díaz.

There were many other such experiments: "el negro" Juan Latino, who published three books of poems in Latin at Granada between 1573 and 1576; Jacobus Capitein, who graduated from the University of Leyden in 1742 and whose thesis was published in Latin and in Dutch that same year; and Phillis Wheatley, who in 1773 became the first African to publish a book of poems in English. All three, among several others, were the subject of

experiments in literature mastery, whose lives and works came
to serve as black figures for the idea of progress and the perfectibility of man, as well as human synecdoches for the capacity of
the African to assume a parallel rank with the European on the
Great Chain of Being.

Amo and his fellow writers, Othello's countrymen, suffered
under the sheer burden of literacy: to demonstrate that the person
of African descent was indeed a human being. Amo was not
competing, as it were, with Newton; he was distinguishing himself
from the apes. How curious, how arbitrary that the written word,
as early as 1700, signified the presence of a common humanity
with the European. Any serious theory of the nature and function
of writing in the Western tradition must, to put it bluntly, take
the critical reception to this unique genre into full account. What
more meaningful example of the eighteenth century's theories of
writing can possibly exist? What a profoundly burdensome task
to impose upon the philosopher such as Amo—indeed, to impose
upon the human being. What an ironic origin of a literary tradition! If Europeans read the individual achievements of blacks in
literature and scholarship as discrete commentaries of Africans
themselves upon the Western fiction of the "text of blackness,"
then the figure of blackness as an absence came to occupy an
ironic place in the texts of even the most sober European philosophers. In the next section of this chapter, I wish to outline the
repetition of the relationship between blackness and writing, so
that I may begin to demonstrate how the strategies of negation,
so central to Black Aesthetic criticism, were locked in a relation
of thesis to antithesis to a racist discourse embedded in Western
philosophy.

II

Considering the crucial role that blacks believed the creation of
art would bear upon their dubious political status, it is not
surprising that the first predictions of a renaissance of black
literature and art, made by William Stanley Braithwaite in 1901,
precisely overlap W. E. B. Du Bois's efforts to form an organization dedicated to lobbying for black civil rights. The origin
of this received association of political salvation and artistic
genius—which we have seen from Amo to the slave narratives—

can be traced back even farther, at least to the seventeenth century. What we arrive at by extracting this black and slender thread from among the philosophical discourse of the Renaissance and Enlightenment is a reading of another side of the philosophy of enlightenment, indeed its nether side. Writing in *The New Organon* in 1620, Sir Francis Bacon, confronted with the problem of classifying the people of color which a sea-faring Renaissance Europe had only recently "discovered," turned to the arts as the ultimate measure of place in nature. "Again," he wrote, "let a man only consider what a difference there is between the life of men in the most civilized province of Europe, and in the wildest and most barbarous districts of New India; he will feel it be great enough to justify the saying that 'man is a good man,' not only in regard to aid and benefit, but also by comparison of condition. And this difference comes not from soil, not from climate, not from race, but from the arts." Eleven years later, Peter Heylyn, in his *Little Description of the Great World,* used Bacon's formulation to relegate the blacks to a subhuman status: The black African, he wrote, lacked completely "the use of Reason which is peculiar unto man; [he is] of little Wit; and destitute of all arts and sciences; prone to luxury, and for the greatest part Idolators." All subsequent commentaries on the matter were elaborations upon Heylyn's position.

The idea of literacy as a technology is useful in understanding the commodity relation implicit in formal Western literature. At least since Purchas published his *Pilgrimage* in 1611, Europeans sought to measure the "sublimity" of the Africans by their progress in the so-called arts and sciences. Although the comparison can be found scattered throughout two centuries of accounts of African discovery, William Bosman in 1705 gave the matter the sanction of a myth of origins, complete with a central opposition between culture and nature, the physical and the metaphysical, sublime refinement and base lust. Writing in *A New and Accurate Description of the Coast of Guinea,* Bosman records the following account of a West African myth of creation:

> A great part of the *Negroes* believe that Man was made by *Anasie,* that is, a great Spider: the rest attribute the Creation of Man to God, which they assert to have happened in the following manner: they tell us, that in the beginning God created Black

as well as White men; thereby not only hinting but endeavoring to prove that their Race was as soon in the World as Ours; and to bestow a yet greater Honour on themselves, they tell us that God having created these sorts of men, offered two sorts of Gifts, viz. Gold, and the knowledge of arts of Reading and Writing, giving the Blacks the first Election, who chose Gold, and left the knowledge of Letters to the White. [Bosman's footnote: "The *Negroes* believe, that there is no Gold in any other Countries besides their own; and that no Blacks have any knowledge of the Arts or Letters; nor have they any notion of the extent of the World but what they recollect from our Informations."] God granted their Request, but being incensed at their Avarice, resolved that the Whites should ever be their masters, and they obliged to wait on them as their slaves.[14]

Bosman's myth of origins, cast as it is within the frame of writing on the one hand and gold on the other,* renders the commodity relation explicitly, just as Morgan Godwyn had suggested in 1680 that same relation implicitly, when he urged forcefully that black people were human beings indeed because they had demonstrated mastery of *"Risibility and Discourse* (Man's Peculiar Faculties)." By 1680, Heylyn's keywords, "Reason" and "Wit," had been reduced to "Reading and Writing," as Morgan Godwyn's summary of received opinion attests:

[A] disingenuous and unmanly *Position* had been formed; and privately (and as it were *in the dark*) handed to and again, which is this, That the Negro's though in their figure they carry some resemblances of manhood, yet are indeed *no* men. . . . [The] consideration of the shape and figure of our Negro's Bodies, their Limbs and members; their Voice and Countenance, in all things according with other mens; together with their *Risibility* and *Discourse* (Man's Peculiar Faculties) should be sufficient Conviction. How should they otherwise be capable of *Trades,* and other no less manly imployments; as also of *Reading and Writing,* or show so much Discretion in management of Business; . . . but wherein (we know) that many of our own People are *deficient,* were they not truly men?[15]

* I have analyzed the import of this opposition and its impact on the rhetorical strategies of the pre-1815 slave narrative in Chapter 4 of *The Signifying Monkey.*

Such a direct correlation of political rights and *literacy* helps us to understand both the transformation of writing into a commodity and the sheer burden of received opinion that both motivated the black slave to seek his or her text and defined the frame against which each black text would be read. The following 1740 South Carolina statute was concerned to make it impossible for black literacy mastery even to occur:

> *And whereas* the having of slaves taught to write, or suffering them to be employed in writing, may be attending with great inconveniences;
> *Be it enacted,* that all and every person and persons whatsoever, who shall hereafter teach, or cause any slave or slaves to be taught to write, or shall use or employ any slave as a scribe in any manner of writing whatsoever, hereafter taught to write; every such person or persons shall, for every offense, forfeit the sum of one hundred pounds current money.[16]

Learning to read and to write, then, was not only difficult; it was a violation of a law. That Frederick Douglass, Thomas Smallwood, William Wells Brown, Moses Grandy, James Pennington, Harriet Jacobs, and John Thompson, among several others, all rendered statements about the direct relationship between freedom and discourse as central scenes of instruction and as repeated fundamental structures of their larger rhetorical strategies only emphasizes the dialectical relation of black text to a context, defined here as other racist texts against which the slave's narrative, by definition, was forced to react.

Bosman's fabrication, of course, was a myth of origins designed to sanction through mythology a political order created by Europeans. It was David Hume, writing at midpoint in the eighteenth century, who gave Bosman's myth the sanction of Enlightenment philosophical reasonings.

Hume's comments about blacks were an unacknowledged elaboration upon those made by Bernard Fontenelle in his *Digression on the Ancients and Moderns*. In this work, Fontenelle, in the midst of a discussion of the relation of climate to genius, suggests that "nature" might have restricted "advancements in knowledge" to the confines of "the Atlas Mountains and the Baltic Sea" and that "it remains to be known . . . if one can ever hope to see [either] great Lapp or Negro authors." Voltaire, writing in 1773, would cite Phillis Wheatley's *Poems* as a refutation of Fontenelle; nevertheless, it is Hume's opinion that seems to have been most widely shared.

In a major essay, "Of National Characters" (1748), Hume discusses the "characteristics" of the world's major divisions of human beings. In a footnote added to his original text in 1753 (at the margins of his discourse), Hume posited with all of the authority of philosophy the fundamental identity of complexion, character, and intellectual capacity:

> I am apt to suspect the negroes and in general all the other species of men (for there are four or five different kinds) to be naturally inferior to the whites. There never was a civilized nation of any other complexion than white, nor even any individual eminent either in action or speculation. No ingenious manufacturers amongst them, *no arts, no sciences.* . . . Such a uniform and constant difference could not happen, in so many countries and ages, if *nature* had not made our original distinction betwixt these breeds of men. Not to mention our colonies, there are Negroe slaves dispersed all over Europe, of which none ever discovered any symptoms of ingenuity. . . . In Jamaica, indeed they talk of one negroe as a man of parts and learning [Francis Williams, the Cambridge-educated poet who wrote verse in Latin]; but 'tis likely he is admired for very slender accomplishments, like a parrot who speaks a few words plainly.

Hume's opinion on the subject, as we might expect, became prescriptive.[17]

Writing in 1764 in *Observations on the Feeling of the Beautiful and the Sublime,* Immanuel Kant elaborates upon Hume's essay in a fourth section entitled "Of National Characteristics, as far as They Depend upon the Distinct Feeling of the Beautiful and the Sublime." Kant first claims that "so fundamental is the difference between [the black and white] races of man, and it appears to be as great in regard to mental capacities as in color." Kant, moreover, is one of the earliest major European philosophers to conflate color with intelligence, a determining relation he posits with dictatorial surety. The excerpt bears citation:

> Father Labat reports that a Negro carpenter, whom he re-
> proached for haughty treatment toward his wives, answered:
> "You whites are indeed fools, for first you make great conces-
> sions to your wives, and afterward you complain when they drive
> you mad." And it might be that there was something in this
> which perhaps deserved to be considered; but in short, this fel-
> low was *quite black* from head to foot, a clear proof that what
> he said was *stupid* [emphasis added].[18]

Kant posits the correlation of blackness and stupidity as if self-
evident. In the same year in which Jefferson criticized Wheatley,
Kant, basing his observations on the absence of published writing
among blacks, noted as if simply obvious that "Americans [In-
dians] and blacks are lower in their mental capacities than all
other races." A few years later Hegel, echoing Hume and Kant,
noted the absence of history among black people and derided
them for failing to develop indigenous African scripts, or even to
master the art of writing in modern languages.

Hegel writes about the relation of the African to culture and
to history in *The Philosophy of History*. It is the absence of writing that he takes to be the most salient indication that Africa is
the land of ultimate difference. "Africa proper," he writes, "as
far as History goes back, has remained—for all purposes of connection with the rest of the World—shut up; it is the Goldland
compressed within itself—the land of childhood, which lying beyond the *day of self-conscious history,* is enveloped in the dark
mantle of Night" (emphasis added). We cannot "know" the "African character," he continues, expanding upon both Hume and Kant,
because the African himself has not demonstrated the capacity to
make it "objective," neither by admitting of a self-consciousness of
"an absolute Being, an Other and a Higher than his individual
self" nor by evincing the ultimate of human awareness of itself,
the writing of history. "The peculiarly African character is difficult to comprehend," Hegel argues, so "we must quite give up
the principle which naturally accompanies all *our* ideas—the category of Universality." The African, rather, is grounded in the
true prison of particularity, a drastic particularity that separates
him or her from the rest of the human community, precisely because the black "consciousness has not yet attained to the real-

ization of any substantial objective existence . . . in which the
interest of man's volition is involved and in which he realizes
his own being." The African, moreover, cannot distinguish between "himself as an individual and the universality of his
essential being"; this crucial difference "the African in the
uniform, underdeveloped oneness of his existence has not yet
attained." Because of this, Hegel concludes, "there is nothing
harmonious with humanity to be found in this type of character."

Hegel maintains that there is no "culture" in Africa, and only
"Mahommedianism" seems to have been capable of bringing "the
Negroes within the range of culture." The African lacks "all that
we call feeling," and his "Fetiches" lack any "aesthetic independence as a work of art." For Africans, "cannibalism is looked
upon as quite customary and proper," as an extension of their
"perfect *contempt* for humanity, which in its bearing on Justice
and Morality is the fundamental characteristic of the race." Again
echoing Jefferson and Kant, Hegel argues that "among the Negroes moral sentiments are quite weak, or more strictly speaking,
non-existent."

In this degraded state, Hegel explains, the African "is capable of
no development or culture, and as we see them at this day, such
have they always been." Their saving grace, however, shall be
that peculiar institution of slavery. It is Western slavery that
serves the African as "a phase of *education*—a mode of becoming
participant in a higher morality and the culture connected with
it." For this reason, Hegel advocates the "gradual abolition of
slavery" rather than "its sudden removal."

Africa, ultimately for Hegel,

> is no historical part of the World; it has no movement or devel-
> opment to exhibit. Historical movements in it—that is in its
> northern part—belong to the Asiatic or European world. . . .
> What we properly understand by Africa, is the Unhistorical, Un-
> developed Spirit, still involved in the conditions of mere nature,
> and which had to be presented here only as on the threshold of
> the World's History.[19]

Hegel's strictures on the African about the absence of "history" presume a crucial role of memory—of a collective, cultural
memory—in the estimation of a civilization. Metaphors of the

childlike nature of the slaves, of the masked, puppetlike* personality of the black, all share this assumption about the absence
of memory. Mary Langdon, writing in 1855 in her novel *Ida
May: A Story of Things Actual and Possible,* says that "but then
they *are* mere children. . . . You seldom hear them say much
about anything that's past, if they only get enough to eat and
drink at the present moment." Without writing, there could exist
no repeatable sign of the workings of reason, of mind; without
memory or mind, there could exist no history; without history,
there could exist no "humanity," as defined consistently from
Vico to Hegel.

The sheer pervasiveness in Western letters of this equation of
"the rights of man" and the ability to write affected even those
vehemently opposed to slavery. Writing in 1832, in William Lloyd
Garrrison's *Liberator,* a journal created the year before expressly
to agitate for the abolition of slavery, an essayist wrote that "till
[the blacks] are equal to other people in knowledge and cultivation, they will not and cannot rank as equals." Emerson, speaking in 1844 on the anniversary of the emancipation of Haiti,
summarized the challenge facing black people determined to end
their own enslavement. Nature, he said, "deals with men after
the same manner. If they are rude and foolish, down they must
go. When at last in a race a new principle appears, an idea—that
conserves it; ideas only save races. If the black man is feeble
and not important to the existing races, not on a parity with the
best race, the black man must serve, and be exterminated. But
if the black man carries in his bosom an indispensable element
of a new and coming civilization, for the sake of that element,
he will survive and play his part."[20] This "idea," of course, could
be communicated only in written form. By 1896, the association
of freedom and literacy had such a long heritage that William
Dean Howells repeated it in his key review of Paul Laurence
Dunbar's book of poems, *Majors and Minors,* as we shall see
below.

These readings of blackness as a trope of absence adumbrate
the very properties of property. In fact, what we discover here
is a correlation between property and properties and between

* On the relation of the mask of blackness to metaphors of childhood, see
Chapter 6.

character and characteristics, which proved so pervasive in the latter half of the nineteenth century that Booker T. Washington's *Up from Slavery,* for example, becomes after its seventh chapter the autobiography of an institution, thereby detaching itself somewhat from the slave narrative tradition, where the rhetorical movement was from institution and property to the shaping of the human subject.

This relationship between essence and value, between ethics and aesthetics, became as late as Howells's review of Dunbar's *Majors and Minors,* a correlation between a metaphysical blackness and a physical blackness. Howells emphasizes almost immediately Dunbar's appearance:

> the face of a young negro, with the race's traits strangely accented: the black skin, the wooly hair, the thick, out-rolling lips, and the mild, soft eyes of the pure African type. One cannot be very sure, ever, about the age of those people, but I should have thought that this poet was about twenty years old; and I suppose that a generation ago he would have been worth, apart from his literary gift, twelve or fifteen hundred dollars, under the hammer.

Howells makes a most remarkable, and literal, shift from Dunbar's properties to his possible value as property. Moreover, he outlines and prefigures the still prevalent notion that treats black art as artifact:

> He is, so far as I know, the first man of his color to study his race objectively, to analyze it to himself, and then to represent it in art as he felt it and found it to be; to represent it humorously, yet tenderly, and above all so faithfully that we know the portrait to be undeniably like. A race which has reached this effect in any of its members can no longer be held wholly uncivilized; and intellectually Mr. Dunbar makes a stronger claim for the negro than the negro yet has done.

Howells then makes the leap so crucial to this discussion and so crucial to the aesthetics of the Black Arts movement:

> If his Minors [the dialect pieces] had been written by a white man, I should have been struck by their very uncommon quality; I should have said that they were wonderful divinations. But since they are expressions of a race-life from within the race, they seem to me infinitely more valuable and significant. I have

sometimes fancied that perhaps the negroes *thought* black, and *felt* black: that they were racially so utterly alien and distinct from ourselves that there ever could be common intellectual and emotional ground between us, and that whatever eternity might do to reconcile us, the end of time would find us far asunder as ever. But this little book, has given me pause in my speculation. Here in the artistic effect at least, is white thinking and white feeling in a black man, and perhaps the human unity and not the race unity, is the precious thing, the divine thing, after all. God hath made of one blood all nations of men: perhaps the proof of this saying is to appear in the arts, and our hostilities and prejudices are to vanish in them.[21]

Here we find suggestions of imperatives for the cultural renaissance that Du Bois would outline in the *Crisis* just fifteen years later. Here, in Howells, we find the premise that would assume a shape in the fiction of a "New Negro." Here we find the sustained apocalyptic notion of the Negro arts, about which Carl Van Vechten and James Weldon Johnson would correspond at length. Here we find the supposition, elaborated on by Du Bois and even William Stanley Braithwaite, by Langston Hughes and Claude McKay, that while blacks and whites are in essence the same, they bear apparent differences, and these differences can be mediated through the media of art. The Black Christ, in short, would be a poetaster.

And what of somewhat more contemporary critical movements and their reflections on black literature? I shall cite briefly three instances, involving two exponents of "formalist" theories and the other of Marxist theory, to suggest that the curious line that I have drawn from the eighteenth to the early twentieth centuries continued at least to midcentury. I. A. Richards, writing in 1920 in the preface to Claude McKay's book of poems, *Spring in New Hampshire,* describes the author as "a pure blood negro" and as "the first instance of [black] success in poetry," due no doubt to "the difficulties presented by modern literary English as an acquired medium." McKay's place in the world of art, Richards concludes, is one next to the sculptures from Benin and the music of the "Spirituals," a major event, therefore, in the Negro's search for equality.

Two years later, Max Eastman, the American Marxist, writing

in the introduction to McKay's *Harlem Shadows,* would elaborate
upon Richards's remarks in what we can safely assume to have
been one of the few occasions on which these two dissimilar
critics agreed. "These poems have a special interest for all the
races of man," Eastman writes, "because they are sung by a pure-
blooded Negro." Eastman the socialist, like Richards the practical critic, equates the normative with the biological: McKay's
poems are of special import because they are the product of a
"pure-blooded Negro" mind.

At midcentury, Allen Tate refined the terms of the equation,
in a preface to Melvin B. Tolson's *Libretto for the Republic of
Liberia,* to make of the concern for the color of the black author
a concern for the poetic diction he or she imitated. Significance,
in the sense that we have been using the term here, lay in a black
face imitating (in the sense of mimesis) what Tate called "the
full poetic language of his time and, by implication, the language
of the Anglo-American poetic tradition." That Tolson is, according to Tate, the black poet who achieved this "for the first time"
is the source of Tate's enthusiasm, for this feat implies, once
again, something major about the intellectual "progress of the
race."

Richards, Tate, and Eastman are not exceptions; their range
of theoretical concerns makes them salient examples merely.
Comments by Karl Shapiro and Louis B. Simpson on black
poetry, Irving Howe on black narrative, and especially Theodor
Adorno's curious psychosocial critiques of jazz could serve just
as well to suggest that when members of one sort of critical
school or another did indeed turn to black literature or culture,
often their results were discouraging. As often, explicating the
"black difference" led to judgments inconsistent with the principles of the aesthetic system with which each critic was closely
identified. Let us consider how this tradition of prefaces to blackness affected the shape of the Afro-American literary tradition
and the image of the black in American art.

III

I would hope that it is obvious that the creation of formal literature could be no mean matter in the life of the slave, since the

sheer literacy of writing was the very commodity that separated animal from human being, slave from citizen, object from subject. Reading, and especially writing, in the life of the slave represented a process larger than even "mere" physical manumission, since mastery of the arts and letters was Enlightenment Europe's sign of that solid line of division between human being and thing.

The letters of attestation of authorship that preface Phillis Wheatley's *Poems* of 1773 are an aspect of the commodity function of black writing, just as surely as we can describe the curious attempts of George Moses Horton's master in 1829 to raise his slave's manumission price by publishing and selling his slave's poetry through subscriptions advertised in Northern black and reform antebellum newspapers. Any theory of the origins of American literature, for example, must account for this process of the reification of the activity of writing into a commodity, which I have traced above from Samuel Purchas in the seventeenth century to Fontenelle, Hume, Kant, Jefferson, and Hegel in 1813, down to William Dean Howells at the turn of the century, and beyond. Race and reason, ethnocentrism and logocentrism, together were used by the enlightened to deprive the black of his or her humanity.

Unlike almost every other literary tradition, the Afro-American literary tradition was generated as a response to eighteenth- and nineteenth-century allegations that persons of African descent did not, and could not, create literature. Philosophers and literary critics, such as Hume, Kant, Jefferson, and Hegel, seemed to decide that the absence or presence of a written literature was the signal measure of the potential, innate humanity of a race. The African living in Europe or in the New World seems to have felt compelled to create a literature both to demonstrate implicitly that blacks did indeed possess the intellectual ability to create a written art and to indict the several social and economic institutions that delimited the humanity of all black people in Western cultures.

So insistent did these racist allegations prove to be, at least from the eighteenth to the early twentieth centuries, that it is fair to describe the subtext of the history of black letters as this urge to refute the claim that because blacks had no written traditions

they were bearers of an inferior culture. The relationship between
European and American critical theory, then, and the development of African and Afro-American literary traditions, can readily be seen to have been ironic indeed. Even as late as 1911,
when J. E. Casely-Hayford published *Ethiopia Unbound* (called
the first African novel), that pioneering author felt compelled
to address this matter in the first two paragraphs of his text. "At
the dawn of the twentieth century," the novel opens, "men of
light and leading both in Europe and in America had not yet
made up their minds as to what place to assign to the spiritual
aspirations of the black man. . . . Before this time, it had been
discovered that the black man was not necessarily the missing
link between man and ape. It has even been granted that for
intellectual endowments he had nothing to be ashamed of in an
open competition with the Aryan or any other type." *Ethiopia
Unbound,* it seems obvious, was concerned to settle the matter
of black mental equality, which had remained something of an
open question for two hundred years. Concluding this curiously
polemical exposition of three paragraphs, which precedes the
introduction of the novel's protagonist, Casely-Hayford points
to "the names of men like [W. E. B.] Du Bois, Booker T. Washington, [Edward Wilmot] Blyden, [Paul Laurence] Dunbar, [Sam-
uel] Coleridge-Taylor, and others" as prima facie evidence of
the sheer saliency of what Carter G. Woodson once termed "the
public Negro mind." These were men, the narrative concludes,
"who had distinguished themselves in the fields of activity and
intellectuality," men who had demonstrated conclusively that the
African's first cousin was indeed the European rather than the
ape.

That the presence of a written literature could assume such
large proportions in several Western cultures from the Enlightenment to this century is only as curious as the fact that blacks
themselves, as late as 1911, felt the need to speak the matter
silent, to end the argument by producing literature. Few literary
traditions have begun or been sustained by such a complex and
ironic relation to their criticism: allegations of an absence led
directly to a presence, a literature often inextricably bound in a
dialogue with its potentially harshest critics.

In Spanish and English, in Latin and French, in German and

Dutch, the writings of blacks in the Enlightenment came under scrutiny not primarily literary, giving rise to an implicit theory of writing itself, at least of black writing, and its relation to what we have come to think of as the innate rights of a people to political freedom. Indeed, we can only begin to understand the resistance to theory in the Afro-American tradition if we qualify these terms somewhat and call this tendency the resistance to *Western* theory. Black writers and critics, since Amo, have been forced to react against an impressive received tradition of Western critical theory which not only posited the firm relation among writing, "civilization," and political authority, but which also was called upon by various Western men of letters to justify various forms of enslavement and servitude of black people. It is no surprise that black people have been theory-resistant. Because the history of this relationship between blacks and theory involves many Western philosophers, because its threads of influence have not been defined before, and because it has had such a determining effect upon black critics and writers since the eighteenth century, I have sketched its contours to begin to suggest its implications. Let us next consider how black writers and critics reacted to the racism of Western writings about the relationship between the written arts and the status of the black human being.

Hume, Kant, Jefferson, and Hegel's stature demanded response: from black writers, refutations of white doubts about their very capacity to imagine great art and hence to take a few giant steps up the Great Chain of Being; from would-be critics, encyclopedic and often hyperbolic replies to these disparaging generalizations. The critical responses include Thomas Clarkson's Prize Essay, written in Latin at Cambridge in 1785 and published as *An Essay on the Slavery and Commerce of the Human Species, Particularly the African* (1788), and the following rather remarkable volumes: Gilbert Imlay's *A Topographical Description of the Western Territory of North America* (1793); the Marquis de Bois-Robert's two-volume *The Negro Equalled by Few Europeans* (1791); Thomas Branagan's *Preliminary Essay on the Oppression of the Exiled Sons of Africa* (1804); the Abbé Grégoire's *An Enquiry Concerning the Intellectual and Moral Faculties, and Literature of Negroes . . .* (1808); Samuel Stanhope Smith's *An Essay on the Causes of the Variety of the Hu-*

man Complexion and Figure in the Human Species (1810); Lydia
Maria Child's *An Appeal in Favor of That Class of Americans
Called Africans* (1833); B. B. Thatcher's *Memoir of Phillis
Wheatley, a Native American and a Slave* (1834); Abigail Mott's
*Biographical Sketches and Interesting Anecdotes of Persons of
Color* (1838); R. B. Lewis's *Light and Truth* (1844); Theodore
Hally's *A Vindication of the Capacity of the Negro Race* (1851);
R. T. Greener's urbane long essay in *The National Quarterly
Review* (1880); Joseph Wilson's rather ambitious *Emancipa-
tion: Its Course and Progress from 1481 B.C. to A.D. 1875*
(1882); William Simmon's *Men of Mark* (1887); Benjamin
Brawley's *The Negro in Literature and Art* (1918); and Joel A.
Rodgers's two-volume *The World's Great Men of Color* (1946).
There are well over 150 encyclopedias of black intellection, pub-
lished to disprove racist aspersions cast upon the mind of "the
race."

Even more telling for our purposes here is that the almost
quaint authenticating signatures and statements that prefaced
Wheatley's book became, certainly through the period of Dunbar
and Chesnutt and even until the middle of the Harlem Renaissance, fixed attestations of the "specimen" author's physical
blackness. This sort of authenticating color description was so
common to these prefaces that many late nineteenth- and early
twentieth-century black reviewers, particularly in the *African
Methodist Episcopal Church Review,* the *Southern Workman,*
the *Voice of the Negro, Alexander's Magazine,* and *The Colored
American,* adopted it as a political as well as rhetorical strategy
to counter the intense and bitter allegations of African inferiority
popularized by journalistic accounts and "colorations" of social
Darwinism. Through an examination of a few of these prefaces,
I have tried to sketch an ironic circular thread of interpretation
that commences in the eighteenth century but does not reach its
fullest philosophical form until the decade between 1965 and
1975: the movement from blackness as a physical concept to
blackness as a metaphysical concept. Indeed, this movement became the very text and pretext of the "Blackness" of the recent
Black Arts movement, a solidly traced hermeneutical circle into
which we all found ourselves drawn.

The confusion of realms, of art with propaganda, plagued the

Harlem Renaissance in the twenties. A critical determination—a mutation of principles set in motion by Matthew Arnold's *Culture and Anarchy,* simplified thirty years later into Booker T. Washington's "toothbrush and bar of soap" and derived from Victorian notions of "uplifting" spiritual and moral ideals that separated the savage (noble or not) from the realm of culture and the civilized mind—meant that only certain literary treatments of black people could escape community censure. The race against social Darwinism and the psychological remnants of slavery meant that each piece of creative writing became a political statement. Each particular manifestation served as a polemic: "another bombshell fired into the heart of bourgeois culture," as *The World Tomorrow* editorialized in 1921. "The black writer," said Richard Wright, "approached the critical community dressed in knee pants of servility, curtseying to show that the Negro was not inferior, that he was human, and that he had a gift comparable to other men." As early as 1921, W. E. B. Du Bois wrote of this in the *Crisis:*

> Negro art is today plowing a difficult row. We want everything that is said about us to tell of the best and highest and noblest in us. We insist that our Art and Propaganda be one. We fear that evil in us will be called racial, while in others it is viewed as individual. We fear that our shortcomings are not merely human.[22]

And as late as 1925, even as sedate an observer as Heywood Broun argued that only through art would the Negro gain freedom: "A supremely great negro artist," he told the New York Urban League, "who could catch the imagination of the world, would do more than any other agency to remove the disabilities against which the negro now labors." Further, Broun remarked that this artist—redeemer could come at any time, and he asked his audience to remain silent for ten seconds to imagine that coming![23] Ambiguity in language, then, and "feelings that are general" (argued for as early as 1861 by Frances E. W. Harper) garnered hostility and suspicion from the critical minority; ambuiguity was a threat to "knowing the lines." The results for a growing black literature were disastrous, these perorations themselves dubious. Black literature came to be seen as a cultural artifact (the product of unique historical forces) or as a document that bore witness to

the political and emotional tendencies of the Negro victim of
white racism. Literary theory became the application of a social
attitude.

By the apex of the Harlem Renaissance, then, certain latent
assumptions about the relationships between art and life had become prescriptive canon. In 1925, Du Bois outlined what he
called "the social compulsion" of black literature, built as it was,
he contended, on "the sorrow and strain inherent in American
slavery, on the difficulties that sprang from emancipation, on the
feelings of revenge, despair, aspiration, and hatred which arose as
the Negro struggled and fought his way upward."[24] Further, he
made formal the mechanistic distinction between "method" and
"content," the same distinction that allowed James Weldon Johnson to declare with glee that, sixty years after slavery, all that
separated the black poet from the white was "mere technique"!
Structure, by now, was atomized. Form was merely a surface for
a reflection of the world, the world here being an attitude toward
race; form was a repository for the disposal of ideas; message was
not only meaning but value; poetic discourse was taken to be literal, or once removed; language lost its capacity to be metaphorical in the eyes of the critic; the poem approached the essay, with
referents immediately perceivable; literalness precluded the view
of life as allegorical; and black critics forgot that writers approached things through words, not the other way around. The
functional and didactic aspects of formal discourse assumed primacy in normative analysis. The confusion of realms was complete: the critic became social reformer, and literature became
an instrument for the social and ethical betterment of the black
person.

So, while certain rather conservative notions of art and culture
wove themselves into F. R. Leavis's *Scrutiny* in Cambridge in the
thirties, blacks borrowed whole the Marxist notion of base and
superstructure and made of it, if you will, race and superstructure.
Here, as in Wright's "Blueprint for Negro Literature," for example, race in American society was held to determine the social
relations that determine consciousness, which in turn determines
actual ideas and creative works. "In the beginning was the
deed," said Trotsky in an attack on the Formalists; now the
deed was *black*. The brilliant critical work of Sterling Brown and

Zora Neale Hurston ran counter to these trends but did not predominate.

This notion of race and superstructure became, during the forties and fifties, in one form or another the mode of criticism of black literature. As would be expected, critics urged the supremacy of one extraliterary idea after another, as Ralph Ellison challenged Richard Wright on one front and James Baldwin on another. But race as the controlling mechanism in critical theory reached its zenith of influence and mystification when LeRoi Jones metamorphosed himself into Imamu Baraka and his dai-shiki-clad, Swahili-named "harbari gani" disciplines "discovered" they were black. With few exceptions, black critics employed blackness-as-theme to forward one argument or another for the amelioration of the Afro-American's social dilemma. Yet the critical activity altered little, whether that message was integration or whether it was militant separation. Message was the medium; message reigned supreme; form became a mere convenience or, worse, a contrivance.

The commonplace observation that black literature with very few exceptions has failed to match pace with a sublime black music stems in large measure from this concern with statement. Black music, by definition, could never utilize the schism between form and content, because of the nature of music. Black music, alone of the black arts, has developed free of the imperative, the compulsion, to make an explicit political statement. Black musicians, of course, had no choice: music groups masses of non-representational material into significant form; it is the audible embodiment of form. All this, however, requires a specific mastery of technique, which cannot be separated from "poetic insight." There could be no "knowing the lines" in the creation of black music, especially since the Afro-American listening audience had such a refined and critical aesthetic sense. Thus, Afro-America has a tradition of masters, from Bessie Smith through John Coltrane, unequaled perhaps in all of modern music. In literature, however, we have no similar development, no sustained poignancy in writing. In poetry, where the command of language is indispensable if only because poetry "thickens" language and thus draws attention from its referential aspect, we saw in the sixties the growth of what the poet Ted Joans calls the "Hand-Grenade" poets, who concern themselves with futile attempts to make poetry preach, which poetry is not capable of doing so well. And the glorification of this poetry (especially the glorification of Baraka and Don Lee's largely insipid rhetoric), in which we feel the unrelenting vise of the poet's grip upon our shoulders, became the principal activity of the "New Black" critic. The suppositions on which this theory of criticism rests are best explicated through a close reading of four texts that, conveniently, treat poetry, literary history, and the novel.

Stephen Henderson's *Understanding the New Black Poetry* is the first attempt at a quasi-formalistic analysis of black poetry.[25] It is of the utmost importance to the history of race and superstructure criticism because it attempts to map a black poetic landscape, identifying inductively those unique cultural artifacts that critics, "especially white critics," have "widely misunderstood, misinterpreted, and undervalued for a variety of reasons—aesthetic, cultural, and political." Henderson's work is seminal insofar as he is concerned with discrete uses of language, but in the course of his study he succumbs to the tendency of advancing specific ideological prerequisites.

Henderson readily admits his bias: he equates aesthetics and ethics. "Ultimately," he says, "the 'beautiful' is bound up with the truth of a people's history, as they perceive it themselves." This absolute of truth Henderson defines in his fifth definition of what "black poetry is chiefly": "Poetry by any identifiably Black person whose ideological stance vis-à-vis the history and aspirations of his people since slavery [is] adjudged by them to be 'correct.' " Hence, an ideal of truth, which exists in fact for the black poet to find, is a "Black" truth. And "Black" is integral to the poetic equation, since "if there is such a *commodity* as 'blackness' in literature (and I assume that there is), it should somehow be found in concentrated or in residual form in the poetry" (emphasis added).

Had Henderson elaborated on "residual form" in literary language, measured formally, structurally, or linguistically, he would have revolutionized black literary criticism and brought it into the twentieth century. But his theory of poetry is based on three sometimes jumbled broad categories that allow the *black* critic to define "norms" of blackness." The first of these is an oversimplified conception of *theme:* "that which is spoken of, whether the specific subject matter, the emotional response to it, or its intellectual formulation." The second is *structure,* by which Henderson intends "chiefly some aspects of the poem such as diction, rhythm, figurative language, which goes into the total makeup." (At times, he notes, "I use the word in an extended sense to include what is usually called genre.") His third critical tool, the scale by which he measures the "commodity" he calls "Blackness," is *saturation.* He means by this "several things, chiefly the comunication of 'Blackness' and fidelity to the observed or intuited truth of the Black Experience in the United States."

Now, the textual critic has problems with Henderson's schema not only because it represents an artificial segmentation of poetic structure (which can never, in fact, be explicated as if one element existed independently of the rest) but also because that same scheme tends to be defined in terms of itself and hence is tautological. Henderson defines *theme,* for example, as "perhaps the simplest and most apparent" of the three. By *theme,* however, he means a poem's paraphrased level of "meaning." To illustrate this, he contrasts a George Moses Horton quatrain with a couplet from Countee Cullen. The "ambiguity" of the former lines, he concludes, defined for us insofar as "it might evoke a sympathetic tear from the eye of a white [Jewish] New York professor meditating upon his people's enslavement in ancient Egypt, does make it a less precise kind of ["Black"] statement than Cullen's, because in the latter the irony cannot be appreciated without understanding the actual historical debasement of the African psyche in America." Thus, the principal corollary to the theorem of "black themes" is that the closer a theme approaches cultural exclusivity, the closer it comes to a higher "fidelity." Moreover, Henderson allows himself to say, had Shakespeare's Sonnet 130 "been written by an African at Elizabeth's court, would not the thematic meaning change?" That leap of logic is difficult to comprehend, for a poem is above all atemporal and must cohere at a symbolic level, if it coheres at all. Perhaps Henderson's problem is the poetry prompting his theory; he has only followed that poetry's lead and in that way left himself open to Wittgenstein's remonstration: "Do not forget that a poem, even though it is composed in the language of information, is not used in the language of giving information."

The most promising of Henderson's categories is *structure,* and yet it is perhaps the most disappointing. By *structure,* he means that "Black poetry is most distinctly Black" whenever "it derives its form from two basic sources, Black speech and Black music." At first glance, this idea seems exciting, since it implies a unique, almost intangible use of language peculiar to Afro-Americans. On this, one could build—nay, one *must* build—that elusive "Black Aesthetic" the race and superstructure critics have sought in vain. But Henderson's understanding of speech as referent is not linguistic; he means a literal referent to nonpoetic discourse and unfortunately makes no allowances for the manner in which poetic discourse differs from prosaic discourse or "instances" of speech. He provides us with an elaborate and complicated taxonomy of reference to speech and to music, yet unaccountably ignores the fact that the "meaning" of a word in a poem is derived from its context within that poem, as well as from its context in our actual, historical (un)consciousness. But a taxonomy is a tool to knowledge, not knowledge itself. The use of language is not a stockpile of referents or forms, but an activity.

Henderson remarks with some astonishment that "Black speech in this country" is remarkable in that "certain words and constructions seem to carry an inordinate charge of emotional and psychological weight." These he calls "mascon" words, borrowing the acronym from NASA, where it is employed to describe a massive concentration of matter beneath the lunar surface. What he is describing, of course, is not unique to black poetic discourse; it is common to all poetic uses of language in all literatures and is what helps to create ambiguity, paradox, and irony. This, of course, has been stated adamantly by the "practical critics" since the twenties—those same "New Critics" Henderson disparages. These usages, however, do make black poetic language unique and argue strongly for a compilation of a black dictionary of discrete examples of specific signification, where "Black English" departs from "general usage." They are not, I am afraid, found only in the language of black folks in this country. Had Henderson identified some criteria by which we could define an oral tradition in terms of the "grammar" it superimposes on non-literary discourse, then shown how this comes to bear on literary discourse, and further shown such grammars to be distinctly black, then his contribution to our understanding of language and literature would have been no mean thing indeed.

His final category, *saturation,* is the ultimate tautology: poetry is "Black" when it communicates "Blackness." The more a text is saturated, the "Blacker" the text. One imagines a daishiki-clad Dionysus weighing the saturated, mascon lines of Countee Cullen against those of Langston Hughes, as Paul Laurence Dunbar and Jean Toomer are silhouetted by the flames of our own black Hades. The blacker the berry, the sweeter the juice.

Should it appear that I have belabored my reading of this theory, it is not because it is the weakest of the three theories of black literature. In fact, as I will try to show, Henderson's is by far the most imaginative of the three and has, at least, touched on areas critical to the explication of black literature. His examination of form is the first in a race and superstructure study and will most certainly give birth to more systematic and less polemical studies. But the notions implicit and explicit in Henderson's ideas were shared by Houston A. Baker, Jr., and Addison Gayle as well.

In the first essay of *Long Black Song: Essays in Black American Literature and Culture,* Houston A. Baker proffers the considerable claim that black culture, particularly as measured" through black folklore and literature, serves in intent and effect as an "index" of "repudiation" not only of white Western values and white Western culture but of white Western literature as well.[26] "In fact," he writes, "it is to a great extent the culture theorizing of whites that has made for a separate and distinctive black American culture. That is to say, one index of the distinctiveness of black American culture is the extent to which it repudiates the culture theorizing of the white Western world." Repudiation, he continues, "is characteristic of black American folklore; and this is one of the most important factors in setting black American literature apart from white American literature." Further, "black folklore and the black American literary tradition that grew out of it reflect a culture that is distinctive both of white American and of African culture, and therefore neither can pro-

vide valid standards by which black American folklore and literature may be judged." A text becomes "blacker," it surely follows,
to the extent that it serves as an index of repudiation. Here we
find an ironic response to Harold Bloom's *Anxiety of Influence*
in what we could characterize as an "animosity of influence."

Baker discusses this notion of influence between black and
white American culture at length. "Call it black, Afro-American,
Negro," he writes, "the fact remains that there is a fundamental,
qualitative difference between it and white American culture."
The bases of this "fundamental, qualitative difference" are, first,
that "black American culture was developed orally or musically
for many years"; second, that black American culture was characterized by a "collective ethos"; and, finally, that "one of [black
American culture's] most salient characteristics is an index of
repudiation." Oral, collectivistic, and repudiative, Baker concludes, "each of these aspects helps to distinguish black American
culture from white American culture."

These tenets suggest that there must be an arbitrary relationship between a sign and its referent, indeed that all meaning is
culture-bound. Yet what we find elaborated here are rather oversimplified, basically political criteria, which are difficult to verify,
partly because they are not subject to verbal analysis (that is, can
this sense of *difference* be measured through the literary uses of
language?), partly because the thematic analytical tools employed
seem to be useful primarily for black naturalist novels or for
the mere paraphrasing of poetry, partly because the matter of
influence is almost certainly too subtle to be traced in other than
close textual readings, and finally because Baker's three bases of
"fundamental, qualitative difference" seem to me too unqualified.
There is so much more to Jean Toomer, Zora Hurston, Langston
Hughes, Sterling Brown, Ralph Ellison, Leon Forrest, Ishmael
Reed, Toni Morrison, and Alice Walker than their "index of
repudiation," whatever that is. Besides, at least Toomer, Ellison,
and Reed have taken care to discuss the complex matter of literary ancestry, in print and without. It is one of the ironies of the
study of black literature that our critical activity is, almost by
definition, a comparative one, since many of our writers seem to
be as influenced by Western masters, writing in English as well
as outside it, as they are by indigenous, Afro-American oral or

even written forms. That the base for our literature is an oral one is certainly true; but, as Fillman Parry and Albert Lord have amply demonstrated, so is the base of the whole of Western literature, commencing with the Hebrews and the Greeks. Nevertheless, Baker does not suggest any critical tools for explicating the oral tradition in our literature, such as the formulaic studies so common to the subject. Nor does he suggest how folklore is displaced in literature, even though, like Henderson, he does see it at "the base of the black literary tradition." The claim that black culture is characterized by a collective ethos most definitely demands some qualification, since our history, literary and extra-literary, often turns on a tension, a dialectic, between the private perceptions of an individual and the white public perceptions of that same individual.

Nor does Baker's thought-provoking contention that black imaginative culture is deprived of the American frontier stand to prove this thesis:

> When the black American reads Frederick Jackson Turner's *The Frontier in American History,* he feels no regret over the end of the Western *frontier.* To black America, frontier is an alien word; for, in essence, all frontiers established by the white psyche have been closed to the black man. Heretofore, later, few have been willing to look steadily at America's past and acknowledge that the black man was denied his part in the frontier and his share of the nation's wealth.

At least Ralph Ellison has written extensively on the fact of the frontier (physical and metaphysical) and its centrality to his sensibility, and Ishmael Reed uses the frontier again and again as a central trope.

Part of the problem here is not only Baker's exclusive use of thematic analysis to attempt to delineate a literary tradition but also his implicit stance that literature functions primarily as a cultural artifact, as a repository for ideas. "It is impossible to comprehend the process of transcribing cultural values," he says (in his essay "Racial Wisdom and Richard Wright's *Native Son*"), "without an understanding of the changes that have characterized both the culture as a whole and the lives of its individual transcribers." Further, "Black American literature has a human immediacy and a pointed relevance which are obscured by the over-ingenious methods of the New Criticism, or any other school that attempts to talk of works of art as though they had no creators or of sociohistorical factors as though they did not filter through the lives of individual human beings." (How ironic this sentence seems today, since Baker by his own admission is now a post-structuralist critic.*) Here we find the implicit thesis in *Long Black Song,* the rather Herderian notion of literature as primarily the reflection of ideas and experiences outside it. It is not, of course, that literature is unrelated to culture, to other disciplines, or even to other arts; it is not that words and usage somehow exist in a vacuum or that the literary work of art occupies an ideal or reified, privileged status, the province of some elite cult of culture. It is rather that the literary work of art is a system of signs that may be decoded with various methods, all of which assume a fundamental relationship between form and content and all of which demand close reading. Baker seems to be reading black texts in a particular fashion for other than literary purposes. In *Singers of Daybreak: Studies in Black American Literature,* he suggests these purposes. "What lies behind the neglect of black American literature," he asserts, "is not a supportable body of critical criteria that includes a meaningful definition of *utile* and *dulce,* but a refusal to believe that blacks possess the humanity requisite for the production of works of art."[27] Baker finds himself shadow-boxing with the ghostly judgments of Jefferson on Phillis Wheatley and Ignatius Sancho; his blows are often telling, but his opponent's feint is deadly.

If Baker's early pre-theoretical criticism taught us more about this attitude toward being black in white America than it did about black literature, then Addison Gayle, Jr., in *The Way of the New World,* does not even teach us that.[28] Gayle makes no bones about his premises:

> To evaluate the life and culture of black people, it is necessary that one live the black experience in a world where substance is more important than form, where the social takes precedence over the aesthetic, where each act, gesture, and movement is po-

* See Baker's very important book, *Blues, Ideology, and Afro-American Literature: A Vernacular Theory* (Chicago: University of Chicago Press, 1984).

litical, and where continual rebellion separates the insane from the sane, the robot from the revolutionary.

Gayle's view of America, and of the critic, means that he can base his "literary judgments" on some measure of ideology; and he does. Regrettably, he accuses James Baldwin of "ignorance of black culture." His praise of John A. Williams seems predicated on an affinity of ideology. He praises John Killens's *And Then We Heard the Thunder* because Killens "creates no images of racial degradation." For Gayle, the "central flaw" of the protagonist is *Invisible Man* ("an otherwise superb novel") is "attributable more to Ellison's political beliefs than to artistic deficiency." In Gayle, we see race and superstructure criticism as its basest: not only is his approach to literature deterministic, but his treatment of the critical activity demonstrates an alarming disrespect for the diversity of the black experience itself and for the subtleties of close textual criticism.

What is wrong with employing race and superstructure as a critical premise? This theory of criticism sees language and literature as reflections of "Blackness." It postulates "Blackness" as an entity, rather than as metaphor or sign. Thus, the notion of a signified black element in literature retains a certain impressiveness insofar as it exists in some mystical knigdom halfway between a fusion of psychology and religion on the one hand and the Platonic Theory of Ideas on the other. Reflections of this "Blackness" are more or less literary according to the ideological posture of the critic. Content is primary over form and indeed is either divorced completely from form, in terms of genesis and normative value, or else is merely facilitated by form as a means to an end. In this criticism, rhetorical value judgments are closely related to social values. This method reconstitutes message, when what is demanded is an explication of a literary system.

The race and superstructure critics would have us believe that the function of the critic is to achieve an intimate knowledge of a literary text by re-creating it from the inside: critical thought must become the thought criticized. Only a black man, therefore, can think (hence, rethink) a black thought. Consciousness is predetermined by culture and color. These critics, in Todorov's phrase, "recreate" a text either by repeating its own words in their own order or by establishing a relationship between the work and some system of ideas outside it. They leave no room for the idea of literature as a system. Normative judgments stem from how readily a text yields its secrets or is made to confess falsely on the rack of "black reality."

Yet perceptions of reality are in no sense absolute; reality is a function of many variables. Writers present models of reality rather than a description of it, though obviously the two may be related variously. In fact, fiction often contributes to cognition by providing models that highlight the nature of things precisely by their failure to coincide with received ideas of reality. Such, certainly, is the case in science fiction. Moreover, the thematic studies so common to black criticism suffer from a similar fallacy. Themes in poetry, for instance, are rarely reducible to literal statement; literature approaches its richest development when its "presentational symbolism" (as opposed by Suzanne Langer to its "literal discourse") cannot be reduced to the form of a literal proposition. Passages of creative discourse cannot be excerpted and their meaning presented independent of context. For Ralph Ellison, for example, invisibility was not a matter of not being seen but rather a refusal to run the gamut of one's own humanity.

"Blackness," as these critics understand it, is weak in just the decisive area where practical criticism is strong: in its capacity to give discrete accounts of consciousness rather than a scheme or a generalization. And the reason for this weakness is not difficult to discern; it lies in the received formula of race and superstructure, which reduces far too readily to the simple repetition of ideology. The critical method, then, is reductionist; literary discourse is described mechanically by classifications that find their ultimate meaning and significance somewhere else, outside the texts at hand.

Ultimately, black literature is a verbal art like other verbal arts. "Blackness" is not a material object, an absolute, or an event, but a trope; it does not have an "essence" as such but is defined by a network of relations that form a particular aesthetic unity. Even the slave narratives offer the text as a world, as a system of signs. The black writer is the point of consciousness of his or her language. If the writer does embody a "Black Aesthetic," then it can be measured not by content but by a complex structure of meanings. The correspondence of content between a writer and his or her world is less significant to literary criticism than is a correspondence of organization of structure, for a relation of content may be a mere reflection of prescriptive, scriptural canon, such as those argued for by Baker, Gayle, and Henderson. A relation of structure, on the other hand, according to Raymond Williams, "can show us the organizing principles by which a particular view of the world, and from that the coherence of the social group which maintains it, really operates in consciousness." If there is a relationship between social and literary "facts," it must be found here.[29]

To paraphrase Rene Wellek, black literature may well be dark, mysterious, and foreboding, but it is certainly not beyond careful scrutiny and fuller understanding. The tendency toward thematic criticism implies a marked inferiority complex: afraid that our literature cannot sustain sophisticated verbal analysis, we view it from the surface merely and treat it as if it were a Chinese lantern with an elaborately wrought surface, parchment-thin but full of hot air. Black critics enjoyed such freedom in our discipline that we found ourselves with no discipline at all. This set of preconceptions brought readers and writers into a blind alley. Literary images, even black ones, are combinations of words, not of absolute or fixed things. The tendency of black criticism toward an ideological absolutism, with its attendant inquisition, had to come to an end. A literary text is a linguistic event; its explication must be an activity of close textual analysis. Simply because Bigger Thomas kills Mary Dalton and tosses her body into a furnace, *Native Son* is not necessarily a "blacker" novel than *Invisible Man*—Gayle notwithstanding. We urgently need to direct our attention to the nature of black figurative language, to the nature of black narrative forms, to the history and theory of Afro-American literary criticism, to the fundamental relation of form and content, and to the arbitrary relationships between the sign and its referent. Finally, we must begin to understand the nature of intertextuality, that is, the nonthematic manner by which texts—poems and novels—respond to other texts. After all, all cats may be black at night, but not to other cats.

V

Black literature and its criticism, then, have been put to uses that were not primarily aesthetic; rather, they have formed part of a larger discourse on the nature of the black and his or her role in the order of things. The integral relation between theory and a literary text, therefore, which so often in other traditions has been a sustaining relation, in our tradition has been an extraordinarily problematical one. The relationship among theory, tradition, and integrity within the black literary tradition has not been, and perhaps cannot be, a straightforward matter at all.

Let us consider the etymology of the word *integrity,* which I take to be the keyword in the subject of the relationship between the black tradition and theory. *Integrity* is a curious keyword to address in a period of bold and sometimes exhilarating speculation and experimentation, two other words that aptly characterize literary criticism generally, and Afro-American criticism specifically, at the present time. The Latin origin of the English word, *integritas,* connotes wholeness, entireness, completeness, chastity, and purity, most of which are descriptive terms that made their way frequently into the writings of the American "New Critics," who seem not to have cared particularly for or about the literature of Afro-Americans. Two of the most common definitions of *integrity* elaborate upon the sense of wholeness, derived from the Latin original. Let me cite these here, as taken from the *Oxford English Dictionary:*

1. The condition of having no part or element taken away or wanting; undivided or unbroken state; material wholeness, completeness, entirety; something undivided; an integral whole.
2. The condition of not being marred or violated; unimpaired or uncorrupted condition; original perfect state; soundness.

It is the second definition of *integrity*—that is to say, connoting the absence of violation and corruption, the preservation of an initial wholeness or soundness—which I would like to consider in this deliberation upon theory and the black tradition, or more precisely upon that relationship which ideally should obtain between Afro-American literature and the theories we fabricate to account for its precise nature and shape.

It is probably true that critics of Afro-American literature (which, by the way, I employ as a less ethnocentric designation than "the black American critic") are more concerned with the complex relationship between literature and literary theory than we have ever been before. There are many reasons for this, not the least of which is our increasingly central role in the profession, precisely when our colleagues in other literatures are engulfed in their own extensive debates about the intellectual merit of so very much theorizing. Theory, as a second-order reflection upon a primary gesture such as literature, has always been viewed with deep mistrust and suspicion by those scholars who find it presumptuous and perhaps even decadent when criticism claims the right to stand as discourse on its own, as a parallel textual universe to literature. Theoretical texts breed other, equally decadent theoretical responses, in a creative process that can be remarkably far removed from a poem or a novel.

For the critic of Afro-American literature, this process is even more perilous precisely because the large part of contemporary literary theory derives from critics of Western European languages and literatures. Is the use of theory to write about Afro-American literature, we might ask rhetorically, merely another form of intellectual indenture, a form of servitude of the mind as pernicious in its intellectual implications as any other form of enslavement? This is the issue raised, for me at least, not only by the notion of the word *integrity* in this context but also by my own work in critical theory over the last ten years. Does the propensity to theorize about a text or a literary tradition mar, violate, impair, or corrupt, the soundness of an "original perfect state" of a black text or of the black tradition? This is the implied subject of this book, which I try to address in several ways.

To be sure, this matter of criticism and integrity has a long and ironic history in black letters. It was Hume, we recall, who called the Jamaican poet of Latin verse, Francis Williams, "a parrot who merely speaks a few words plainly"; and Phillis Wheatley has for far too long suffered from the spurious attacks of black and white critics alike for being the original *rara avis* of a school of so-called mockingbird poets, whose use and imitation of received European and American literary conventions has been regarded, simply put, as a corruption itself of a "purer" black expression, privileged somehow in black artistic forms such as the blues, Signifyin(g), the spirituals, and the Afro-American dance. Can we, as critics, escape the mockingbird trap? Can we signify only as critical monkeys?

These are some of the questions that have been debated heatedly by critics of Afro-American literature in the past few years. For example, a conference of twenty-eight college professors, grouped together at Yale for two weeks during the summer of 1977, prefaced their summarizing statement (which outlined the nature and function of black literary criticism) with the premise that "Afro-American literature is, above all, an act of language." The conference itself, funded by the National Endowment for the Humanities, sponsored by the Modern Language Association, and jointly directed by Robert Burns Stepto, Assistant Professor of English at Yale, and Dexter Fisher, then Program Coordinator of the MLA's Commission on Minority Literatures, seemed determined to refute certain received notions of the relationship between black art and black social and political status within American society. Among these presuppositions are the following formulations: that black literature is primarily raw data or cultural artifact for the social scientist determined to explicate the "true nature" of black people; that there is a correlation between a people's artistic excellence and its political authority; and, especially, that the corpus of creative writing by Africans and Afro-Americans, dark and mysterious and foreboding as it might be, is not open to legitimate literary analysis by critics of any "intellectual complexion" employing all of the remarkably sophisticated tools of explication now at their disposal. Further and most crucially, the conference seemed to argue, just as we read and reread Joyce's *Ulysses* more to discover the art of the novel than to remark at the manners and morals of a Dublin Jew, so too must we read the works of black authors as discrete manifestations of form and genre and as implicit commentaries on the white literature of similar structure. The conference itself, in short, represented an attempt to take the "mau-mauing" out of the black literary criticism that defined the "Black Aesthetic Movement" of the sixties and transform it into a valid field of intellectual inquiry once again.

That the conference boldly and successfully addressed these

matters is as remarkable as the very need to speak at all. Only ten years ago, the shared polemic of black criticism was that "blackness" existed as some mythical and mystical absolute, an entity so subtle, sublime, and unspeakable that only the "very black" racial initiate could ever begin to trace its contours, let alone force it to utter its darkest secrets. As I have argued above, our critics' hermeneutical circle was a mere tautology; only black people could think black thoughts, and therefore only the black critic could rethink, and hence criticize, a black text.

Not only the theory but also the practice of black literature has, for two hundred years, grown stunted within these dubious ideological shadows. The content of a black work of art has, with few but notable exceptions, assumed primacy in normative analysis, at the expense of the judgment of form. What's more, many black writers themselves seem to have conceived their task to be the creation of an art that reports and directly reflects brute, irreducible, and ineffable "black reality," a reality that in fact was often merely the formulaic fictions spawned by social scientists whose work intended to reveal a black America dehumanized by slavery, segregation, and racial discrimination, in a one-to-one relationship of art to life. Black literacy, then, became far more preoccupied with the literal representation of social content than with literary form, with ethics and thematics rather than poetics and aesthetics. Art, therefore, was argued implicitly and explicitly to be essentially referential. This theory assumed, first of all, that there existed a common, phenomenal world, which could be reliably described by the methods of empirical historiography or else by those of empirical social science. It assumed, second, that the function of the black writer was to testify to the private world of black pain and degradation, determined by a pervasive white and unblinking racism. Not only would creative writing at last make visible the face of the victimized and invisible black person, but it would also serve notice to the white world that individual black people had the requisite imagination to create great art and therefore to be "equal," an impetus, again, that we have traced to the eighteenth century.

To signify upon Henry James, the House of Black Fiction has many windows, but many are cracked and jagged. Haunted by archetypal Running Men who wrestle in dream-and-nightmare sequences with the unmediated Specter of White Racism, our House of Black Fiction is strewn with dead rats and cockroaches that feed off the ashen-pale bodies of dumb and, of course, wealthy white girls. Only the odor of chittlins and collard greens, steaming on gas burners, mitigates the certain stench of death. Nowhere can the critic unravel James's "figure in the carpet," and not only because "the city's" welfare checks are too paltry to afford the luxury. And the kitchen linoleum is worn thin, we fear, from overuse, buried, we suspect, beneath a growing mound of garbage, and purchased, we assume, on some usurious Easy Payment Plan. It is a house in tatters, created by novelists who fail to realize that by the very act of writing—the language of which is not reality but a system of signs—they commit themselves to the construction of coherent, symbolic worlds related to but never relegated to be merely plausible reproductions of the real world, not even the nightmare land of the inner city.

VI

If theories of race and superstructure criticism did not prove to be fertile grounds in which Afro-American criticism could blossom, it nevertheless remains incumbent upon critics of black literature to extend their pioneering search *within the black idiom* for principles of criticism.

The Afro-American literary tradition has not yet produced a coherent theory of the texts that comprise it. We have benefited little from this absence of theories that are specific to black texts. What a fecund field awaits our attention. Perhaps the last black scholar to write a purely theoretical text was Amo, one of the first persons of African descent to publish a book in a European language. Amo may well have been the first, and remains one of the few writers of African descent to theorize about the integrity of literature as an ideal institution. Amo was concerned, moreover, with the nature of analysis, of interpretation itself, rather than with containing an ideological stance about oppression in the guise of criticism. True, there are ideological presuppositions implicit in any critical judgment; for Amo, we recognize his explicit formalism as a reaction against eighteenth-century correlations between the race of an author and the value of his or her work. The import, if not the stance, of his work does reflect the world of ideas and economic relations that surround him. Nevertheless, Amo's treatise is a philosophical discourse upon the role of the reader as he or she interacts with text and author to produce meaning.

To underscore Amo's formalism is not merely to emphasize his uniqueness in a critical tradition that, consistently since Amo and until the last half-decade, has privileged the political function of a work of art at the expense of what it has described as sterile flirtation with "decadent" or "bourgeois" or "white" notions of art for art's sake. To underscore Amo's concern for the text is to emphasize the irony of eighteenth-century European theorizing about the nature and function of writers of African descent publishing texts in European languages. As I hope I have demonstrated above, these Enlightenment theorists privileged the fact of public writing—the literacy of literature, as it were—as the signal criterion for demonstrating the innate mental equality of the African with the European. Contrary to our assumptions that the Western philosophical tradition privileged the spoken over the written text, close readings of the evidence suggest strongly that the written word was privileged, not only above the spoken word but among all of the other representational arts as well. Had polyrhythms in music been privileged, for instance, our history in the West could have been a drastically different one. But it was the literacy of literature that, arbitrarily, was used as a commodity to measure the black's humanity. Amo, we know, was acutely aware of all of this. For Amo, as we have seen, was the very product of one such Enlightenment experiment designed to measure the mental capacity of the African by his ability to master the European arts and letters.

How are we to escape this trap of our own literature mastery, as well as the trap of the mindless imitation of the monkey? Are we doomed as critics of a noncanonical literature merely to cut monkeyshines, or can signifying monkeys decode the signs that comprise our black structures of literature? It seems to me that finding metaphors for black literary relations from within the Afro-American tradition, and combining these with that which is useful in contemporary literary theory, is the challenge of Afro-

American literary history. At least two other critics of black
literature have developed meaningful metaphors of Afro-American
literary history. Houston A. Baker, Jr., and Robert Burns Stepto
have defined "repudiation" and "authentication," respectively, as
metaphors of literary history.*[30]

Baker's theory of repudiation establishes an inverse relationship
between a nonblack text and its black repudiation. This repudiation is essentially thematic, epistemological, and ontological.
Baker's metaphor for literary relationships between black and
white texts concerns itself with the signified, and not especially
with the signifier. Stepto's metaphor of authentication draws upon
strategies of legitimacy employed by black authors and their white
"prefacers," since Phillis Wheatley published her poems in 1773,
to attest to the claims of authorship of the black subject. Stepto's
work traces this theme of "authorial control," of subject–object
dialectics, from its most patent form in the slave narratives to
Ralph Ellison's subtle refiguration in *Invisible Man*. Above all
else, Stepto is concerned with the capacity of a narrator to tell
his or her own tale.

Both Baker and Stepto, curiously enough, have developed
metaphors of literary history that are implicitly ideological and
antagonistic, turning as they do on notions of power and autonomy, which we may read as themes of racial and individual self-
hood. If only in these broad senses, the two metaphors share
similar presuppositions about the will to power as the will to
write. I have tried to supplement these creative theories by locat-
ing a metaphor for literary history that arises from within the
black idiom exclusively, that is not dependent upon black–white
power or racial relations, and that is essentially rhetorical. I call
it critical signification, and I take it from the black rhetorical
strategy called Signifyin(g). *Signifyin(g)* is a rhetorical strategy
that is indigenously black and that derives from the Signifying
Monkey tales. The figure of the Signifying Monkey, in turn, is
the profane counterpart of Esu-Elegbara, the Yoruba sacred
trickster who is truly Pan-African, manifesting himself among the

* Baker's brilliant theory of the black vernacular, the blues idiom, and its
relation to literary structure is fundamentally related to my theory of signifying. Although Baker graciously acknowledges my influence on his work,
I would argue that ours is a reciprocal relationship.

Cubans, the Haitians, and the Fon as Legba, among the Brazilians as Exu, among the believers of Vodun as Papa Legba, and among the believers of Hoodoo as Papa LaBas. Hermes is his closest Western counterpart. As Hermes is to hermeneutics, so is Esu to the black art of interpretation, *Esu-'tufunaalo*.

I use Esu as the metaphor for the critical activity of interpretation and Signifyin(g) as my metaphor for literary history because these are idiomatically black. I have not had to strain or reinterpret these figures. The discursive, or signifying, structures from which I take them define them in these ways: Esu the Yoruba call the figure of indeterminacy and the figure of interpretation. Signifyin(g) is a uniquely black rhetorical concept, entirely textual or linguistic, by which a second statement or figure repeats, or tropes, or reverses the first. Its use as a figure for intertextuality allows us to understand literary revision without resource to thematic, biographical, or Oedipal slayings at the crossroads; rather, critical signification is tropic and rhetorical. Indeed, the very concept of Signifyin(g) can exist only in the realm of the intertextual relation.

We are able to trace such complex intertextual Signifyin(g) relations by explicating what I like to think of as the Discourse of the Black Other in the eighteenth and early nineteenth centuries. By "Discourse of the Black" I mean to say the literature that persons of African descent created as well as the nonblack literature that depicts black characters. The phrase, then, suggests both how blacks figured language and how blacks and their blackness were figured in Western languages, especially in English and French. I am speaking here of the black as both subject and object of literature.

Because the discourse of the black occupied a fundamental polemical place in the fight against slavery, literary historians have tended to dismiss or ignore the hundreds of poems, plays, and novels about blacks that Europeans and Americans published between the seventeenth and the mid-nineteenth centuries. This literature contains only a few noble blacks, and even these are rendered ambiguously. Aphra Behn renders Oronooko, for example, as a noble African, but only at the expense of his fellow Africans: they are short, while he is tall; they speak an African language, while he speaks French; they have African features, while his are aquiline; they are weak and cowardly, while he is strong. The "Dying Negro" poems made popular by the English Romantics attempt to elicit pity and sentiment for the insufferable plight of the unfortunate slave. These, too, like the noble Negro tales, draw upon received racist images of the African, even if they intend to arouse the conscience of the European.

We can think of the slave narratives as a reaction to these sentimental figurations. The generic expectations of this aspect of the discourse of the black had a profound effect on the shape of that discourse which we call the slave's narrative, as did the sentimental novel and more especially the particularly American transmutation of the European picaresque. The slave narratives, in turn, spawned their formal antithesis, the Confederate romance. It is useful to think of this curious, dialectical relation of the slave narratives to the confederate romance as that of repetition and reversal. It is as if the figure of the North Star in the slave narratives becomes the figures of moonbeams and magnolia blossoms in the plantation novel. Structurally, the two modes of figuration are opposite, mirror images, in a relation of archetype and stereotype. Furthermore, all of those so-called illegitimate slave narratives, anathema to the historian, are merely novels that refigure tropes and conventions of both genres, often masking themselves as authentic first-person slave narratives, both pro- and anti-slavery, such as Mattie Griffiths's *Autobiography of a Female Slave,* or Richard Hildreth's *Archy Moore* and my absolute favorite, *Peculiar,* published in 1863, the protagonist of which is called Peculiar Institution.

The hundreds of slave narratives and Confederate romances published before 1865 have been documented and analyzed by scholars such as Charles Nichols, Marion Wilson Starling, Margaret Young Jackson, Frances Smith Foster, John W. Blassingame, Vernon Loggins, John Herbert Nelson, Sterling A. Brown, and Jean Fagan Yellin. Moreover, Charles T. Davis, Leslie Fielder, and Harry Levin have explicated the interplay of figures of light and darkness in the works of Hawthorne, Melville, and Poe. No one, to my knowledge, has yet discussed the relationship among the slave narratives, the Confederate romance, and the American Romantics, which we may think of as the three terms of the dialectic—thesis, antithesis, synthesis—wherein the themes of black and white, common to the bipolar moment in which the slave narratives and the plantation novel oscillate, inform the very structuring principles of the great gothic works of Hawthorne, Melville, and Poe. The intertextual relations that obtain here are formal ones; indeed, the use of the power of blackness as a structuring principle in many ways assumes the function of any mythic structure, reconciling the two otherwise irreconcilable forces. Narration here is the trick of mediation.

We can illustrate this set of relationships in literary history by considering that curious relationship between the figures of Harlequin and the American Minstrel Man. Many scholars have discussed myths of origins of Harlequin which attribute the blackness of his mask and its patently "negroid" features to the mask of blackness of the African. Marmontel wrote in 1787 that "it is likely that an African slave was the first model for this character." Florian, a few years later, argued that "the most realistic opinion is that [Harlequin] was originally an African slave. His black face and shaved head seem to indicate this." Harlequin's tricolored clothing, moreover, Florian attributes to the clothing of this same orphaned African by three sons of a cloth merchant, who pieced together "three half-ells" to clothe the stranger. Ducharte, writing in this century, suggests that "the ancient Harlequin was a phallophore, and, inasmuch as some of the phallophores of the ancient theatre played the part of African slaves, it is thought that Harlequin might be their direct descendant," thereby explaining his black mask. Harlequin's authentic mask, he continues, suggests "a cat, a satyr, and the sort of negro that the Renaissance painter portrayed." When we recall that early Harlequin figures wore a phallus, the connections between him and Western representations of the African are even stronger.[31]

These are all, of course, myths of origins. Nevertheless, the visual evidence does suggest at least the myth of an African connection with the origins of Harlequin's mask, in terms of both its features and its color. So stylized did Harlequin's role become that he could simply point to one of the black patches on his suit and become invisible, a trope that has become central to the black literary tradition. The following three figures, from the late seventeenth and early eighteenth centuries, suggest this African connection (illustrations appear after this chapter):

1. Illustration 1, "Harlequin in Love," is a frontispiece to *Le bon ménage* in J. P. C. de Florian's *Théâtre* (Paris, 1786). Note the "negroid" profile of Harlequin.
2. Illustration 2 is the frontispiece to C. Cotolendi's *Arliquiniana*, a work printed at Paris in 1694, from the British Museum.
3. Illustration 3 is an eighteenth-century German watercolor, now at the McGill University Library.

It is this watercolor that suggests a connection with minstrelsy, just as Illustration 1 underscores Harlequin's "African" origins; those peculiar English harlequinades performed and published between 1783 and 1870 and which contain figures of the black as Harlequin combine both blackness and minstrelsy. I am thinking here especially of *Harlequin Mungo; or Peep into the Tower* (1789); *Furibond, or Harlequin Negro* (1807); and *Cowardy, Cowardy, Custard; or Harlequin Jim Crow and the Magic Mustard Pot* (1836). In the first two harlequinades, a black slave, about to commit suicide, is transformed into Harlequin by a wizard, marries the master's daughter (who is or becomes Columbine), and after long and confusing chases lives happily ever after. In the third harlequinade, however, the figure of Jim Crow from the American minstrel stage makes his appearance. In a lithograph dated 1819 called "Four and Twenty Hobby Horses," a close-up reveals the connections between the figures of Harlequin and of Minstrel Man to be explicit, although minstrelsy was not officially "born" until a few years later. (Illustrations 4a and 4b.) A cartoon from *Judge Magazine* of 1888 makes the Harlequin-minstrelsy connection explicit. (Illustrations 5, 6, 7, 8.)

We have seen here the inherent nobility of Harlequin the Black Clown transformed by degrees into the ignoble black minstrel figure. Their relationship is that of archetype to stereotype, translated through repetition and reversal in a dialectical relationship analogous to that of the slave narratives and the Confederate romance. (Illustration 9.) The black and white mask of Harlequin, then, is split into the masks of Bones and Tambo, the two characters central to minstrelsy. These stand as examples of what I call Signifyin(g) textual relations, or critical signification.

Critical signification is a useful concept in explaining these black–white relations. The relation of Phillis Wheatley's poetry to that of Milton and Pope, and to the aesthetic theories of Kant and Hume, is a Signifyin(g) relation. The intertextual relationship between the slave narrative as a body of discourse and its counter-genre, the Confederate romance or the plantation novel, is also a relation of Signifyin(g) structures. The body of literature through which we define the New Negro Renaissance repeats and reverses the racist presuppositions of turn-of-the-century American pseudo-science and social Darwinism. Minstrel Man and Bones's bifurcated presence is a signification upon the half-black, half-white mask of Harlequin, as mediated through the dozen harlequinades in which a wizard transforms a black slave into Harlequin and sets him free. It is through such formal textual relations that we begin to understand the arbitrariness of both the signifier and the signified, the latter of which divides reality arbitrarily, culture by culture, language by language, discourse by discourse. But it is this very chiastic imperative in Afro-American literature that helps us to understand the tautology at the heart of Black Aesthetic criticism and the need of subsequent critics of black literature to relate their project to what is vaguely known as contemporary literary theory.

In the final chapter of this book, on the Signifying Monkey and on *Mumbo Jumbo,* I supplement my analysis of race and superstructure with an analysis of the idea of a transcendent signified, a belief in an essence called blackness, a presence our tradition has tried of late to will into being, in order to negate two and a half millennia of its figuration as an absence. As healthy politically as such a gesture was, as revealing as it was in this country and abroad of the very arbitrariness of the received sign of blackness itself, we must also criticize the idealism, the notion of essence, implicit in even this important political gesture. To think of oneself as free simply because one can claim—one can utter—the negation of an assertion is not to think deeply enough. *Négritude* already constituted such a claim of blackness as a transcendent signified, of a full and sufficient presence; but to make such a claim, to feel the necessity to make such a claim, is already to reveal too much about perceived absence and desire. It is to take the terms of one's assertion from a discourse whose universe has been determined by an Other. Even the terms of one's so-called spontaneous desire have been presupposed by the Other. I render this critique of blackness as a transcendent signified in order to help break through the enclosure of negation.

The enclosure of negation is only one trap. That sort of intellectual indenture, which we might call, after Jean Price-Mars, "bovarysme collectif," is quite another, and equally deadly, trap. Jules De Gaultier, expanding upon Price-Mars, defines bovarysme as the phenomenon of being "fated to obey the suggestion of an external milieu, for lack of auto-suggestion from within."[32] The challenge of black literary criticism is to derive principles of literary criticism from the black tradition itself, as defined in the idiom of critical theory but also in the idiom that constitutes the language of blackness, the Signifyin(g) difference that makes the black tradition our very own. To borrow mindlessly, or to vulgarize, a critical theory from another tradition is to satisfy de Gaultier's definition of bovarysme; but it is also to satisfy, in the black idiom, Ishmael Reed's definition of "The Talking Andriod." The sign of the successful negotiation of this precipice of indenture, of slavish imitation, is that the black critical essay refers to two contexts, two traditions, the Western and the Black. Each utterance, then, is "double-voiced."

In a 1925 review of James Weldon Johnston's *The Book of American Negro Spirituals,* W. E. B. Du Bois argued that evidence of critical activity is a sign of a tradition's sophistication, since criticism implies an awareness of the process of art itself and is a second-order reflection upon those primary texts that define a tradition and its canon. Insofar as we, critics of the black tradition, master our craft, we serve both to preserve our own traditions and to shape their direction. All great writers demand great critics. The imperatives of our task are clear.

The chapters of this book, ranging from theoretical to practical criticism, exemplify various modes of reading. The black literary and critical traditions need all sorts of close readings; the body of practical criticism that enabled new theories of reading to emerge in the Western tradition has yet to be created in the black traditions. The tradition needs readings of several kinds before it can move into the mainstream of critical debate in the profession. Such a move, it seems to me, is a desirable one, since ultimately our subject is literary discourse and not the blackness of blackness. Nevertheless, I am not advocating a new form of de Gaultier's "bovarysm," in which we seek to imitate, from the critics we have decided to be most "like," "all that can be imitated, everything exterior, appearance, gesture, intonation, and dress." To do so would be to repeat the mistake of a neo-Romantic poet such as Countee Cullen, for whom form was a container into which he could pour a precious and black content. Rather than proselytizing for one warring faction of criticism or another, or vulgarizing this or that theory by reducing it to summary or method, this book seeks to encourage a plurality of readings, as various as the discrete texts in our literary tradition, and as black. These essays address issues fundamental to critical theory and to the nature of black literary discourse. My subject is the interpretation of literature.

This book attempts to achieve its unity from the stress each chapter brings to bear upon the play of the signifier, and from the belief that, as Rene Girard puts it,

> great writers apprehend intuitively and concretely, through the medium of their art, if not formally, the system in which they were first imprisoned together with their contemporaries. Literary interpretation must be systematic because it is the continuation of literature. It should formalize implicit or already half explicit systems. . . . The value of a critical thought depends not on how cleverly it manages to disguise its own systematic nature or on how much literary substance it really embraces, comprehends, and makes articulate. The goal may be ambitious but it is not outside the scope of literary criticism. Failure to reach it should be condemned but not the attempt. Everything else has already been done.[33]

In an essay called "For Whom Does One Write?" collected in *What Is Literature?* Jean-Paul Sartre asks none too rhetorically, "To whom does Richard Wright address himself?" Sartre's answer helps us to answer our own central question, "For Whom Does the Critic of Black Literature Write?"

> Each of Wright's works contains what Baudelaire would have called "a double simultaneous postulation"; each word refers to two contexts; two forces are applied simultaneously to each phrase and determine the incomparable tension of his tale. Had he spoken to the whites alone, he might have turned out to be

more prolix, more didactic, and more abusive; to the negroes alone, still more elliptical, more of a confederate and more elegiac. In the first case, his work might have come close to satire; in the second, to prophetic lamentations. Jeremiah spoke only to the Jews. But Wright, a writer for a split public, has been able to maintain and go beyond this split. He has made it the pretext for a work of art.[34]

How does this split readership affect the work of criticism? The most obvious way, it seems to me, is in exactly what one can take for granted. While a reader from within the black tradition might need no footnote on T. Thomas Fortune, *Cane,* or *Signifying,* that same reader may need data about "The Lyrical Ballads," "East Coker," or John Donne. The problem is compounded by the need I feel to establish the very texts I explicate, to make available to the reader *my* text milieu. Only footnoting and extensive quotation works only where a readership shares familiarity with a common body of texts. Not even other critics of black texts share the sort of familiarity we assume when interpreting canonical texts; we are still in the process of recovering and establishing the texts in the tradition, a process necessarily preceding canon formation.

What we are able to assume about our readers is related to the complex matter of "originality." How "original" is the use of contemporary theory to read black texts? Perhaps only critics who are familiar with black texts can ascertain this, since only they understand the received interpretations that serve as discourse on that text. What is "original" about Edward Said's use of post-structuralist theory to analyze representations of "the Oriental" is his "application"; indeed, the application of a mode of reading to explicate a black text changes both the received theory and received ideas about the text. When this occurs, the results are "original."

We write, it seems to me, primarily for other critics of literature. Through shared theoretical presuppositions, the arduous process of "cultural translation," if not resolved, is most certainly not hindered. To maintain yet go beyond this split text milieu is our curse and, of course, our challenge, as is the fact that we must often resurrect the texts in our tradition before we can begin to explicate them. To render major contributions to contemporary theory's quest to "save the text," in Hartman's phrase, is our splendid opportunity. Unlike critics in almost every other literary tradition, almost all that we have to say about our literature is new. What critics of the Western tradition can make an even remotely similar claim? Jeremiah could speak only to the Jews; we, however, must address two audiences, the Jews and the Babylonians, whose interests are distinct yet overlapping in the manner of interlocking sets.

I would say that the most conscious presupposition of my work is that one repeats, as it were, in order to produce a black and critical difference, to echo Barbara Johnson. As Said argues in "On Repetition" about Marx's narrative strategy in the *Eighteenth Brumaire of Louis Bonaparte,* Marx's intention is "not to validate Bonaparte's claims but to give facts by emending their apparent direction." We are able to achieve difference through repetition, as Ralph Ellison put it, we "change the joke and slip the yoke." Marx himself in *Eighteenth Brumaire* states the process in this way: "The beginner who has learned a new language always retranslates it into his mother tongue: he can only be said to have appropriated the spirit of the new language and to be able to express himself in it freely when he can manipulate it without reference to the old, and when he forgets his original language while using the new one." Does this sort of repetition, Said asks at the end of his essay, "enhance or degrade a fact?" His creative response bears repetition here: "But the question brings forth consciousness of two where there had been repose in one; and such knowledge of course, like procreation, cannot really be reversed. Thereafter the problems multiply. Naturally or not, filiatively or affiliatively, is the question." The speculative and interpretive chapters of this book chart one critic's adventure through the jungle of criticism, as he wrestles eagerly with that dense and compelling terrain, and with Said's rhetorical question.[35]

If I had to define my relationship to contemporary criticism, I would turn, as I frequently do, to Ralph Ellison. As Ellison said to Ishmael Reed in an interview published in 1978:

> So that's the way it continues to go: anywhere I find a critic who has an idea or concept that seems useful, I grab it. Eclecticism is the word. Like a jazz musician who creates his own style out of the styles around him, I play by ear.[36]

Although all theory is text-specific and can tend to break down when mechanically applied outside its own tradition, other aspects of theory are more broadly relevant than to one text milieu. Free indirect discourse is free indirect discourse, no matter in what literary tradition it appears. Just as Zora Neale Hurston, for example, imitated the story-telling devices of the black oral tradition, so too is her lyrical novel, *Their Eyes Were Watching God* (1937), drawn after the manner of Flaubert and Woolf. Her text, in this sense, is double-voiced. The critic of her text, moreover, must also be double-voiced. The challenge of the critic of comparative black literature is to allow contemporary theoretical developments to inform his or her readings of discrete black texts but also to generate his or her own theories from the black idiom itself. The challenge of theorists generally is to realize that what we have for too long called "the tradition" is merely one tradition of several and that we have much to learn from the systematic exploration of new canons. That which unites those of us whose canonical texts differ is the shared concern with theory that arises from these texts. It is here that we are to find common ground; it is here that we can bridge text milieus. It is here that the hegemony of the Western tradition at last can be seen to be the arbitrary and ideological structure that it is.

I end this chapter with a quote from great blues artist Junior Parker: "Anybody can boil up some greens, but a good cook—a good one—has a special way of seasoning 'em that ain't like nobody else's. So anybody can do it, but it's only somebody who can do it their own way."[37] I have tried to do it my own way; this, after all, is the imperative of all literary criticism. Perhaps critics of other literatures can find something useful in my metaphors of Esu and signification for interpretation and literary history.

1. "Harlequin in Love." From Allardyce Nicoll, *The World of Harlequin* (New York: Cambridge University Press, 1963). Reprinted by permission of Cambridge University Press.

2. "L'Harlequino Bergamasco." From Allardyce Nicoll, *The World of Harlequin* (New York: Cambridge University Press, 1963). Reprinted by permission of Cambridge University Press.

3. "Harlequin." From Allardyce Nicoll, *The World of Harlequin* (New York: Cambridge University Press, 1963). Reprinted by permission of Cambridge University Press.

4A. "Four and Twenty Hobby Horses," litho, 1819. From the collection of Brooke Baldwin.

4B. "Four and Twenty Hobby Horses," detail.

5. "Harlequin." *Judge Magazine,* January 21, 1888. From the collection of Brooke Baldwin.

6. "Harlequin," frame 1.

7. "Harlequin," frame 2.

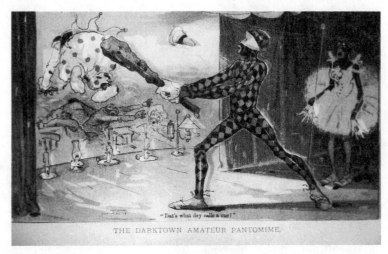

"Dat's what dey calls a cue!"

THE DARKTOWN AMATEUR PANTOMIME

8. "Harlequin," frame 3.

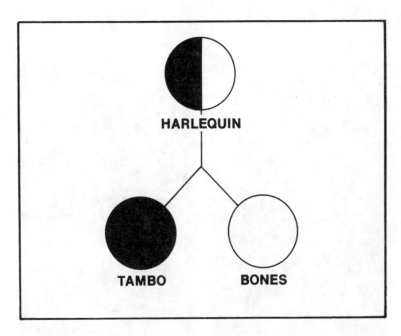

HARLEQUIN

TAMBO   BONES

9. Harlequin's black and white mask splits into the masks of Tambo and Bones, the two central characters of minstrelsy.

The Literature
of the Slave

[If one can establish] that the negro intellect is fully equal to that of the white race . . . you not only take away the best argument for keeping him in subjection, but you take away the possibility of doing so. *Prima facie,* however, the fact that he *is* a slave, is conclusive against the argument for his freedom, as it is against his equality of claim in respect of intellect. . . . Whenever the negro shall be fully fit for freedom, he will make himself free, and no power on earth can prevent him.

William Gilmore Simms

Were I to state here, frankly and categorically, that the primary purpose of this book is to write the negro out of America and the secondary object is to write him (and manifold millions of other black and bicolored caitiffs, little better than himself) out of existence, God's simple truth would be told.

Hinton Helper

· 2 ·

Phillis Wheatley and the "Nature of the Negro"

It is difficult to begin to understand the political and social import that the literature of the African bore in the eighteenth century. A fairly detailed study of the critical reception of Phillis Wheatley by her contemporaries perhaps can enable us to understand the curious extraliterary uses to which black literacy has been put in French and English critical discourse *and* in the texts of the Afro-American tradition as well.

I

The matter of the nature of the Negro was one of intense speculation and enthusiastic surmise during and after "the case of James Somersett, a Negro."[1] Samuel Estwick, the assistant agent for the island of Barbados,[2] was so enraged by Lord Mansfield's judgment in the case that he, by his own admission, dashed off an impassioned, open reply near the end of 1772.[3] He significantly expanded a second edition so that his argument might be a more cogent one. Estwick's anonymous first edition was meant essentially to rebut Lord Mansfield's verdict in favor of the Negro by demonstrating that Negro slavery was an innovation in the history of human institutions, one unknown to common law and "totally different" from ancient villeinage. His second edition, however, contained this argument, expanded to address what he now decided was to be the crux of Hargray's argument.[4]

In what must stand as one of the most peculiar assortments of popular and philosophical speculation on the matter, Estwick, by way of Soame Jenyns, John Locke, David Hume, and Pope, among others, structures a carefully considered affront on the nature of the Negro. Estwick's tract reveals tellingly the peculiar fashion in which romance, myth, and metaphor, coupled with rather imaginative anatomical and philosophical disquisitions, meet in the vulgar practical application of the metaphor of a chain of being as a rigid construct of nature, which somehow is held to exist in fact.

The urge to draw distinctions, Estwick argues, is perhaps the fundamental urge of modern science, uniting human reason and imagination in a grand synthesis as noble and as old as Aristotle. Nevertheless, modern man somehow flinches when confronted with the awful truth about his own condition. Why should that same principle found in nature, which allows man to separate both "vegetable and mineral kingdoms of this world" into "systems morally perfect," comprised of hundreds of subdivisions, not hold true for the varieties of man? The suggestion that mankind is above the principles of nature, profoundly uniform and "democratic" in every particular, can be folly, Estwick concludes, or else a species of hubris resoundingly aberrant.

Not only is this supposition an affront to reason; it defies that divine sanction accorded the great chain itself:

> Does this not seem to break in upon and unlink the great chain of Heaven, which in due gradations joins and unites the whole with all its parts? May it not be more perfective of the system to say, that human nature is a class, comprehending an order of beings, of which man is the genus, divided into distinct and separate species of man? All other species of the animal kingdom have their marks of distinction: why should man be universally indiscriminate one to the other?[5]

The crux of the issue at hand, Estwick argues, is with what measure philosophy should determine that elusive "characteristic difference" between man and man. That which makes man a distinct creature from beasts, according to "the great Mr. Locke," is the exercise of reason. The measure, Estwick suggests, must not be reason, since Locke suggests that beasts to some degree share in the exercise of reason; it is, rather, the existence of a "moral sense." Estwick reasons that the single "faculty of the human mind," shared by all manner of the varieties of men, is "the capacity of perceiving moral relations." Further, and quite crucially, the "compound ratio of its exercise" must stand as nature's own way for men to draw distinctions among men. Where the faculty of reason serves "to raise [man] from the tenth to the ten thousandth link of the chain," so too does the "compound ratio" of the exertion of moral sense mark man from man. These differences are nature's, Estwick maintains, and signify a "purpose" for which the varieties of man must be best suited, just as surely as nature has signified distinct inherent functions for the elephant and the flea.

The disquisition proceeds by citing Hume's theory of tropical degeneration of the human mind. The tropical climate leaves the mind "utterly incapable of all the higher attainments."[6] Moreover, Hume maintains, "there are four or five different *kinds* of men," by which he meant species.[7] The idea of multiple human species of men proved compelling to Estwick but, perhaps surprisingly, only because he found it hyperbolic. "In order to have different *species* of men," Estwick comments on Hume's suggestion, it did not seem to him to be "at all necessary to have four or five different kinds."[8] There is "but one" genus or "kind," that is, "mankind," comprised of "sorts" or "species" of men.[9] Then, citing Hume fully on the metonymic relationship between "white" and "civilization"—"no arts, no sciences"—Estwick contrasts that by which Hume "marks the difference betwixt the several species of men," with that by which Estwick does.[10] Hume, as did Locke, distinguished man one from another "by their natural capacity or incapacity of exerting in degree the rational powers, or faculties of understanding."

Such was the distinction Locke employed to distinguish "between man and brutes."[11] Estwick, on the other hand, draws his boundaries with "the moral sense or moral powers." The exercise of reason, called for as a privileged category by Locke and Hume, was an unsatisfactory one because blacks could obviously read and write, skills learned through imitation and repetition:

Nor have I been able to find one author, by whom I could discover that there was any sort of plan or system of morality conceived by these tribes of Africa, or practised among them. Their
barbarity to their children debases their nature even below that
of brutes. Their cruelty to their aged parents is akin to this. They
have a religion, it is true; but it is a religion, [not] in kind, but in
species; and verifying that unerring truth of Mr. Pope, that
    "Order is heaven's first law; and this contest,
    Some are, and must be, greater than the rest."[12]

In sum, Estwick concludes, these physical and metaphysical "in-
superable barriers" demonstrate conclusively that the Negro is a
man apart from "the inhabitants of Europe" and destined to remain so. His proper place in European society is to serve "as
articles of its trade and commerce only." The African, therefore,
was consigned a slave by nature.

That Estwick's *Consideration on the Negro Cause* is emblem-
atic of shared concerns of European and American philosophers
wrestling with the unreconcilable contradictions of human enslavement can be gleaned from a reading of the pamphlet debate
over African mental capacity which raged in Philadelphia later
that same year, and especially in the curious history of Phillis,
Negro servant to John Wheatley of Boston, and the curious history of the critical reception to her slim volume of *Poems on
Various Subjects, Religious and Moral.*

Perhaps it is appropriately ironic that Phillis Wheatley—who
contained so painstakingly her poetic concerns within highly con-
trived and classically structured decasyllabic lines of closed heroic
couplets, which seem in retrospect to have been about the direct
imitation of neoclassical poetic models rather than the imitation
of nature or the fanciful invention of peculiarly American forms—
would be judged by critics whose poetics seemed to be grounded
not in the praise of imitation and artifice but in the praise of a
supposed unmediated relation between genius and nature. A
major shift in the first principles of neoclassical poetics involved a
fundamental reorientation of emphasis from what was, in the
most general and inclusive terms, called "art" to its equally abstract and inclusive opposite, "nature."[13] In Sir William Temple's
essays "Upon Poetry" and "Upon Ancient and Modern Learning" (1690), Dryden's "Origin and Progress of Satire" (1693),

key passages in Pope's *Essay on Criticism,* Voltaire's *Essay upon Epic Poetry* (1727), Thomas Blackwell's *Enquiry into the Life and Writings of Homer* (1735), Johnson's "Prefaces to Shakespeare" (1765), Vico's *Princippi d'una scienza nuova* (1744), and Herder's "Briefweschsel uber Ossian und die lieder alter Volker" (1773), "neoclassical" historians and critics

> began increasingly to examine the special rhetorical circumstances, environmental causes, and historical setting of the author's production—his gifts, education, life, audience, geographic location, climate, nationality, language, and the spirit or condition of his age—thus providing, in general, a variety of explanations and justifications of the peculiar forms and qualities of the works of poets in different social conditions, ages, and nations.[14]

A second profound shift of emphasis, which occurred concomitantly with a shift from the concern with art to nature, involved a marked concern for the nature of the poet which often entailed attempted correlations between untutored, natural "genius" and "imagination" on the one hand,[15] and the effects of temperature, geography, and race on the other. This direct relationship between environment and genius had been made in English neoclassical criticism as early as 1690. Sir William Temple's "theory about the concentration between the variable English weather and the odd humor of Englishmen was one of the earliest instances of the explanation of literature by climatic conditions."[16] Joseph Wharton, in his essay on Pope published in 1756, formalized this relationship into a maxim; the proper critic could "never completely relish, or adequately understand, any author, especially any ancient, except we constantly keep in our eye, his climate, his country, and his age."[17] Three years later, Oliver Goldsmith, writing in his *Enquiry into the Present State of Polite Learning,* argued adamantly that criticism must "understand the nature of the climate and country &c. before it gives rules to direct taste. In other words, every country should have a national system of criticism."[18] But both Hume and Lord Kames (Hume in 1748 in his essay "Of National Characters"[19] and Kames in 1774 in his *Sketches of a History of Man*[20]) expressed skepticism of the role of climate or geographical conditions as the paramount variable in the forging of genius. Robert Wood's *An Essay on the Original*

Genius and Writing of Homer,[21] published first in 1769, related
his study of the topography of the site of Troy to Homer's depictions. Robert Lowth, in *De sacra poesi Hebraeorum,*[22] published
in 1753, attempted much the same thing by comparing the character of Hebrew poetry with the Palestinian landscape as well as
the imagery of the Old Testament. These late eighteenth-century
neoclassical impulses, combined with a dramatically increased
degree of speculation by "Americans" on the effects of environment on political, religious, and cultural institutions, determined
the character of the critical response to the writing of African
slaves between 1773 and 1831.[23]

Locke's denial of the existence of innate ideas, along with the
discovery first by explorers and then by anatomists that the human
species existed in a number of variations, "necessitated the assumption that variations within the species derived from some
less august sponsorship" than from God's design.[24] The variability
of humans arose, then, of necessity, from variations in their environment. Rather than the soul, the environment could be and
need be transformed to usher in either the inner or, more importantly, the outer drama of "salvation." Human nature, however,
as Benjamin Rush put is so bluntly in 1773, is everywhere "the
same."

The assertions of the sameness of human nature presupposed
not only that the distinctions between peoples were circumstantial
and arbitrary but also that these distinctions could well be
changed. "This postulation of quintessential human nature," Winthrop Jordan maintains, "formed the critical point of contact
between environmentalist thinking and the political ideology of
the Revolution."[25] The idea of "natural" rights, then, was one that
had as a corollary the idea that humans were everywhere in essence the same, although their environments might somehow
make them appear to be different, and that they were entitled by
this very fact to all of the attendant "natural" rights of humanity.
As early as 1764, James Otis's *The Rights of the British Colonies
Asserted and Proved* declared boldly that "the Colonists are by
the law of nature free born, as indeed all men are, white or
black."[26] Thus, John Wesley could declare in 1774 that the sus-
pected "stupidity therefore in our plantations is not natural; otherwise than it is the natural effect of their condition."[27] Similarly,

Levi Hart could in the same atmosphere denounce racial slavery as "a flagrant violation of the law of nature, of the natural rights of mankind,"[28] rather than as a violation of some unwritten covenant between God and man. The ramifications of environmentalism and the natural rights of man are outlined sharply in the Quaker David Cooper's summation of the larger implications of the continued existence of slavery and the colonists' declaration of certain self-evident truths:

> If these solemn truths, uttered at such an awful crisis, are self-evident: unless we can shew that the African race are not men, words can hardly express the amazement which naturally arises on reflecting, that the very people who make these pompous declarations are slaveholders, and, by their legislative conduct, tell us, that these blessings were only meant to be the rights of *white-men* not of all men.[29]

By the time of publication of Phillis Wheatley's *Poems* in September 1773, discussions over innate and acquired mental and moral qualities had become the subject of an impassioned and bitter controversy which reached the public in the form of a pamphlet debate carried along by argument and rebuttal in Philadelphia.

In an anonymously published pamphlet, printed at least four times in 1773 under the title of *An Address to the Inhabitants of the British Settlement in America, Upon Slave-Keeping*, Benjamin Rush, a noted Philadelphia physician, not only served to focus the philosophical problems of racial slavery in the British settlements of America on the matter of the nature of the African but also became the first antislavery advocate to cite the poetry of Phillis Wheatley as an irrefutable proof of the African's mental equality with the European and of the African's fundamentally human nature. Rush's argument not only intends to refute David Hume's "Of National Characters" but also serves as a powerful summation of the philosophy of natural rights which had, notwithstanding James Otis and the implacable Anthony Benezet, been wanting a solid context for its application. If Estwick's hurriedly revised second edition had been a sign of a profound recasting of the terms of the debate against slavery, then Rush's modest essay would determine the contours of a debate that would involve Richard Nisbet and Edward Long, Thomas Jefferson and the Abbé Grégoire, Voltaire and Benjamin Franklin, Henri Christophe and Ralph Waldo Emerson. It is a debate, glibly described journalistically today, in the coded terms of nature versus nurture, but which had its origins in the complex quandary of the supposed composition of human nature and the suggested scales by which this commodity would be measured.

Rush situates his argument in Africa initially, then accounts for any "debasement" from the European ideal as being "occasioned by climate," and any debasement from the African "ideal" as being the result of the institution of slavery.

> And here I need hardly say anything in favor of the intellects of the Negroes, or of their capacities for virtue and happiness, although these have been supposed by some to be inferior to those of the inhabitants of Europe. The accounts which travellers give us of their ingenuity, humanity, and strong attachment to their parents, relations, friends, and country, show us that they are equal to the Europeans, when we allow for the diversity of temper and genius which is occasioned by climate.[30]

To allow for "the diversity of temper and genius," which is virtually determined by "climate," was an unusually liberal and sophisticated rebuttal of the idea of an absolute system of aesthetics, such as had been espoused in early neoclassical poetics. Rush's thesis is a seminal one, based as it is on a quasi-aesthetic relativism and its corollary environmentalism.

Citing *The Spectator*[31] as his reference, Rush maintains that already "we have many well attested anecdotes of as sublime and disinterested virtue among them as ever adorned a Roman or Christian character." Again, in a footnote, he cites as evidence the example of "a free Negro Girl":

> There is now in the town of Boston a free Negro Girl, about eighteen years of age, who has been but nine years in the country, whose singular genius and accomplishments are such as not only do honour to her sex, but to human nature. Several of her poems have been printed, and read with pleasure by the public.[32]

Well before her book of verse was to appear, Phillis, "a free Negro Girl," had been called upon as a living refutation of the charge of innate Negro inferiority and, concomitantly, as an ideal example of the miraculous effects of a shift in environment. Not only was Phillis a "Negro," but a "Girl" as well, whose "singular genius" did "honour to her sex." As the "free Negro Girl" in Boston demonstrates, even the Africans brought to the British settlements expressly for slavery can transcend their condition within an ideal environment. Rush's solution to the problem of the fate of the slaves, once manumitted, reflects his concern for this crucial role of environment in shaping character. The matter will be resolved through literacy. The functions of literacy, and the role of the arts, are meant to be essential to the ascertaining of the nature of the African's "civilization" and, therefore, of the nature of the African. Too rooted in eternal verities to be labeled romantic, Benjamin Rush nevertheless epitomizes a major reorientation of values in early American aesthetic theory, which in turn reflects the increased demand for the protection of "natural" rights as well as the marked secularization of the "equality" of man.

Perhaps because of the refreshingly novel terms in which Rush had cast his brief against the enslavement of human beings, there is no little irony in the fact that a passing remark about the sanction by scripture of slavery[33] should have become the premise for a strident rebuttal of Rush's pamphlet. Richard Nisbet, "an emotionally unstable West Indian living in Pennsylvania who later turned to the Negro's defense and closed his life in tragic insanity,"[34] undertook "a defense of the West Indian Planters" in a pamphlet published as a direct response to Rush's *Address*.

Published anonymously, *Slavery Not Forbidden by Scripture: Or, a Defense of the West Indian Planters*[35] struck hard. After citing the Old Testament chapter and verse to reveal the scriptural sanction of slavery, Nisbet addresses Rush's contentions of innate African mental capacity.

In a remark which he employs rhetorically to introduce in a long footnote Hume's estimation of the national character of the blacks, Nisbet explicitly concedes Rush's suggestion that environment could affect "intellect":

> It is impossible to determine, with accuracy, whether their intellects or ours are superior, as individuals, no doubt, have not the same opportunities of improving as we have: However, on the whole, it seems probable, that they are a much inferior race of men to the whites, in every respect.[36]

Individual differences can be accounted for, Nisbet confesses, by
"the same opportunities of improving." Yet individual exceptions
do not alter the balance: "on the whole," the Africans "are a
much inferior race of men to the whites."

The debate, Nisbet proceeds, must be settled in terms of the
"general character" of their "genius." Only here can it be ascertained fairly if their enslavement runs counter to "natural" law,
since a biblical sanction is evident. The problem is one of exception and the rule:

> A few instances may be found, of African negroes possessing
> virtues and becoming ingenious; but still, what I have said, with
> regard to their general character, I dare say, most people ac-
> quainted with them, will agree. [Referring the reader to a foot-
> note, in much the same manner and at the identical place in his
> argument as had Rush, Nisbet concludes that the author of the
> address gives a single example of a Negro girl writing a few silly
> poems to prove that the blacks are not inferior to whites in under-
> standing.][37]

The blacks, unlike the remainder of the world's people of color,
have alone failed to cut "a figure in history." Not only had the Africans failed visibly to make a figure in history; they indeed had no
history and, the "few silly poems" of a Negro girl in Boston notwithstanding, no arts. The Africans' "natural rights," Nisbet concludes, center on their place on the scale of nature, a place determined by their lack of "genius."

Nisbet's pamphlet demanded a rebuttal. Rush's *A Vindication
of the Address, To the Inhabitants of the British Settlements, on
the Slavery of the Negroes in America, In Answer to a Pamphlet*
appeared just as anonymously as had his and Nisbet's earlier essays.[38] Premise by premise, Rush redresses Nisbet's argument with
travelers' accounts, eyewitness testimony of brutality to slaves,
and even the direct quotation of the clergy. The subjective biases
of European travelers, along with certain blatant barriers to the
meaningful exchange of knowledge, make our knowledge of the
Africans little more than a motley array of rumor and hearsay.

Despite the role of the observer in recording the nature of African civilizations, however, Rush outlines in a brilliant summation the fundamental premise on which all natural rights philoso-

phy was based, as well as those elements by which the distinctions among men could be explained:

> Human nature is the same in all Ages and Countries; and all the difference we perceive in its Characters in respect to Virtue and Vice, Knowledge and Ignorance, may be accounted for from Climate, Country, Degrees of Civilization, form of Government, or other accidental causes.[39]

In a rather rhetorical flourish, Rush concludes his rebuttal of the "African Genius" by devoting four pages to exemplifying the subjectivity of judgment and the relativity of meaning and value. His argument turns on the idea of an absolute and constant human nature, one infinitely adaptable and plastic. Echoing Beattie's *Essay,* Rush contends that were we able to free ourselves of the prejudices of our point in history, then we would be free of the illusion of unbridgeable human differences and distinctions which are merely veiled appearances.

Rush's position on the exigencies of interpretation, on the role of the interpreter in the determination of meaning, was an unprecedented one in the American discourses on African aesthetics. His was a position rooted in the biological sciences, but rooted as well in the theory of those "rights" which were "natural" to man. For these rights to exist, they must be applicable to all varieties of man. To place the blacks below the whites because of color or custom was to abnegate the very concept of natural rights. The idea of hierarchy, in this sense, Rush implied, reflected the fiction of an unchanging universe, in which no demands were made of the past and no more demands could be made against the prevailing order of society.[40] As the anonymous author of *Personal Slavery Established* attested on his title page, in a famous epigraph from Pope, "Whatever is, is right."[41]

Profoundly, Rush suggests that what passes for visible indications of an uncommon humanity between the African and the European is merely a distinct relation each bears to nature and to art. "Where is the difference," he asks, "between the African savage, whose scanty wants are supplied by Nature; and the European Nobleman, whose numerous wants are supplied by Art?"[42] Importantly, Rush viciously attacks the idea of using "genius" or "the arts" to measure man's place in nature; this is what constitutes the ultimate hubris, because it is a crime against nature it-self. Nisbet's hubris, Rush concludes with great passion, was "the Attack you have made upon the Rights of Mankind."[43]

Impassioned and detailed biblical exegeses, which for two and a half centuries had tried to fit the rapidly proliferating kinds of persons into an order ordained by God; the wildly speculative natural philosophy which clung, rather perilously, to the metaphor of the chain; the bemused arrangements, by cranial capacity, of the "progressively" larger skulls of ape and man; the creative and imaginative descriptions of black humanity repeated with such enthusiasm by the European discoveries of Africa; and a received metaphorical system which had consistently made the color black analogous with the shade of evil—all these complex matters lay buried beneath the debate over the natural rights of the African and his or her fitness for enslavement. As surely as the temporalization of the chain of being had led eventually to its demise as a valid construct by which philosophy could account for the order of things, so too had the American colonists' fundamental belief in a quantity they could call "the rights of man" led them to declare a belief in the determining power of environment on the reshaping of a human nature which had to be, by definition, "everywhere the same."[44]

As crucial as the year 1773 proved to be to the American colonists' struggle for independence from the crown, it also proved to be the determining year for speculation of the Negro's place in nature as well as for the manner in which the arts were to figure in the debate over slavery, a debate no longer seriously thought to be resolvable by scripture. It is ironic that Phillis Wheatley, who so painstakingly located her poetry within a larger and peculiarly Puritan tradition of Christian piety, would have her slim volume of verse utilized as prima facie evidence in a fundamentally secular debate over the rights of man.

II

For reasons as various as they are complex, it would appear that, had Phillis Wheatley not published, another African slave's poetry would have served equally well as a refutation of certain commonly repeated assumptions about the nature of the Negro.

Although the word would reappear in the reviews of Wheatley's *Poems*, "genius" was not her province to occupy. The formal gap between Milton, Pope, Gray, Addison, Watts, and Wheatley would appear to be profound, although she rather self-consciously assumed these as her models.[45]

Although viewers seem to have found much in her work that is genuinely "poetic," her verse, criticized rarely, seems to have been read primarily in nonliterary terms and for other than literary purposes. The nature of the function Wheatley served between 1773 and 1831 can be described usefully but analogously by two tropes. Wheatley and her poems bore a relation of metaphor and metonymy in the language of the criticism her verse elicited. Metaphors of her blackness—a blackness both spiritual and physical—punctuate her critics' essays as they do her own poetry, as in "To Maecenas," for example, and in "On Being Brought from Africa to America,"[46] which was often quoted in the earliest reviews of her book.[47] When Bernard Romans,[48] writing about the "capacity" of Africans to be other than slaves, terms Wheatley a mere exception, the figure he utilizes to characterize her is that of "a Phaenix of her race," which bears a certain resonance to Wheatley's own lines on the mutability of blackness:

> 'Twas mercy brought me from my *Pagan* land,
> Taught my benighted soul to understand
> That there's a God, that there's a Saviour too:
> Once I redemption neither sought nor knew,
> Some view our race with scornful eye,
> "Their Colour is a diabolic die."
> Remember, *Christians, Negroes,* black as *Cain,*
> May be refin'd, and join th'Angelic train.[49]

After 1831, however, the metaphorical functions Wheatley is made to serve shift somewhat.[50]

Metonymically, however, her relation to the potential of other black people to assume "cultivation" remained consistent in critical writings well into the twentieth century, in part because of Jefferson's use of her as the written record of the sum total of the African's potential for "civilization," followed by the manifestly felt need of blacks and their sympathizers to refute Jefferson's claims.[51] Metonymically, Wheatley bears a relation to Africa and

to the mental capacity of all other African people in a manner remarkably similar to that which Aristotle and Alexander, Milton,
and Newton bear to the white race in the tropes frequently repeated in the practical criticism of her work, and in numerous
disquisitions on the nature of the Negro.[52] It would not be incor-
rect to characterize the relation of Phillis Wheatley to the black
race and the relation of her *Poems* to "black art" as a relation of
synecdoche.[53] Because the history of the criticism of the poetry of
slaves and ex-slaves published in English between 1773 and 1831
is in large part the history of the critical reception of Phillis
Wheatley, a short reading of her poetry could be of sufficient relevance to sustain a digression from an explication of her critics'
judgments.

That Wheatley's verse could become cited so frequently as
"the" example of the mental and aesthetic capacity of the African slave can be explained somewhat by the curious circumstances of her enslavement in Africa as well as by the condition
of her servitude to Mr. and Mrs. John Wheatley of Boston.[54]
Perhaps because of the extensive citations of her achievement and
her poetry by both ardent supporters and opponents of racial
slavery, the Wheatley scholarship is rather extensive, although
her biographical facts are more highly refined than is the criticism
of her verse.[55]

After 1770, Wheatley's own history, except for accounts of her
trip to London in 1773,[56] her tragic marriage to John Peters in
1778, and her untimely death in 1784,[57] has been the history of
her publications, a history as curious as her biography. In 1770,
she published a broadside in Boston called *An Elegiac Poem, on
the Death of that Celebrated Divine, and eminent Servant of Je-
sus Christ, the late Reverend, and pious George Whitefield, Chap-
lain to the Right Honourable the Countess of Huntingdon*. The
poem was published in the *Massachusetts Spy* on October 11,
1770, and was republished in 1770—once in Newport, four times
again in Boston, once in New York, and once in Philadelphia.[58]
Wheatley's broadside was appended the following year to Ebenezer Pemberton's *Heaven the Residence of Saints*.[59] As Julian Mason rightly concludes, the *Elegiac Poem's* "several reprintings gave
Phillis her first fame as a poet."[60]

A recurrent suggestion has been that Wheatley remained aloof from matters that were in any sense racial or, more correctly, "positively" racial.[61] Although much of the misreading[62] of Wheatley must certainly arise from a blatant unfamiliarity with the conventions of neoclassical verse as well as with the various forms of the elegy she used, there is another reason why Wheatley's verse has suffered sophisticated critical neglect. As William H. Robinson demonstrates rather passionately, there exists no edition of her complete works; further, "until 1935 perhaps no more than 12 or 14 of Phillis's poems had been anthologized in excerpted and complete versions,"[63] a remarkable statistic considering the extensive amount of criticism devoted to Wheatley since 1773. Although variants of her *Poems* have been reprinted frequently, they remain incomplete and inconsistent, as in the reprinting of her signature piece, "On the Death of the Rev. Mr. George Whitefield," in the 1770 Boston broadside and in the 1773 American edition of the *Poems*. The 1770 broadside contains sixty-two lines. Another broadside version, likely published in London in 1771, contains sixty-four lines, including the otherwise deleted word "free" in reference to the relationships between the "Impartial Saviour" and "ye Africans":

> Take him, ye Wretched, for your only Good;
> Take him, ye hungry Souls, to be your Food;
> Take him, ye Thristy, for your cooling Stream;
> Ye Preachers, take him for your joyful Theme;
> Take him, my dear *Americans,* he said,
> Be your Complaints in his kind Bosom laid;
> Take him, ye Africans, he longs for you,
> Impartial Saviour is his Title due.
> If you will walk in Grace's heavenly Road,
> He'll make you free, and Kings, and Priests to God.[64]

In addition to errors of this sort, in the sixty published poems and twenty-two extant letters there exist a number of apparently overlooked poems and letters in which Wheatley discusses the horrors of racial slavery and reveals, to a surprising degree, the quality of concern she felt for Africans, which certainly cannot be said to be diminished by her affiliation to the idea of Christian beneficence and, always for Wheatley, its concomitant "way of true felicity."[65] These poems include "To the University of Cambridge, in New England" (1767), "An Address to the Deist"

(1767), "America" (1768–70),[66] and especially "To Maecenas," the first title in her *Poems*. Here Wheatley queries the Muse about the relation of the poet and poetry to "Afric's sable race":

> Not you, my Friend, these plaintive strains become,
> Not you, whose bosom is the *Muses* home;
> When they from tow'ring *Helicon* retire,
> They fan in you the bright immortal fire,
> But less happy, cannot raise the song,
> The fault-ring music dies upon my tongue.
> The happier Terence all the *choir* inspir'd,
> His soul replenished, and his bosom fir'd;
> But say, ye Muses, why this partial grace,
> To one alone of *Afric's* sable race;
> From age to age transmitting thus his name
> With the first glory in the rolls of fame?[67]

Similarly, her "Reply" to an anonymous response ("The Answer") to Wheatley's poem, "To a Gentleman in the Navy,"[68] demonstrates an uncommon amount of emotion in her "Afric's blissful plain":

> In fair description are thy powers displayed
> In artless grottos, and the sylvan shade;
> Charm'd with thy painting, how my bosom burns!
> And pleasing Gambia on my soul returns,
> With native grace in spring's luxuriant reign,
> Smiles the gay mead, and Eden blooms again,
> The various bower, the tuneful flowing stream,
> The soft retreats, the lovers golden dream,
> Her soil spontaneous, yields exhaustless stores;
> For phoebus revels on her verdent shores.
> Whose flowery births, a fragrant train appears,
> And crown the youth throughout the smiling year,
>   There, as in Britain's favour'd isle, behold
> The bending harvest ripen into gold!
> Just are thy views of Afric's blissful plain,
> On the warm limits of the land and main.
>   Pleas'd with the theme, see sportive fancy play,
> In realms devoted to the God of day![69]

Phillis Wheatley shared her antislavery sentiment in a compelling letter to Samuel Occom, the famous Mohegan Indian Presbyterian preacher,[70] who that same year published *A Choice Collection of Hymns and Spiritual Songs*. The letter was written to Occom in Boston on February 11, 1774, and published in *The Massachusetts Spy* on March 24, 1774; the *Boston Post Boy* on March 21, 1774; and the *Connecticut Journal* on April 1, 1774.[71] A headnote from the editors attests that they "are desired to insert [the letter] as a Specimen of her Ingenuity."[72] The letter is a subtle and controlled but passionate and eloquent address on the sheer evil of racial slavery:

> I have this Day received your obliging kind Epistle, and am greatly satisfied with your Reasons respecting the Negroes, and think highly reasonable what you offer in Vindication of their Natural Rights: Those that invade them cannot be insensible that the divine Light is chasing away the thick Darkness which broods over the Land of Africa; and the Chaos which has reign'd so long, is converting into beautiful Order, and reveals more and more clearly, the glorious Dispensation of civil and religious Liberty, which are so inseparably united, that there is little or no Enjoyment of one without the other: Otherwise, perhaps the Israelites had been less solicitous for their Freedom from Egyptian Slavery; I don't say they would have been contented without it, by no means, for in every human Breast God has implanted a Principle, which we call the love of Freedom; it is impatient of Oppression, and pants for Deliverance; and by the Leave of our modern Egyptians I will assert that the same principle lives in us. God grant Deliverance in his own Way and Time, and get him honor upon all those whose Avarice impels them in countenance and help forward the Calamities of their fellow Creatures. This I desire not for their Hurt, but to convince them of the strange Absurdity of their Conduct whose Words and Actions are so diametrically opposite. How well the cry for Liberty, and the reverse Disposition for the exercise of oppressive Power over others agree,—I humbly think it does not require the Penetration of a Philosopher to determine.

For what reasonable being, Wheatley asks, could hold in mind any doubt that slavery is evil incarnate: the matter is as simple as that.

The letter to Occom and a few others,[73] when considered with the poems in which Wheatley does address Africa or Africans, suggest strongly that the nature of Wheatley's poetry remains to be ascertained, as does her role in Afro-American literary history, and even her nonrole as a poet of "racial sentiment."

Imitating Pope in rhythm and meter, Wheatley wrote in decasyllabic lines of closed heroic couplets. There is much use of invocation, hyperbole, and inflated ornamentation, and an overemphasis of personification, all of which characterize neoclassical poetry.

Seventeen, or one-third, of her extant poems are elegies, fourteen of which appeared in the first edition of *Poems on Various Subjects, Religious and Moral* and five of which have been revised from earlier published elegies. In one of the few close readings of Wheatley's verse, Gregory Rigsby[74] demonstrates conclusively that her elegies are a creative variation of the "English Elegy" and the "Puritan Elegy."[75] Wheatley's elegies are threnodic after the fashion of the "Renaissance Elegy," in that they are meant "to praise the subject, to lament the death, and to comfort the bereaved."[76] Yet they are "Medieval" rather than "Elizabethan"[77] insofar as they prefer a sublime resignation to an unrestrained death force, and seem to avoid the protest against it.[78] The medieval resignation toward death, the function of the "Renaissance Elegy,"[79] and the form of the threnody as it developed in Elizabethan poetry were fused together in the "Puritan Funeral Elegy," a form peculiar to colonial America.

The Puritan funeral elegy, in turn, derived its specific shape and tone from the early American funeral sermon, based as it was on energetic exhortation.[80] But, as Rigsby argues, Wheatley utilized the triple function of the Renaissance elegy within "her own elegiac structure and established more elaborate conventions."[81] Rigsby then identifies these elements to be the underlying "structure of a Wheatley elegy": (1) the deceased in Heaven, (2) the deceased "winging" his way to Heaven, (3) an appreciation of the deceased's work on earth, (4) seraphic strains of heavenly bliss, (5) consolation of the living, (6) exhortation.[82] The identification of the conventions of her elegies indicates that Wheatley was an imaginative artist to a degree largely unrecognized in critical literature. Although her remaining occasional verse lacks the irony, the contrast, and the balance of Pope's poetry, which she cited as her conscious model, her critical reception since the eighteenth century has failed in a remarkably consistent way to read her verse in comparison with the various literary traditions that she so obviously attempted to imitate and by which she just as obviously sought to measure herself. Curiously, all of her extant poems, except five, utilize the heroic couplet.[83] Vernon Loggins traces, albeit vaguely, the influence of Milton in her hymns to morning and evening,[84] as well as in her poem to General Lee,[85] as he does Gray's influence on her elegy to Whitefield and Addison and Watt's presence in "Ode to Neptune" and "Hymn to Humanity."[86] But these, again, are suggestions of influence rather than practical criticism.

As William Cairns recognized as early as 1912, the criticism of Wheatley's poetry has been a matter centered primarily around exactly what the existence of the poeisis faculty signifies about a far more problematical inquiry. Phillis Wheatley's verses, Cairns writes,

> are good conventional work in the forms then popular, devoid of originality, but really remarkable considering the history of the author. That they have been remembered is partly due, however, to the fact that in the days of the abolitionists they were often cited to prove the intellectual capability of the negro.[87]

The peculiar history of Wheatley's reception by critics has, ironically enough, largely determined the theory of the criticism of the creative writings of Afro-Americans from the eighteenth century to the present time.

Binary Oppositions in Chapter One of *Narrative of the Life of Frederick Douglass an American Slave Written by Himself*

I was not hunting for my liberty, but also hunting for my name.

William Wells Brown

Whatever may be the ill or favored condition of the slave in the matter of mere personal treatment, it is the chattel relation that robs him of his manhood.

James Pennington

The white race will only respect those who oppose their usurpation, and acknowledge as equals those who will not submit to their rule. . . . We must make an issue, create an event and establish for ourselves a position. This is essentially necessary for our effective elevation as a people, directing our destiny and redeeming ourselves as a race.

Martin R. Delany

Autobiographical forms in English and in French assumed narrative priority toward the end of the eighteenth century; they shaped themselves principally around military exploits, court intrigues, and spiritual quests. As one scholar has outlined, "Elizabethan sea dogs and generals of the War of the Spanish Succession wrote of the strenuous campaigns, grand strategy, and gory battles. The memoirs of Louis XIV's great commander, the Prince of Conde, for example, thrilled thousands in Europe and America, as did the 'inside stories' of the nefarious, clandestine doings of the great European courts. The memoirs of the Cardinal de Retz, which told of the Machiavellian intrigues of French government during Louis XIV's minority and of the cabal behind the election of a Pope, captivated a large audience. Even more titillating were personal accounts of the boudoir escapades of noblemen and their mistresses. Nell Gwyn, Madame Pompadour, and even the fictitious Fanny Hill were legends if not idols in their day. More edifying but no less marvelous were the autobiographies of spiritual pilgrimage—such as the graphic accounts of Loyola, John Bunyan, and the Quaker George Fox. Their mystical experiences and miraculous deliverances filled readers with awe and wonder."[1] It is no surprise, then, that the narratives of the escaped slave became, during the three decades before the Civil War, the most popular form of written discourse in the country. Its audience was built to order. And the expectations created by this peculiar autobiographical convention, as well as by two other literary traditions, had a profound effect on the shape of discourse in the slave narrative. I am thinking here of the marked (but generally unheralded) tradition of the sentimental novel and, more especially, of the particularly American transmutation of the European picaresque. The slave narrative, I suggest, is a countergenre, a mediation between the novel of sentiment and the picaresque, oscillating somewhere between the two in a bipolar moment, set in motion by the mode of the confession. (Indeed, as we shall see, the slave narrative spawned its formal negation, the plantation novel.)

Claudio Guillen's seminal typology of the picaresque, outlined in seven "characteristics" of that form and derived from numerous examples in Spanish and French literature, provides a curious counterpoint to the morphology of the slave narratives and aids remarkably in delineating what he has proved to be an elusive but recurring narrative structure.

The picaro, who is after all a type of character, only becomes one at a certain point in his career, just as a man or woman "becomes" a slave only at a certain (and structurally crucial) point of perception in his or her "career." Both the picaro and the slave narrators are orphans; both, in fact, are outsiders. The picaresque is a pseudo-autobiography, whereas the slave narratives often tend toward quasi-autobiography. Yet, in both, "life is at the same time revived and judged, presented and remembered." In both forms, the narrator's point of view is partial and prejudiced, although the total view of both is "reflective, philosophical, and

critical on moral or religious grounds." In both, there is a general
stress on the material level of existence or indeed of subsistence,
sordid facts, hunger, money. There is in the narration of both a
profusion of objects and detail. Both the picaro and the slave, as
outsiders, comment on, if not parody, collective social institutions.[2]
Moreover, both, in their odysseys, move horizontally through space
and vertically through society.

If we combine these resemblances with certain characteristics of
the sentimental novel such as florid asides, stilted rhetoric, severe
piety, melodramatic conversation, destruction of the family unit,
violation of womanhood, abuse of innocence, punishment of assertion, and the rags-to-riches success story, we can see that the
slave narrative grafted together the conventions of two separate
literary traditions and became its own form, utilizing popular
conventions to affect its reader in much the same way as did
cheap popular fiction. Lydia Child, we recall, was not only the
amanuensis for escaped slave Harriet Jacobs, but also a successful author in the sentimental tradition. (That the plantation novel
was the antithesis or negation of the slave narrative becomes apparent when we consider its conventions. From 1824, when George
Tucker published *The Valley of the Shenandoah,* the plantation
novel concerned itself with aristocratic, virtuous masters; beast-
like, docile slaves; great manor houses; squalid field quarters; and
idealized, alabaster womanhood—all obvious negations of themes
common to the slave narratives. Indeed, within two years of the
publication in 1852 of Harriet Beecher Stowe's *Uncle Tom's Cabin,*
at least fourteen plantation novels appeared.)

It should not surprise us, then, that the narratives were popular,
since the use of well-established and well-received narrative conventions was meant to ensure commercial and hence political success. By at least one account, the sales of slave narratives reached
such high proportions that a critic was moved to complain that the
"shelves of booksellers groan under the weight of Sambo's woes,
done up in covers! . . . We hate this niggerism, and hope it may
be done away with. . . . If we are threatened with any more negro stories—here goes." These "literary nigritudes" [sic] were "stories" whose "editions run to hundreds of thousands."[3] Marion
Wilson Starling recalls Gladstone's belief that not more than about
five percent of the books published in England had a sale of more

than five hundred copies; between 1835 and 1863, no fewer than ten of these were slave narratives.[4] So popular were they in England that a considerable number were published at London or Manchester before they were published in America, if at all. Nor should it surprise us that, of these, the more popular were those that defined the genre structurally. It was Frederick Douglass's *Narrative* of 1845 that exploited the potential and came to determine the shape of language in the slave narrative.

Douglass's *Narrative,* in its initial edition of five thousand copies, was sold out in four months. Within a year, four more editions of two thousand copies each were published. In the British Isles, five editions appeared, two in Ireland in 1846 and three in England in 1846 and 1847. Within the five years after its appearance, a total of some thirty thousand copies of the *Narrative* had been published in the English-speaking world. By 1848, a French paperback edition was being sold in the stalls. *Littells Living Age,* an American periodical, gave an estimate of its sweep in the British Isles after one year's circulation: "Taking all together, not less than one million persons in Great Britain and Ireland have been excited by the book and its commentators."[5]

Of the scores of reviews of the *Narrative,* two especially discuss the work in terms of its literary merits. One review, published initially in the *New York Tribune* and reprinted in *The Liberator,* attempts to place the work in the larger tradition of the narrative tale as a literary form:

> Considered merely as a narrative, we have never read one more simple, true, coherent, and warm with genuine feeling. It is an excellent piece of writing, and on that score to be prized as a specimen of the powers of the black race, which prejudice persists in disputing. We prize highly all evidence of this kind, and it is becoming more abundant.[6]

Even more telling is the review from the *Lynn Pioneer* reprinted in the same issue of *The Liberator;* this review was perhaps the first to attempt to attach a priority to the *Narrative's* form and thereby place Douglass directly in a major literary tradition:

> It is evidently drawn with a nice eye, and the coloring is chaste and subdued, rather than extravagant or overwrought. Thrilling

as it is, and full of the most burning eloquence, it is yet simple and unimpassioned.

Although its "eloquence is the eloquence of truth" and so "is as simple and touching as the impulses of childhood," yet its "message" transcends even its superior moral content: "There are passages in it which would brighten the reputation of any author,— while the book, as a whole, judged as a mere work of art, would widen the fame of Bunyan or De Foe."[7] Leaving the matter of "truth" to the historians,[8] these reviews argue correctly that despite the intention of the author for his autobiography to be a major document in the abolitionist struggle and regardless of Douglass's meticulous attempt at documentation, the *Narrative* falls into the larger class of the heroic fugitive with some important modifications that are related to the confession and the picaresque forms (hence, Bunyan and Defoe), a peculiar blend that would mark Afro-American fiction at least until the publication of James Weldon Johnson's *Autobiography of an Ex-Coloured Man.*

These resemblances between confession and picaresque informed the narrative shape of Afro-American fiction in much the same way as they did that of the English and American novel. As Robert Scholes and Robert Kellogg maintain,

> the similarity in narrative stance between picaresque and confession enables the two to blend easily, making possible an entirely fictional narrative which is more in the spirit of the confession than the picaresque, such as *Moll Flanders* and *Great Expectations.*

But this same blend makes possible a different sort of sublime narrative, "one that is picaresque in spirit but which employs actual materials from the author's life, such as [Wells's] Tono-Bungay." Into this class fall slave narratives, the polemical Afro-American first-person form, the influence of which would shape the development of point of view in black fiction for the next hundred years, precisely because

> by turning the direction of the narrative inward the author almost inevitably presents a central character who is an example of something. By turning the direction of the narrative outward the author almost inevitably exposes weaknesses in society. First-person narrative is thus a ready vehicle for ideas.[9]

It is this first-person narration, utilized precisely in this manner, that is the first great shaping characteristic of the slave narratives. But there is another formal influence on the slave narratives whose effect is telling: the American romance. Stephen Butterfield[10] makes this argument tellingly, and I shall paraphrase it closely.

Like Herman Melville's marvelous romance, *Pierre,* the slave narratives utilize as a structural principle the irony of seeming innocence. Here in American society, both say, is to be found as much that is contrary to moral order as could be found in prerevolutionary Europe. The novelty of American innocence is, however, the refusal or failure to recognize evil while participating in that evil. As with other American romantic modes of narration, the language of the slave narratives remains primarily an expression of the self, a conduit for particularly personal emotion. In this sort of narrative, language was meant to be merely a necessary but unfortunate instrument. In the slave narratives, this structuring of the self couples with the minute explication of gross evil and human depravity, and does so with such sheer intent as to make for a tyranny of point. If the matter of the shaping of the self can come only after the slave is free, in the context of an autobiographical narrative where the slave first posits that full self, then slavery indeed dehumanizes and must in no uncertain terms be abolished, by violence if necessary, since it is by nature a violent institution. The irony here is tyrannically romantic: illusion and substance are patterned antitheses.

As with other examples of romance, the narratives turn on an unconsummated love. The slave and the ex-slave are the dark ladies of the new country destined to expire for unrequited love. Yet the leitmotif of the journey north and the concomitant evolution of consciousness within the slave—from an identity as property and object to a sublime identity as human being and subject—display in the first person the selfsame spirit of the New World's personal experience with titanic nature that Benjamin Franklin's *Autobiography* has come to symbolize. The author of the slave narrative, in his or her flight through the wilderness (recreated in vivid detailed descriptions of the relationship between man and land on the plantation and off), seems to be arguing strongly that one can "study nature" to know oneself. The two great precepts—the former Emersonian and the latter Cartesian—

in the American adventure become one. Further, as with the American symbolists, the odyssey is a process of becoming. Walt Whitman, for instance, is less concerned with explorations of emotion than with exploration as a mode of consciousness. Slave narratives not only describe the voyage but also enact the voyage so that their content is primarily a reflection of their literary method. Theirs is a structure in which the writer and the subject merge into the stream of language. Language indeed is primarily a perception of reality. Yet, unlike the American symbolists, these writers of slave narratives want not so much to adopt a novel stance from which the world assumes new shapes as to impose a new form onto the world. There can be no qualification regarding the nature of slavery; there can be no equivocation.

Butterfield explicates this idea rather well by contrasting the levels of diction in the slave narrative *The Life of John Thompson*[11] with a remarkably similar passage from Herman Melville's *Moby-Dick*. The first is from Thompson:

> The harpoon is sharp, and barbed at one end, so that when it has once entered the animal, it is difficult to draw it out again, and has attached to its other end a pole, two inches thick and five feet long. Attached to this is a line 75 to 100 fathoms in length, which is coiled into the bow of the boat.

Melville follows:

> Thus the whale-line folds the whole boat in its complicated coils, twisting and writhing about it in almost every direction. All the oarsmen are involved in its perilous contortions; so that to the timid eye of the landsman they seem as festooning their limbs.

There is a difference here of rhetorical strategies that distinguishes the two. Melville's language is symbolic and weighted with ambiguous moral meanings: the serpentine rope allows for no innocence; "all the oarsmen" are involved, even those who have nothing to do with coiling the rope in the tub; the crew lives with the serpent and by the serpent, necessarily for their livelihood, unaware of the nature of the coil yet contaminated and imperiled by its inherent danger. Melville thus depicts the metaphysical necessity of evil.

Thompson's language is distinguished formally from the concrete and symbolistic devices in Melville. Thompson allows the imagery of a whaling voyage to carry moral and allegorical meanings, yet he means his narration to be descriptive and realistic; his concern is with verisimilitude. There can be nothing morally ambiguous about the need to abolish slavery, and there can be little ambiguity about the reason for the suffering of the slave. "The slave narrative," Butterfield concludes, "does not see oppression in terms of a symbol-structure that transforms evil into a metaphysical necessity. For to do so would have been to locate the source of evil outside the master–slave relationship, and thus would have cut the ideological ground from under the entire thrust of the abolitionist movement."[12] Thompson means not so much to narrate as to convey a message, a value system; as with the black sermon, the slave's narrative functions as a single sign. And the nature of Frederick Douglass's rhetorical strategy directly reflects this sentiment through the use of what rhetoricians have called antitheses and of what the structuralists have come to call the binary opposition.

In the act of interpretation, we establish a sign relationship between the description and a meaning. The relations most crucial to structural analysis are functional binary oppositions. Roman Jakobson and Morris Halle argue in *Fundamentals of Language* that binary oppositions are inherent in all languages, that they are, indeed, a fundamental principle of language formation itself.[13] Many structuralists, seizing on Jakobson's formulation, hold the binary opposition to be a fundamental operation of the human mind, basic to the production of meaning. Lévi-Strauss, who turned topsy-turvy the way we examine mythological discourse, describes the binary opposition as "this elementary logic which is the smallest common denominator of all thought."[14] Lévi-Strauss's model of opposition and mediation, which sees the binary opposition as an underlying structural pattern as well as a method of revealing that pattern, has in its many variants become a most satisfying mechanism for retrieving almost primal social contradictions, long ago "resolved" in the mediated structure itself.[15] Perhaps it is not irresponsible or premature to call Lévi-Strauss's contribution to human understanding a classic one.

Fredric Jameson, in *The Prison-House of Language,* maintains that the binary opposition is . . . at the outset a heuristic principle, that instrument of analysis on which the mythological hermeneutic is founded. We would ourselves be tempted to describe it as a technique for stimulating perception, when faced with a mass of apparently homogenous data to which the mind and the eyes are numb: a way of forcing ourselves to perceive difference and identity in a whole new language the very sounds of which we cannot yet distinguish from each other. It is a decoding or deciphering device, or alternately a technique of language learning.

How does this "decoding device" work as a tool for practical criticism? When any two terms are set in opposition to each other, the reader is forced to explore qualitative similarities and differences, to make some connection, and, therefore, to derive some meaning from points of disjunction. If one opposes A to B, for instance, and X to Y, the two cases become similar as long as each involves the presence and absence of a given feature. In short, two terms are brought together by some quality that they share and are then opposed and made to signify the absence and presence of that quality. The relationship between presence and absence, positive and negative signs, is the simplest form of the binary opposition. These relationships, Jameson concludes, "embody a tension 'in which one of the two terms of the binary opposition is apprehended as positively having a certain feature while the other is apprehended as deprived of the feature in question.' "[16]

Frederick Douglass's *Narrative* attempts with painstaking verisimilitude to reproduce a system of signs that we have come to call plantation culture, from the initial paragraph of the first chapter:

> I was born in Tuckahoe, near Hillsborough, and about twelve miles from Easton, in Talbot County, Maryland. I have no accurate knowledge of my age, never having seen any authentic record containing it. By far the larger part of the slaves know as little of their ages as horses know of theirs, and it is the wish of most masters within my knowledge to keep their slaves thus ignorant. I do not remember to have ever met a slave who could tell of his birthday, they seldom come nearer to it than planting-time, harvest-time, cherry-time, spring-time, or fall-time. A want of information concerning my own was a source of unhappiness to me even during childhood. The white children could tell their

ages, I could not tell why I ought to be deprived of the same privilege. I was not allowed to make any inquiries of my master concerning it. He deemed such inquiries on the part of a slave improper and impertinent, and evidence of a restless spirit. The nearest estimate I can give makes me now between twenty-seven and twenty-eight years of age. I come to this, from hearing my master say, sometime during 1835, I was about seventeen years old.[17]

We see an ordering of the world based on a profoundly relational type of thinking, in which a strict barrier of difference or opposition forms the basis of a class rather than, as in other classification schemes, an ordering based on resemblances or the identity of two or more elements. In the text, we can say that these binary oppositions produce through separation the most inflexible of barriers: that of meaning. We, the readers, must exploit the oppositions and give them a place in a larger symbolic structure.

Douglass's narrative strategy seems to be this: He brings together two terms in special relationships suggested by some quality that they share; then, by opposing two seemingly unrelated elements, such as the sheep, cattle, or horses on the plantation and the specimen of life known as slave, Douglass's language is made to signify the presence and absence of some quality—in this case, humanity.[18] Douglass uses this device to explicate the slave's understanding of himself and of his relation to the world through the system of the perceptions that defined the world the planters made. Not only does his *Narrative* come to concern itself with two diametrically opposed notions of genesis, origins, and meaning itself, but its structure actually turns on an opposition between nature and culture as well. Finally and, for our purposes, crucially, Douglass's method of complex mediation—and the ironic reversals so peculiar to his text—suggests overwhelmingly the completely arbitrary relationship between description and meaning, between signifier and signified, between sign and referent.

Douglass uses these oppositions to create a unity on a symbolic level, not only through physical opposition but also through an opposition of space and time. The *Narrative* begins, "I was born in Tuckahoe, near Hillsborough, and about twelve miles from Easton, in Talbot County, Maryland." Douglass knows the physical circumstances of his birth: Tuckahoe, we know, is near Hills-

borough and is twelve miles from Easton. Though his place of
birth is fairly definite, his date of birth is not for him to know: "I
have no accurate knowledge of my age," he admits, because "any
authentic record containing it" would be in the possession of his
master. Indeed, this opposition, or counterpoint, between that
which is knowable in the world of the slave and that which is
not abounds throughout this chapter. Already we know that the
world of the master and the world of the slave are separated by
an inflexible barrier of meaning. The knowledge the slave has of
his circumstances he must deduce from the earth; a quantity such
as time, our understanding of which is cultural and not natural,
derives from a nonmaterial source, let us say the heavens. How
do we know a white child from a black child? Douglass's response
is brilliant in its simplicity: "The white children could tell their
ages. I could not."

The deprivation of the means to tell the time is the very structural center of this initial paragraph, in which he defines what it
means to become aware of one's own enslavement: "A want of information concerning my own [birthday] was a source of unhappi-
ness to me even during childhood." This state of disequilibrium—
this absence of choice—motivates the slave's search for his humanity
as well as Douglass's search for his text, the text that will come to
stand for his life in the form of an autobiography. This deprivation
has created that gap in the slave's imagination between self and
other, between lord and bondsman, between black and white.
What is more, this deprivation of time has created an apparent
likeness between the slave and the plantation's animals. "By far,"
Douglass confesses, "the large part of slaves know as little of their
ages as horses know of theirs." This deprivation is not accidental;
it is systematic: "it is the wish of most masters within my knowledge to keep their slaves thus ignorant." Douglass, in his subtle
juxtaposition here of "masters" and "knowledge" and of "slaves"
and "ignorance," again introduces homologous terms. "I do not
remember to have ever met a slave," Douglass emphasizes, "who
could tell of his birthday." Slaves, he seems to conclude, are those
who cannot plot their course by and who stand outside of the linear progression of the calendar. And precisely here Douglass summarizes the symbolic code of this world, which makes the slave's

closest blood relations the horses and which makes his or her very
notion of time a cyclical one, diametrically opposed to the master's linear conception: "They [the slaves] seldom come nearer to
[the notion of time] than planting-time, harvest-time, cherry-time,
spring-time, or fall-time." The slave had arrived, but not in time
to partake at the welcome table of human culture.

For Douglass, the bonds of blood kinship are the primary metaphors of human culture.[19] As an animal would know its mother,
so Douglass knows his. "My mother was named Harriet Bailey.
She was the daughter of Isaac and Betsey Bailey," both of whom
were "colored," Douglass notes, "and quite dark." His mother
"was of a darker complexion" even than either grandparent. His
father, on the other hand, is some indefinite "white man," suggested through innuendo to be his master: "The opinion was also
whispered," he says, "that my master was my father." His master
was his father; his father his master. "Of the correctness of this
opinion," Douglass concludes, "I know nothing," only and precisely because "the means of knowing was withheld from me."
Two paragraphs below, having reflected on the death of his mother,
Douglass repeats this peculiar unity twice again. "Called thus suddenly away," he commences, "she left me without the slightest intimation of who my father was." Yet Douglass repeats "the whisper
that my father was my master" as he launches into a description
of the rank odiousness of a system "that slaveholders have ordained, and by law established," in which the partrilineal succession of the planter has been forcibly replaced by a matrilineal succession for the slave: "the children of slave women shall in all
cases follow the condition of their mothers." The planters therefore make of the "gratification of their wicked desires," spits
Douglass, a thing "profitable as well as pleasurable." Further,
the end result of "this cunning arrangement" is that "the slaveholder, in cases not a few, sustains to his slaves the double relation of master and father." "I know of such cases," he opens his
sixth paragraph, using a declaration of verisimilitude as a transition to introduce another opposition, this one between the fertile
slave–lover–mother and the planter's barren wife.

The profound ambiguity of this relationship between father and
son and master and slave persists, if only because the two terms

"father" and "master" are here embodied in one, with no mediation between them. It is a rather grotesque bond that links Douglass to his parent, a bond that embodies "the distorted and unnatural relationship endemic to slavery."[20] It is as if the usually
implied primal tension between father and son is rendered apparent in the daily contact between father–master–human and
son–slave–animal, a contact that occurs, significantly, only during
the light of day.

Douglass's contact with his mother ("to know her as such," he
qualifies) never occurred "more than four or five times in my
life." Each of these visits, he recalls, "was of short duration," and
each, he repeats over and over, took place "at night." Douglass
continues: "[My mother] made her journey to see me in the night,
travelling the whole distance," he mentions as if an afterthought,
"on foot." "I do not recollect of ever seeing my mother," he repeats one sentence later, "by the light of day. She was with me in
the night." Always she returned to a Mr. Stewart's plantation,
some twelve miles away, "long before I waked," so as to be at the
plantation before dawn, since she "was a field hand, and a whipping is the penalty of not being in the field at sunrise." The slaves
metaphorically "owned" the night, while the master owned the
day. By the fourth paragraph of the narrative, the terms of our
homology—the symbolic code of this world—are developed further
to include relations of the animal, the mother, the slave, the night,
the earth, matrilineal succession, and nature opposed to relations
of the human being, the father, the master, the daylight, the heavens, patrilineal succession, and culture. Douglass, in short, opposes the absolute and the eternal to the mortal and the finite.
Our list certainly could be expanded to include oppositions between
spiritual/material, aristocratic/base, civilized/barbaric, sterile/fer-
tile, enterprise/sloth, force/principle, fact/imagination, linear/
cyclical, thinking/feeling, rational/irrational, chivalry/cowardice,
grace/brutishness, pure/cursed, and human/beastly.

Yet the code, Douglass proceeds to show, stands in defiance of
the natural and moral order. Here Douglass commences as mediator and as trickster to reverse the relations of the opposition. That
the relationship between the slave–son and master–father was an
unnatural one and even grotesque, as are the results of any defile-

ment of order, is reflected in the nature of the relationship between the plantation mistress and the planter's illegitimate off-
spring. "She is ever disposed to find fault with them," laments
Douglass; "she is never better pleased than when she sees them
under the lash." Indeed, it is the white mistress who often compels her husband, the master, to sell "this class of his slaves, out
of deference to the feelings of his white wife." But it is the priority
of the economic relation over the kinship tie that is the true per-
version of nature in this world: "It is often the dictate of humanity for a man to sell his own children to human flesh-mongers,"
Douglass observes tellingly. Here we see the ultimate reversal: it
is now the mistress, the proverbial carrier of culture, who demands
that the master's son be delivered up to the "human flesh-mongers"
and traded for consumption. Douglass has here defined American
cannibalism, a consumption of human flesh dictated by a system
that could only be demonic.

Douglass's narrative demonstrates not only how the deprivation
of the hallmarks of identity can affect the slave but also how the
slaveowner's world negates and even perverts those very values on
which it is built. Deprivation of a birthdate, a name, a family
structure, and legal rights makes of the deprived brute a subhuman, says Douglass, until he comes to a consciousness of these relations; yet, it is the human depriver who is the actual barbarian
structuring his existence on the consumption of human flesh. Just
as the mulatto son is a mediation between two opposed terms, man
and animal, so too has Douglass's text become the complex mediator between the world as the master would have it and the world
as the slave knows it really is. Douglass has subverted the terms of
the code he was meant to mediate; he has been a trickster. As with
all mediations, the trickster is a mediator and his mediation is a
trick—only a trick—for there can be no mediation in this world.
Douglass's narrative has aimed to destroy the symbolic code that
created the false oppositions themselves. The oppositions, all along,
were only arbitrary, not fixed.

Douglass first suggests that the symbolic code created in this
text is arbitrary and not fixed, human-imposed and not divinely
ordained, in an ironic aside on the myth of the curse of Ham,
which comes in the very center of the seventh paragraph of the

narrative and is meant to be an elaboration on the ramifications of "this class of slaves" who are the fruit of the unnatural liaison between animal and man. If the justification of this order is the curse on Ham and his tribe, if Ham's tribe signifies the black African, and if this prescription for enslavement is scriptural, then, Douglass argues, "it is certain that slavery at the south must soon become unscriptural; for thousands are ushered into the world, annually, who, like myself, owe their existence to white fathers, and those fathers," he repeats for the fourth time, are "most frequently their own masters."

As if to underscore the falsity of this notion of an imposed, inflexibly divine order, Douglass inverts a standard Christian symbol, that of the straight and narrow gate to Paradise. The severe beating of his Aunt Hester, who, Douglass advises us parenthetically, "happened to be absent when my master desired her presence," is the occasion of this inversion. "It struck me with awful force," he remembers. "It was the blood-stained gate, the entrance to the hell of slavery, through which I was about to pass. It was," he concludes, "a most terrible spectacle." This startling image suggests that of the archetypal necromancer, Faustus, in whose final vision the usual serene presence of the Cross is stained with warm and dripping blood.

Douglass has posited the completely arbitary nature of the sign. The master's actions belie the metaphysical suppositions on which is based the order of his world. It is an order ostensibly imposed by the father of Adam, yet one in fact exposed by the sons of Ham. It is a world whose oppositions have generated their own mediator, Douglass himself. This mulatto son, half-animal, half-man, writes a text (which is itself another mediation) in which he can expose the arbitrary nature of the signs found in this world, the very process necessary to the destruction of this world. "You have seen how a man was made a slave," Douglass writes at the structural center of his *Narrative,* "you shall see how a slave was made a man."[21] As with all mediation, Douglass has constructed a system of perception that becomes the plot development in the text but results in an inversion of the initial state of the oppositions through the operations of the mediator himself, as indicated in this diagram:

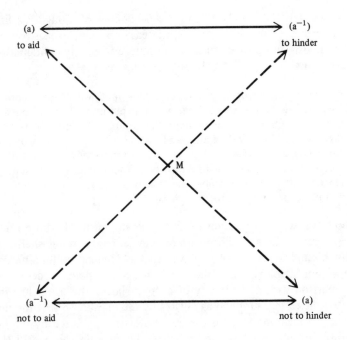

With this narrative gesture alone, slave has become master, creature has become man, object has become subject. What more telling embodiment of Emersonian idealism and its capacity to transubstantiate a material reality! Not only has an idea made subject of object, but creature has assumed self, and the assumption of self has created a race. For, as with all myths of origins, the relation of self to race is a relation of synecdoche. As Michael Cooke maintains concerning the characteristics of black autobiography,

the self is the source of the system of which it is a part, creates what it discovers, and although (as Coleridge realized) it is nothing unto itself, it is the possibility of everything for itself. Autobiography is the coordination of the self as content—everything available in memory, perception, understanding, imagination, desire—and the self as shaped, formed in terms of a perspective and pattern of interpretation.[22]

If we step outside the self-imposed confines of Douglass's first chapter to seek textual evidence, the case becomes even stronger. The opposition between culture and nature is clearly contained in a description of a slave meal, found in Chapter V.[23]

> We were not regularly allowanced. Our food was coarse corn meal boiled. This was called *mush*. It was put into a large wooden tray or trough, and set down upon the ground. The children were then called, like so many pigs, and like so many pigs they would come and devour the mush; some with oyster-shells, others with pieces of shingle, some with naked hands, and none with spoons. He that ate fastest got most; he that was strongest secured the best place; and few left the trough satisfied.

The slave, we read, did not eat food; he ate mush. He did not eat with a spoon; he ate with pieces of shingle, or on oyster shells, or with his naked hands. Again we see the obvious culture–nature opposition at play. When the slave, in another place, accepts the comparison with and identity of a "bad sheep," he again has inverted the terms, supplied as always by the master, so that the unfavorable meaning this has for the master is supplanted by the favorable meaning it has for the slave. There is in this world the planter has made, Douglass maintains, an ironic relationship between appearance and reality. "Slaves sing most," he writes at the end of Chapter II, "when they are most unhappy. . . . The singing of a man cast away upon a desolate island might be as appropriately considered as evidence of contentment and happiness, as the singing of a slave; the songs of the one and of the other are prompted by the same emotion."

Douglass concludes his second chapter with a discourse on the nature of interpretation, which we could perhaps call the first charting of the black hermeneutical circle and which we could take again as a declaration of the arbitrary relationship between a sign and its referent, between the signifier and the signified. The slaves, he writes, "would compose and sing as they went along, consulting neither time nor tune. The thought that came up, came out—if not in the word, [then] in the sound;—and as frequently in the one as in the other."[24] Douglass describes here a certain convergence of perception peculiar only to members of a very specific culture: the thought could very well be embodied nonverbally, in the sound if not in the word. What is more, sound and sense could very well operate at odds to create through tension a dialectical relation. Douglass remarks: "They would sometimes sing the most pathetic sentiment in the most rapturous tone, and the most rapturous sentiment in the most pathetic tone. . . . They would thus sing as a chorus to words which to many would seem unmeaning jargon, but which, nevertheless, were full of meaning to themselves." Yet the decoding of these cryptic messages did not, as some of us have postulated, depend on some sort of mystical union with their texts. "I did not, when a slave," Douglass admits, "understand the deep meaning of those rude and apparently incoherent songs." Meaning, on the contrary, came only with a certain aesthetic distance and an acceptance of the critical imperative. "I was myself within the circle," he concludes, "so that I neither saw nor heard as those without might see and hear." There exists always the danger, Douglass seems to say, that the meanings of nonlinguistic signs will seem natural; one must view them with a certain detachment to see that their meanings are in fact merely the products of a certain culture, the result of shared assumptions and conventions. Not only is meaning culture-bound and the reference of all signs an assigned relation, Douglass tells us, but *how* we read determines *what* we read, in the truest sense of the hermeneutical circle.

Frederick Douglass and
the Language of the Self

A hush is over the teeming lists,
   And there is pause, a breath-space in the strife;
A spirit brave has passed beyond the mists
   And vapors that obscure the sun of life.
And Ethiopia, with bosom torn,
Laments the passing of her noblest born.

* * *

For her his voice, a fearless clarion, rung
   That broke in warning on the ears of men;
For her the strong bow of his power he stung,
   And sent his arrows to the very den
Where grim Oppression held his bloody place
And gloated o'er the mis'ries of a race.

* * *

When men maligned him, and their torrent wrath
   In furious imprecations o'er him broke,
He kept his counsel as he kept his path;
   'Twas for his race, not for himself he spoke.

Paul Laurence Dunbar, "Frederick Douglass"

When it is finally ours, this freedom, this liberty this beautiful
and terrible thing, needful to man as air,
usable as earth; when it belongs at last to all,
when it is truly instinct, brain matter, diastole, systole,
reflex action; when it is finally won; when it is more
than the gaudy mumbo jumbo of politicians:
this man, this Douglass, this former slave, this Negro
beaten to his knees, exiled, visioning a world
where none is lonely, none hunted, alien,
this man, superb in love and logic, this man
shall be remembered. Oh, not with statues' rhetoric,

not with legends and poems and wreaths of bronze alone,
but with the lives grown out of his life, the lives
fleshing his dream of the beautiful, needful thing.
Robert Hayden, "Frederick Douglass"

I

By the end of 1894, Frederick Douglass had begun to prepare for his death. Unbowed and energetic even to the last, Douglass had, however, apparently reconciled himself to "live and rejoice," as he put it in 1881, to occupy with dignity and gravity that peculiar role conferred upon him by friend and foe, black countryman and white, contemporary and disciple alike: he was "The Representative Colored Man of the United States." Despite the unassailable respect he commanded throughout the country, one bit of common knowledge had never been Douglass's to possess, and, as Peter Walker movingly recounts it, the final entry in his *Diary* suggests that it haunted him to death.[1]

On a March 1894 evening, just less than a year before he died, Frederick Douglass left his home at Anacostia and boarded a train for the brief ride from Washington to Baltimore. At Baltimore, Douglass went directly to the home of a physician, Dr. Thomas Edward Sears. After a carefully calculated but leisurely conversation, during which Douglass put to Dr. Sears a series of specifically formulated questions, Douglass returned by train to Washington and then by coach to Anacostia Heights. Early the next morning, he went to his study, took out his *Diary,* and wrote as that day's entry an account of his trip to Baltimore. This was to be the final entry in Douglass's *Diary.* In the final months remaining to him, no other event moved Douglass sufficiently to record another entry in his little *Diary.* Indeed, no other event had moved Douglass to make an entry since he had made an apparently hurried note in the *Diary* he was at London six years earlier. Douglass's visit with Dr. Sears can without hyperbole be called a mission. It was not that these two men bore so very much in common, nor that through their visit they sought to cement a friendship about to end. Rather, Sears, a descendant of Douglass's old master, would be the last contact Douglass was to have with the family that had once owned him. More important, Sears had some information about his slave past that Douglass wanted, and all his self-conscious life Douglass had pursued passionately all concrete information about his lost, or hidden, past.

Douglass's concern for his lost past, a past far beyond the reach of memory and recall, a concern that took him to the home of the Baltimore physician, is, as Walker demonstrates, one of the profoundly subtle yet fundamentally unifying themes in his life. His day's visit with Dr. Sears, in fact, was one of the most revealing and significant acts of Douglass's life. And that this pregnant event remains unmentioned by all of Douglass's biographers is significant in an analysis of the life of Frederick Douglass.

What sort of information about his own past had Douglass been seeking from Dr. Sears that day in March of 1894? What sort of private, compelling quest could have prevailed upon a great statesman, so honored and praised, to make such an odd pilgrimage so near to his own death? Surely it was not to reminisce with Sears about the good old days of slavery, back on Thomas and Lucretia Auld's plantation in Maryland. In Dr. Thomas Edward Sears, Douglass so painfully knew, resided his last opportunity to ascertain once and for all that crucial piece of data about his own origins which had been systematically denied to Douglass and the largest part of all other black slaves, the absence or presence of which marked the terrible terrain that separated the free person from the slave, and the possession of which alone could enable even a "slave" of Douglass's bearing to recapture and master his own elusive past. Douglass had been in search of his birthdate, his lack of certainty about which he called in his *Diary* entry "a serious trouble."

A sense of self as we have defined it in the West since the Enlightenment turns in part upon written records. Most fundamentally, we mark a human being's existence by his or her brith and death dates, engraved in granite on every tombstone. Our idea of the self, it is fair to argue, is as inextricably interwoven with our ideas of time as it is with uses of language. In antebellum America, it was the deprivation of time in the life of the slave that first signaled his or her status as a piece of property. Slavery's time was delineated by memory and memory alone. One's sense of one's existence, therefore, depended upon memory. It was memory, above all else, that gave a shape to being itself. What a brilliant substructure of the system of slavery! For the dependence upon memory made the slave, first and foremost, a slave to himself or herself, a prisoner of his or her own power of recall. Within such a time machine, as it were, not only had the slave no fixed reference points, but also his or her own past could exist only as memory without support, as the text without footnotes, as the clock without two hands. Within such a tyrannical concept of time, the slave had no past beyond memory; the slave had lived at no time past the point of recollection.

As we have seen in Chapter 3, of such subtle yet poignant import is this imposed system of time that Douglass draws upon it in the first paragraph of the first of his three autobiographies as the very first evidence of his personal status as a slave. We recall that although Douglass knows where he was born (in Tuckahoe, near Hillsborough, about twelve miles from Easton, in Talbot County, Maryland), his date of birth is not for him to know. A "slave" was he or she who, most literally, stood outside of time. To the end of his life, the mystery of his birth remained for Douglass what he called "a serious trouble" and helps us to understand why a man in his seventy-sixth year took the trouble to mount one final attempt to obtain facts about his existence. The skeletal facts of Douglass's journal entry, as Peter Walker cites it, suggest the pathos of the unconsummated quest:

> I called yesterday while in Baltimore . . . upon Dr. Thomas Edward Sears, a grandson of Thomas and Lucretia Auld and learned the following facts:
> Capt. Thomas Auld, was born 1795
> Amanda Auld, his daughter was born Jan. 28, 1826
> Thomas, son of Hugh and Sophia Auld was born Jan. 1824
> Capt. Aaron Anthony, Died Nov. 14, 1823.

"The Death of Aaron Anthony," Douglass concluded, "makes me fix the year in which I was sent to live with Mr. Hugh Auld in Baltimore, as 1825." At last, Frederick Douglass possessed a major "fact." From his master's death, Douglass could extrapolate the date he was sent to Baltimore as a boy, that key signpost on his personal road to freedom. Perhaps emboldened by the specificity of Aaron Anthony's date of death, Douglass concluded this curious *Diary* entry by being even more specific about when in

1825 he had come to Baltimore, even if, like the slaves, he once more dated the passage of time by the movements of the animals and the seasons: "I know it must have been in the summer of that year that I went to live in Baltimore because the spring lambs were big enough to be sent to market, and I helped to drive a flock of them from Smith's Dock to Fells Point on the day I landed in Baltimore." With this memory of lambs in summer, Frederick Douglass's *Diary* ends, as did his lifelong quest to locate facts that could bolster the limitations of memory. Beyond 1825 and Baltimore, Douglass was not ever able to verify his own memory.

Frederick Douglass assumed numerous roles in his lifetime: slave and freedman, journalist and scholar, civil servant and politician, diplomat and lecturer, equally articulate advocate of the abolition of slavery and equal rights for women. Indeed, these two later interests, in a sense, "frame" Douglass's life. Metaphorically born in August 1841, while he made his first speech to an abolitionist audience in Massachusetts, fifty-four years later Douglass returned home after attending a women's rights convention to die at his desk. During those fifty-four extraordinarily brilliant years, Douglass advised presidents, edited and owned newspapers, wrote three autobiographies, served as the recorder of deeds and marshal for the District of Columbia, as consul general to Haiti, and as president of the Freedman's Bank. To all and sundry, friend and foe, Frederick Douglass was a great man.

Despite the undisputed magnificence of Douglass's career, it is not his life alone that continues to draw scholars to write about him. There have been more biographies of Douglass printed than of any other Afro-American, including the great Du Bois, whose life seems to loom so large that few scholars have dared attempt to contain it, presenting difficulties of perspective much like the vast West did to the early landscape painters who foolishly dared to try to match its sublime glory. From Harriet Beecher Stowe in 1868, through Charles Chesnutt and Booker T. Washington at the turn of the century, to William Pickens, Arna Bontemps, and Benjamin Quarles in the forties, to Philip Foner, John Blassingame, and Nathan Huggins in the sixties, seventies, and eighties, the life of Douglass continues to compel from the scholar and creative writer verbal account of his life. (At least three historical novels

figure Douglass as their protagonist.) What is curious and somewhat puzzling about this range of over a dozen biographies is that,
in the main, they repeat the same facts in pretty much the same
order. At first thought, we can say that so many scholars write
about Douglass because he was the first Black Representative Man
and, along with Du Bois, perhaps one of the only two truly representative men of letters our people are privileged to have had. Yet,
if to his biographers Douglass was indeed this Representative
Man, then Douglass himself carefully crafted that public image
by which he determined he should be recalled. For, above all,
Douglass was demonstrably concerned with the representation in
written language of his public self, a self Douglass created, manipulated, and transformed, if ever so slightly, through the three fictive selves he posited in his three autobiographies. As the anecdote about his final *Diary* entry makes clear, to his death Douglass
was concerned with the representation of this public self.

When I choose to call these selves fictive ones, I do not mean to
suggest any sense of falsity or ill intent; rather, I mean by fictive
the act of crafting or making by design, in this instance a process
that unfolds in language, through the very discourse that Douglass
employs to narrate his autobiographies. There is no doubt that
Frederick Douglass intended to create his biographer's work, even
from the grave. Except for John Blassingame's slim and virtually
unknown life of Douglass, each of his biographers has turned to
Douglass's three autobiographies to ascertain the contours of his
life. The first was *The Narrative of the Life of Frederick Douglass; an American Slave, Written by Himself,* published in 1845,
which by 1850 had sold thirty thousand copies in English. Ten
years later, *My Bondage and My Freedom* appeared. This work
of 462 pages is three times as long as the 1845 narrative and
even includes a 58-page appendix comprised of extracts from his
speeches. By 1857, two years after it was published, *My Bondage*
had sold eighteen thousand copies. In 1881, Douglass published
The Life and Times of Frederick Douglass, which never sold very
well and which he expanded and republished in 1892. Written and
rewritten over a period of forty-seven years, the three autobiographies present precisely drawn portraits that Douglass intended to
will to history, so that he would be remembered exactly as he
wanted to be. The latter two books are essentially polemical ex-

tensions of the first, containing ever briefer accounts of his life as a slave in exchange for more expansive accounts of the public reformer and his social programs. Indeed, it is fair to say that Douglass, as he aged, increasingly subordinated a conception of self in his autobiographies to an embodiment of an ideology and a social ideal. As Paul Laurence Dunbar writes in "Frederick Douglass," it was "For [Ethiopia] his voice, a fearless clarion, rung . . ."

> When men maligned him, and their torrent wrath
> In furious imprecations o'er him broke,
> He kept his counsel as he kept his path;
> 'Twas for his race, not for himself he spoke.

But the writing of blacks had, since the European Renaissance and the Enlightenment, always assumed larger ideological and social implications than the mere rendering of a life. Perhaps the most remarkable aspect of the Enlightenment is that, by the middle of the eighteenth century, ethnocentrism and logocentrism had been forged together into one irresistible weapon drawn upon to justify the enslavement of the African. The absence and presence of writing, of a collective black voice that could in some sense be overheard, were drawn upon by European philosophers to deprive African slaves of their humanity.

For Hegel, as we have seen, cast into silence by their own loss or absence of voice, Africans could have no history, no meaningful text of blackness itself, since they had no true self-consciousness, no power to present or represent this black and terrible self. Being was here determined as presence, and presence in turn as consciousness. There could be no presence of Africans in history without this power of representation. Possessing no true self-consciousness, as signified by the absence of a voice, and therefore no history, for Hegel blacks lay veiled in a shroud of silence, invisible not because they had no face, but rather because they had no voice. Voice, after all, presupposes a face. That alone which separates the subject from the object is, for Hegel, the absence or presence of the voice, the phenomenological voice; the blackness of invisibility is the blackness of this silence. Without a voice, the African is absent, or defaced, from history. Literacy, in this grand sense, was a figure used to conjure with by the Enlightened philosophers of Europe, at the African's expense. "The Dream of Reason," Goya inscribed as a rubric on his *Caprichos,* "breeds monsters." As Diderot wrote of Samuel Richardson upon reading *Clarissa,* "It is he [the writer] who carries the torch to the back of the cave. . . . He blows upon the glorious phantom who presents himself at the entrance of the cave; and the hideous Moor whom he was masking reveals himself."

As a direct result of this curious, arbitrary critique, of which Hegel's and Diderot's are only emblems, abolitionists and exslaves conspired to break this resounding black silence by publishing the narratives of the ex-slaves. And this written language of the ex-slave, to borrow an idea from Jacques Lacan, "signified for *someone*" even before it signified *something.* For, above all else, every public spoken and written utterance of the ex-slaves was written and published for an essentially hostile auditor or interlocutor, the white abolitionist or the white slaveholder, both of whom imposed a meaning upon the discourse of the black subject. Again to quote Lacan, what seems to be at work in this complex relationship between subject and interlocutor is that "the subject progresses only by whatever integration he attains of his [particular] position in the universal: technically by the projection of his past into a discourse in the process of becoming." To become subjects, as it were, black ex-slaves had to demonstrate their language-using capacity before they could become social and historical entities. In short, slaves could inscribe their selves only in language. Ironically, this selfsame notion of people as subjects and as language, which Europeans and Americans used to displace one sort of enslavement of the blacks for another sort of enslavement, is the very idea that lay at the core of the major innovations of post-structural analysis in contemporary literary theory. The key question, of course, must be "Whose language?" (Using implicitly Hegel's opposition of subject and object, incidentally, Robert Stepto in *From Behind the Veil* has turned Hegel on his head and developed a brilliant and penetrating theory of black narrative, which has as its origins the structure of the texts of the slave narratives and which turns upon Stepto's critique of subject and object as aspects of narration generally and "narrative control" specifically, as objects become subjects and subjects interact with other subjects.)

To Douglass the autobiographer, his life was the vehicle for a social program. Accordingly, he served as editor and censor of even the smallest bits of data about his life until he had rendered them in language as part of the public self that he spent forty-seven years retouching. If Frederick Douglass was the nineteenth century's Representative Man, it was primarily because of his mastery of the literary uses of spoken and written language, a usage he diligently reworked and refined, splendidly. Frederick Douglass was no slave to the English language. Douglass himself seems to have given a priority to the spoken word over the written word. As he wrote in 1849, "Speech! Speech! The live, calm, grave, clear, pointed, warm, sweet, melodious, and powerful human voice is [the] chosen instrumentality" of social reform. While writing served its purpose, some matters were of such urgency that the spoken word was demanded. "Humanity, justice and liberty," wrote Douglass, "demand the service of the living human voice."

We can perhaps begin to understand Douglass's priority of voice through Jacques Derrida's radical critique of voice published in English as *Speech and Phenomena*. As Derrida argues, *"The voice is heard*. . . . The subject does not have to pass forth beyond himself to be immediately affected by his [own speaking voice.] My words are 'alive' because they seem not to leave me: not to fall outside me, outside my breath, at a visible distance; not to cease to belong to me, to be at my disposition without further props." As he continues,

No consciousness is possible without the voice. The voice is the being which is present to itself in the form of universality, as consciousness; the voice *is* consciousness. In colloquy, the propagation of signs does not seem to meet any obstacles because it brings together two phenomenological origins of pure auto-affection. To speak to someone is doubtless to hear oneself speak, to be heard by oneself; but, at the same time, if one is heard by another, to speak is to make him *repeat immediately* in himself the hearing-oneself-speak in the very form in which I effectuated it. This immediate repretition is a reproduction of pure auto-affection without the help of anything external. This possibility of reproduction, whose structure is absolutely unique, *gives itself out* as the phenomenon of a mastery or limitless power over the signifier, since the signifier itself has the form of what is not external. Ideally, in the teleological essence of speech, it would then be possible for the signifier to be in absolute proximity to the signified aimed at in intuition and governing the meaning. The signifier would become perfectly diaphanous due to the absolute proximity to the signified. This proximity is broken when, instead of hearing myself speak, I see myself write or gesture.

His own speaking voice gave Douglass the illusion of a greater control than his writing with which to engage himself in the anti-slavery arena, because by speaking one forces the audience to repeat one's same words over in their same order. Significantly, Douglass appended speeches to two of his three autobiographies. Despite his obvious mastery of the written word, this notion of voice and the illusion of control was of the utmost import for Douglass, as John Blassingame makes clear in his excellent introduction to the first volume of the first series of *The Frederick Douglass Papers,* the fourteen volumes of which will include more speeches than any other form.

Even in his novella, *The Heroic Slave,* Douglass's fictional rendering of the slave revolt aboard the slave ship *Creole* in 1841, led by a black slave called Maddison Washington, Douglass placed a major emphasis on the powers of the human voice, which he calls "that unfailing index of the soul." Indeed, it is Maddison Washington's voice, while delivering a soliloquy deep in the woods on the evils of slavery and his will to be free, which converts into an abolitionist a northern traveler who by chance and in secret overhears his speech. As the narrator describes the effect of this speech, when the converted abolitionist later encounters Maddison at a most propitious moment:

Mr. Listwell at once frankly disclosed the secret; describing the place where he first saw him; rehearsing the language which he [Maddison] had used; referring to the effect which his manner and speech had made upon him; declaring the resolution he there formed to be an abolitionist; telling how often he had spoken of the circumstance, and the deep concern he had ever since felt to know what had become of him; and whether he had carried out the purpose to make his escape, as in the woods he declared he would do.

"Ever since that morning," said Mr. Listwell, "you have seldom been absent from my mind, and though now I did not dare to hope that I should ever see you again, I have often wished that

such might be my fortune; for, from that hour, your face seemed
to be daguerreotyped on my memory."

Not only is this episode a model of the function that all of the
slave narratives were to have upon their American and European
audiences, but also it was just this creation of a face, "daguerreotyped on memory," that the strong black speaking voice was intended to create. Whether speaking or writing, the black slave's
voice performed a major function.

Long after the issues for which he struggled so ardently have
become primarily the concern of the historian, Frederick Douglass will continue to be read and reread. And surely this must be
the literary critic's final judgment of Frederick Douglass: that he
was Representative Man because he was Rhetorical Man, black
master of the verbal arts. Douglass is our clearest example of the
will to power as the will to write. The act of writing for the slave
constituted the act of creating a public, historical self, not only the
self of the individual author but also the self, as it were, of the
race. Indeed, in part because of Douglass's literary successes,
blacks in general compensated to Hegel and his less able dis-
ciples for the absence of a collective written history by writing a
remarkable number of individual histories, which taken together
begin to assume the features of a communal, collective tale. In
literacy was power; as Ishamel Reed puts it in his satirical novel
about slavery, *Flight to Canada,* the slave who was the first to read
and the first to write was the first slave to run away. And as Stepto
perceptively demonstrates, the correlation of freedom with literacy
not only became the central trope of the slave narratives, but it
also formed a mythical matrix out of which subsequent black narrative forms developed. For the critic, Frederick Douglass does
not yet exist as a three-dimensional person; rather, he exists as a
rhetorical strategy primarily, as an open-ended system of rhetorical figures and tropes.

II

What have his biographers done with Douglass? In general, the
Douglass biographers have used him to illustrate and promote
various social programs and ideals, all of which turn upon several
ideas of social equality for blacks. Each uses his idea of Douglass

for a political purpose, making him representative of much more than the nineteenth century. Generally, Douglass biographers see him as he permitted himself to be seen, thus writing authorized biographies, the shape of which has been controlled and determined by Douglass himself even from the grave. Douglass has become for the historian an open-ended emblem which readily fastens itself to both the temper of the biographer's times and as the ideological whims of the biographer. Almost never does Douglass allow us to see him as a human individual in all of his complexity; accordingly, in these biographies Douglass comes to exist only as a historical force or presence and not as the multifaceted and intensely human person he undoubtedly was.

For Booker T. Washington, Frederick Douglass was a John the Baptist who roamed the deserts of antebellum and Reconstruction America clearing the way for that great deliverer, Booker T., sanctioning Washington's social program and Washington himself as the true ideals for turn-of-the-century Afro-America. Washington himself inadvertently reveals his idea of their relationship in his own autobiography, *Up from Slavery:* "Frederick Douglass died in February, 1895. In September of the same year I delivered an address in Atlanta at the Cotton States Exposition." Through this act of language, of course, Washington intends to subsume Douglass, as well as to use him to sanctify the passing of the mantle of black leadership, points that Robert Stepto explicates perceptively.

For Charles Chesnutt, Frederick Douglass is the black man's most cogent response to *fin-de-siècle* America's pseudoscientific social Darwinism. Above all else, Chesnutt draws upon Douglass both to claim the Negro's inherently equal innate capacity and to refute arguments against the role of environment in the shaping of intelligence, a racist discourse in nineteenth-century natural and physical scientific thought so compelling that all of black intellectual thought between 1800 and 1930 can be read as a complex response to it. As Chesnutt writes:

> If it be no small task for a man of the most favored antecedents and the most fortunate surroundings to rise above mediocrity in a great nation, it is surely a more remarkable achievement for a man of the very humblest origin possible to humanity in any country in any age of the world, in the face of obstacles seem-

ingly unsurmountable, to win high honors and rewards, to retain
for more than a generation the respect of good men in many
lands, and to be deemed worthy of enrolment [sic] among his
country's great men. Such a man was Frederick Douglass, and the
example of one who thus rose to eminence by sheer force of character and talents that neither slavery nor caste prescription could
crush must ever remain as a shining illustration of the essential
superiority of manhood to environment.

Of Douglass's poignant descriptions of his painful mastery of
reading and writing, Chesnutt writes that "thus again [he] demonstrated the power of the mind to overleap the bounds that men
set for it and work out the destiny to which God designs it."

Peter Walker's critique of Benjamin Quarles's *Frederick Douglass* and of Philip Foner's *Frederick Douglass* accords with my
own. As Walker writes in *Moral Choices: Memory, Desire, and
Imagination in Nineteenth-Century American Letters,* "In Benjamin Quarles's biography Douglass is a black Ragged Dick. . . .
Indeed, Quarles represents Douglass to be the black incarnation
of Andrew Carnegie's *Wealth*." For Quarles, Douglass is the classic example of the potential of black upward social mobility, un-
fettered by the laws of segregation. "Douglass advocated the gos-
pel of wealth," writes Quarles. "His financial independence was
another illustration of his preachments squaring with his practices." Citing a number of Douglass's notions on this subject,
Quarles concludes with the following citation: " 'Aristotle and
Pericles are all right,' writes Douglass; 'get that, too; *but get money
besides, and plenty of it.'* " Quarles's Douglass is an achiever, and
would have been even had the abolition movement not afforded
him ready access to an international platform.

For Philip Foner, Douglass is the first great black general in the
"Marxian warfare between social classes, a war in which Douglass
enlisted first to free the Negro 'masses' from chattel slavery, then
after emancipation fought to free them from an oppressive capital-
ism." For Foner, Walker concludes, "Douglass must be foresworn
while he was still a slave to undertake a mission that accorded
with the design of history. He must escape slavery in order to lead
a racially defined class struggle for freedom." Foner's Douglass simultaneously accepts a racial and a class identity.

Curiously enough, Quarles's Douglass and Foner's Douglass, as

Walker concludes, both take at face value Douglass's claims in his three autobiographies that his identity, his self-conception, were completely formulated and remained unchanged from the time he escaped from slavery in 1838. This fiction, of course, was forged by Douglass himself, who would have his readers believe that he fully possessed his identity within the matrix of his slave past. Despite a valiant attempt to account for these crucial formulative years in Douglass's life, which he describes in lively, almost novelistic language, Nathan Huggins, a recent Douglass biographer, squeezes a quarter-century of a human life into sixteen factual pages, culled almost to a fact from Douglass's own autobiographies. Huggins, like almost every other Douglass biographer, would have us believe, as Douglass wished, that Frederick Augustus Washington Bailey sprang from slavery full-blown, like Minerva from the brow of Jupiter, completely whole and undiminished by the horrors of slavery. His self-given identity is perfected by 1838, when we know that Douglass escaped from Baltimore to New York at an age no older than twenty. This is perhaps one of the most profound fictions ever shared by subject and biographer alike. As soon as the outward strictures of human bondage are fled or destroyed, the always already free black soul can begin to function in a free society. Never does Douglass allow us to witness his development as a person, precisely because he argues that he was always fully formed despite the horrors and brutalities of slavery. Paradoxically, Douglass argues that the self of the enslaved had suffered no essential damage (and this so that the authority the narrator claimed would not be diminished) and simultaneously that slavery did indeed work great damage upon all who dwelled within it. Douglass's solution was that while slavery stopped slaves from actualizing their capacities, it did not in fact destroy them. Even Walker, who otherwise reads closely, fails to see that Douglass's image of himself as rendered in the 1845 *Narrative,* for example, offers us the most salient refutation of that text's thesis of the coherent, fixed self since, as written, his character's self is both fluid and dynamic. Douglass here is truly the ironic subject, drawing upon an ironic rhetorical strategy, as Kierkegaard says, to feel free, because the subject's "appearance is the opposite of what he himself subscribes to." Kierkegaard most clearly explains the nature of the irony at work here. "With irony

. . . the subject is always seeking to get outside the object, and
this he attains by becoming conscious at every moment that the
object has no reality. . . . With irony the subject constantly re-
tires from the field and proceeds to talk every phenomenon out of
its reality in order to save himself, that is, in order to preserve
himself in his negative independence of everything."

For Huggins, whose title—*Slave and Citizen: The Life of
Frederick Douglass*—echoes both Frank Tannebaum's *Slave and
Citizen* and Ralph Korngold's *Citizen Toussaint,* his life of Frederick Douglass is of the questing man of color and consciousness,
in the public arena. For Huggins, Douglass himself saw his life
as a sublime revelation of the "potential within other black men
and women. . . . Through the story of this life one could glimpse
human potentialities, and indeed human perfectibility, a testament
for an American faith." As Huggins concludes, Douglass "lived
his life, even as an agitator and radical so as to exemplify the perfectibility of the black man and the slave, and to expose the idiocy
of a social system that would treat him, and people like him, as
pariahs." To what end this exemplification of perfectibility? Nothing less than "recognition of citizenship rights for Afro-Americans
throughout the country." This, above all else, is Huggins's Douglass, the pragmatic black nationalist fighting consistently for the
full perquisites of American citizenship from 1841 to 1895.

It is fairly simple to show that these lives of Douglass have at
their foundation the idealist premise of the individual belonging to
the realm of the transcendent, beyond further analysis. Repeating
Douglass's same words in their same order, Douglass's meaning,
to them, can only be understood as what Douglass the individual
intends. It is therefore the individual's intention that produces
meaning, the specific relations of difference. This idea, in turn, is
predicated upon an idea of a unified and consistent subject, the
assumption on which Western metaphysical thought has rested at
least since the Enlightenment. All of the biographies of Douglass
share this fiction of Douglass as a unified and consistent subject,
precisely because they take Douglass at his word—or rather they
fail to take him to task for altering his words—about his life as a
slave generally, and more specifically about his relationships with
his mother and with his father, and finding and losing his voice.

The sign of a great biography of Douglass is the space devoted to his life as a slave, from his birthdate in 1818 to his escape from slavery in 1838. If Nathan Huggins's concern is with the public Douglass, with that proposed opposition between slave and citizen, then Dickson J. Preston's concern is with the private Douglass as slave, with the life and times of Frederick Augustus Washington Bailey, which was the name his mother, Harriet Bailey, gave to him at his birth and by which Douglass was known until his escape from slavery in 1838.

Writing in *Young Frederick Douglass: The Maryland Years,* Dickson J. Preston, an amateur historian, has at last been able to re-create in convincing detail "the Maryland years" of Frederick Douglass's youth and adolescence, experiences and seminal influences that have eluded even the most diligent and well-trained historians. Indeed, Preston's feat—which consists of the most rigorous documentation of even seemingly insignificant events in the life of the slave—is that sort of labor of love generally characterized by the English gentleman of leisure who "happens" to discover Troy. Preston's is the first biography of Douglass to presume that Douglass's several social programs, coupled with the human limits of memory, render his depictions of slave life on the eastern shore of Maryland suspect, at the least, and sheer fictions rather frequently.

Preston's work is full of remarkably detailed and documented names and dates and places and events, within the matrix of which young Frederick evolved. These details answer questions that have plagued Douglass historians for almost a century. We know now that he was born in 1818; we know that he moved to Fells Point in Baltimore in March 1826 and that in November of that year the white man who most probably was his father died. We know that he was sent from Baltimore to Hillsborough to be included with the other slaves as part of Captain Anthony's estate on October 18, 1827. We know that Sophia Auld taught him his letters in 1827 and that in 1831 he underwent a profound religious conversion and bought the book from which he would learn the fine art of rhetoric, *The Columbian Orator.* These and a hundred other chronological details, which eluded both Douglass and his biographers, Preston now firmly establishes.

Most profoundly of all, Preston publishes as an appendix the "Genealogy of Frederick Douglass," which he has pieced together sleuthlike from the records of the Anthony, Sinner, and Rice families of Talbot County, Maryland. Remarkably, Preston's genealogy begins with Douglass's great-great-grandparents, born in 1701 and 1720, and traces the Bailey family to its sixth generation, the generation of Frederick Douglass's five children. As Preston concludes of Douglass's heritage, "he had not sprung full-grown out of nowhere, as his contemporaries seemed to think; his black ancestors, for a century or more before his birth, had been a strong and closely knit kin group with family pride and traditions that were handed on to him by his part-Indian grandmother, Betsey Bailey. His roots were anchored deeply in the earliest American experience." Indeed, when the newly free Frederick Augustus Washington Bailey renamed himself first Frederick Bailey, then Frederick Stanley, then Frederick Johnson, and ultimately Frederick Douglass, he self-consciously and ironically abandoned a strong matrilineal black heritage of five stable generations and embraced with equal irony a Scottish character named Douglass in Scott's *The Lady of the Lake.* Booker T. Washington suggests that this naming process was common among ex-slaves: "after the coming of freedom there were two points upon which practically all the people on our place were agreed, and I find that this was generally true throughout the South: that they must change their names, and that they must leave the old plantation for at least a few days or weeks in order that they might really feel that they were free."

Despite a tendency to wax overpoetic about the splendors of the eastern shore of Maryland, and despite an equally disturbing tendency to diminish speculation on the suffocating atmosphere of even the most benign prisonhouse of slavery, Preston has given us in his major biography a more three-dimensional, more human Frederick Douglass than has any other biographer. He succeeds where others could not, essentially because he "tried to look behind [Douglass's] own account to see how much of what he said could be verified—or disproved—by independent evidence." To detailed family and county records, Preston adds the marginalia written in Douglass's autobiographies by descendants of his master's family, thus recording "dialogue" between Douglass and his white owners. One, Harriet Lucretia Anthony, wrote in the margin of *Bondage and Freedom* that "several years before Fred's death

I sent him from my great grandfather's records the date of his birth," which means that Douglass's trip to Dr. Thomas Edward Sears could only have been to verify Lucretia's date of 1818 or his own estimate of 1817. Preston's remarkably thorough skills as a biographer now make every other account of the first quarter of Frederick Douglass's life either suspect or inaccurate.

III

What is serious in Preston's fact-finding mission is that it proves for the historian that Frederick Douglass took wide liberties with the order and narrating of the "facts" about his experiences as a slave, and that it reinforces a more subtle reevaluation of Douglass as a language-using, social, historical, and individual entity; indeed, for both literary critics and a few historians, "Frederick Douglass" has at last come to be seen and explicated as his language itself. In Dexter Fisher and Robert Stepto's edited volume, *Afro-American Literature: The Reconstruction of Instruction* (1979), three literary critics undertake careful, close readings of Douglass's 1845 *Narrative*. If their findings are not so very surprising in light of developments in post-structural and hermeneutic theory generally, then fairly comparable work by two historians, not commonly known for their concern with the ironies of history making, are rather surprising and suggest major innovations in the historiography of the Afro-American experience. Both Peter Walker's three stunning chapters on Douglass in *Moral Choices* and John W. Blassingame's brilliant introduction to the first volume of the *Douglass Papers* clearly define Douglass first and last by uses of spoken and written language.

Why is this such a remarkable development in black historiography? Because the single most pervasive and consistent assumption of all black writing since the eighteenth century has been that there exists an unassailable, integral, black self, as compelling and as whole in Africa as in the New World, within slavery as without slavery. What's more, this self was knowable, retrievable, recuperable, if only enough attention to detail were displayed.

Perhaps the one unshakable assumption of historians of Afro-Americans has been the belief that great black men and women have made great black history. Accused by Hegel and others of having no history, Afro-Americans created the genre of the slave narratives, autobiographical accounts of lordship, bondage, and escape, to render in fascinating detail both the unspeakable horrors of human enslavement and the exact features of a single, transcendent, black, and sufficient self. The sheer narrative and polemical force of these autobiographies, which stood in relation to the lives of every black countryman as the part stands for the whole, helps to explain the growth of the black encyclopedic dictionary, some three hundred of which have been published since 1808. Not only has the fundamental integrity of the speaking black subject undergirded all theories of black cultural nationalism, but it has also remained the great unspoken and unchallenged fiction even of contemporary black literary and historiographical scholarship.

This critique of the black subject, which is only an extension of an idealist notion of self, arises not from historians eager to dispel the notion of individual actors in black history, but rather from those eager to render the very complexity of black history and the actors who played crucial roles in it. Preston, Blassingame, and Walker are concerned with a Frederick Douglass as defined by his uses of language. Through close readings of Douglass's texts, they have for the first time called into question the myth of the eternally knowable and unchanging black and integral self. This is a major innovation in black scholarship, which for all sorts of reasons has generally avoided metacommentary on its own mechanisms.

It is not so surprising that these critiques of received notions of the subject begin with Frederick Douglass. For it is Douglass, above all other black historical selves, who most openly invites, indeed demands, a close reading of his three autobiographies. Anyone, after all, who writes more than one autobiography must be acutely aware of the ironies implicit in the re-creation of successive fictive selves, subject to manipulation and revision in written discourse. Douglass furthermore invites such a critique because each of the selves he renders in each of his biographies is a distinctly different self with distinctly different origins, invented in 1845 and reinvented in 1855 and in 1881 to make consistent the "Frederick Douglass" he intended to reveal to his readers.

Every autobiography, after all, is a figure of a figure, the repetition in language of a human figure. All sorts of pregiven "essences" were attributed by Europeans since the Latin Middle Ages to the "nature" of blacks. To put the matter in terms of a black folk rhyme, "to figure like a nigger" in European discourse was not to figure at all. This runs contrary to the idea of Douglass's legacy that Robert Hayden put forth in his poem, "Frederick Douglass":

> this man, this Douglass, this former slave, this Negro
> beaten to his knees, exiled, visioning a world
> where none is lonely, none hunted, alien,
> this man, superb in love and logic, this man
> shall be remembered. Oh, not with statues' rhetoric,
> not with legends and poems and wreaths of bronze alone,
> but with the lives grown out of his life, the lives
> fleshing his dream of the beautiful, needful thing.

Douglass's legacy to contemporary black letters is his masterful use of the trope of irony. American liberalism since the abolitionists has fastened the myth of equality upon the ideas of the properly speaking subject. To speak properly was to be proper. But to attempt to employ a Western language to posit a black self is inherently to use language ironically. The relation of the speaking black subject to the self figured in these languages must by definition be an ironical relation, since that self exists only in the "non-place of language," and since these languages encoded figuratively the idea that blackness itself is a negative essence, an absence. To refute these pregiven essences, Douglass substitutes his own myth of essence, and of origins, by altering dramatically key elements in his lost past. By rejecting the name his mother gave him, Douglass not only rejected his most concrete and binding linkage with five generations of a black but enslaved past, but he also made of his past a tabula rasa on which he could inscribe critically whatever name or face he chose to, at any point in his life.

Blassingame's contribution to this critique of the black subject is as major as it is subtle and indirect. Not only have Blassingame and his fellow editors of the *Douglass Papers* project re-created the hundreds of speeches that Douglass delivered, but Blassingame's masterful introduction is nothing less than a full treatment of what he calls "Douglass's rhetorical theory." Perhaps the most remarkable feature of Volume One is its "partial itinerary" of Douglass's public speaking engagements between 1841 and 1846, which reveals that Douglass appears to have been an indefatigable servant of the antislavery cause. Juxtaposed with the texts of these speeches, literally pieced together from thousands of press reports, and with detailed "headnotes" that provide all sorts of factual contexts for the speeches, we begin to understand in splendid detail how fully Douglass worked and reworked his text of antislavery, and how often different commentators took the occasion of Douglass's eloquence to remark upon its implications in a new assessment of the "Negro's place in nature," as the cliché went. Acutely aware of this function of language, Douglass calls attention throughout these speeches to his own mastery of language and its ramifications for all subsequent evaluations of the black slave and ex-slave. As Blassingame writes, "Lecturing on the unity of the races in Cincinnati, Douglass 'claimed that the Negro exhibited all the elements of a man—he laughed, he wept, he walked, he knew the use of fire and he acquired and retained knowledge. No animal but man had these qualities. Even the dogs saw it, and followed the Negro as they did the white man, and in these days of doubt, a dog's testimony was worth something.' " As Douglass put the relationship between language acquisition and freedom, "all the education I possess, I may say, I have stolen while a slave. I did manage to steal a little knowledge of literature, but I am now in the eyes of American law considered a thief and robber, since I have not only stolen a little knowledge of literature, but have stolen my body also." And as one Edward Smith maintained in his introduction of Douglass to an English audience, Douglass's rhetorical skills alone would make unnecessary "any further argument to convince them whether or not the slave is endowed with powers of intellect." Blassingame's essay on Douglass, combined with the unparalleled reassembly of Douglass's spoken words, brings together the sophisticated and rigorous scholarship that characterizes both *The Slave Community* and *Black New Orleans* with an attention to the complexities of language as sensitive as that of any literary critic.

Dickson Preston and Peter Walker join the literary critics in Fisher and Stepto's volume in examining what Douglass writes about his mother and his father. Of the two, Walker's treatment is the most sustained, if somewhat bold, a reading of passages from the three autobiographies which he supplements by a revealing analysis of Douglass's accounts of finding and losing his voice with the white Garrisonian abolitionists between 1841 and 1847.

Walker's argument about Douglass's voice is complex but can be summarized. Douglass, in each of his autobiographies, consistently argues that he escaped from slavery both completely whole and fully formed, knowing exactly the contours of his identity. Walker argues that this assertion is a rhetorical strategy designed to establish

> the former slave as a functioning member of a free labor society; that is, it argues that the slavery experience, regardless of its brutalities and deprivations, did not inhibit the development of a slave's essential characteristics as a human being. . . . He is not psychologically crippled. Second, it permits Douglass to move straightway to attack social conditions in the free society that inhibit the former slave from being what he already is.

What Walker does not say is that this rhetorical strategy enables Douglass to displace a negative and received idea of identity—of the slave as lazy and debased—with an equally fictitious idea of identity that exists *before* the individual enters the social relations of a free society. Douglass here substitutes one ideal essence for another: "idealism depends upon notions of 'human essence' which somehow transcend and operate (indeed, cause) the social systems," and are not constructed within this system; to refute the slave's pregiven, negative essence, Douglass posits his own myth of essence, his own myth of origins. Despite the fact that we can critique this gesture as we would any other aspect of idealism, Douglass here most obviously is claiming the authority to define his own and the black person's "essential self."

What Walker's analysis reveals, however, is much of the irony implicit in Douglass's successive myths of origins. Significantly, Douglass, writing in the 1845 *Narrative,* describes his moment of true freedom not as his escape from Baltimore to New York, but rather when, in Robert Stepto's apt phrase, the first "rose and found his voice." The setting was an antislavery convention at Nantucket in August 1841, three years after his escape from Balti-

more. Called upon and "strongly moved to speak," Douglass gives
this account of his conversion experience: "It was a severe cross,
and I took it up reluctantly. *The truth was, I felt* myself a slave,
and the idea of speaking to white people weighed me down. I
spoke but a few moments, *when I felt a degree of freedom,* and
said what I desired with considerable ease. From that time until
now, I have been engaged in pleading the cause of my brethren."
When he rewrote the description for *Bondage and Freedom*
(1855), Douglass expanded on it in this way and allowed it to
stand in the *Life and Times* (1881, 1892): "Young, ardent and
hopeful, I entered upon this new life in the full gush of unsus-
pecting enthusiasm. The cause was good, the men engaged in it
were good, the means to attain its triumph, good. . . . For a
time I was made to forget that my skin was dark and my hair
crisped." Juxtaposed with his rejection of his mother's name and,
as we shall see, her memory, Walker reads Douglass's conversion
as his own escape not only from slavery but from his black mother's heritage, thereby grafting himself onto his nameless white
father's heritage, here displaced in the white Garrisonians. As
Walker concludes accurately, "it is the passive, not the active,
voice that speaks in this keening passage. . . . All of a sudden,
and very briefly, he becomes the passive participant in his own
drama. Power over self was lost and control over his life—the
very definition of self—passes to others, in this case the Garrisonians." As if warding off attacks against his method of reading,
Walker cites a curious phenomenon that happened to Douglass
when at last he broke openly with Garrison. Just as he had found
his voice at Nantucket six years earlier in the full company of
Garrison and the Garrisonians, so too did he now lose his voice,
remaining unable for an extended time to utter even one syllable.
Douglass's oratorical career extended from 1841 to 1895, yet
Walker was unable to find any other example of this sort of loss
of voice.

An even more remarkable example of the manner by which
Douglass manipulated his own blank past as "a representation of
the present," as the consistent extension backwards in time of the
particular self he was forging in each autobiography, are Douglass's accounts of the identity of his mother and father. Three
times in the first chapter of his 1845 *Narrative* Douglass writes

that "my master was my father": "My father was a white man. He was admitted to be such by all I ever heard speak of my parentage. The opinion was also whispered that my master was my father; but of the correctness of that opinion, I know nothing; the means of knowing was withheld from me." Just ten years later, writing in *My Bondage and My Freedom,* Douglass qualifies the unequivocal claim made in the *Narrative:* "I say nothing of father, for he is shrouded in a mystery I have never been able to penetrate. Slavery does away with fathers, as it does away with families. . . . The order of civilization is reversed here. The name of the child is not expected to be that of its father, and his condition does not necessarily affect that of the child. . . . My father was a white man, *or nearly white* [emphasis added]. It was sometimes whispered that my master was my father." A few pages later, Douglass comments on his father again: "My mother died without leaving me a single intimation of *who* my father was. There was a whisper, that my master was my father; yet it was only a whisper, and I cannot say that I ever gave it credence. Indeed, I now have reason to think he was not." In the two editions of the *Life and Times,* Douglass has this to say: "Of my father I know nothing." As Walker concludes, "as an identifiable man his father had ceased to exist."

If Douglass's diminishment of his father from his white master to an invisible nonpresence is curious, his narrative accounts of his mother are even more remarkable. In the 1845 *Narrative,* Douglass can barely recall his mother, from whom he was "separated when I was but an infant. . . . I never saw my mother, to know her as such, more than four or five times in my life; and each of these times was very short in duration, and at night. . . . I do not recollect of ever seeing my mother by the light of day. She was with me in the night. . . . Never having enjoyed, to any considerable extent, her soothing presence, her tender and watchful care, I received the tidings of her death with much the same emotions I should have probably felt at the death of a stranger."

In *Bondage and Freedom,* however, Douglass just ten years later repeats that his knowledge of his mother is "very scanty" but notes that it has also become "very distinct." Douglass writes, "Her personal appearance and bearing are ineffaceably stamped upon my memory. She was tall, and finely proportioned; of deep black, glossy complexion; had regular features, and, among the other slaves, was remarkably sedate in her manners." He concludes in 1855, "It has been a life-long, standing grief to me, that I knew so little of my mother; and that I was so early separated from her. The counsels of her love must have been beneficial to me. The side view of her face is imaged on my memory, and I take few steps in life, without feeling her presence; *but the image is mute, and I have no striking words of her treasured up.*" [emphasis added]. Not only has Douglass fairly suddenly recalled his mother's appearance, but he also has come to feel for her death "life-long, standing grief," when just ten years earlier her death struck him as would the death of a total stranger.

Perhaps even more remarkably, Douglass, in these ten intervening years, has stumbled upon a picture of a person that he claims resembles his mother. This reference to the picture, which is to be found on page 157 of James Prichard's *Natural History of Man,* remained throughout the final editions of his autobiographies. As Douglass himself states, he found in Prichard "the head of a figure . . . the features of which so resemble those of my mother, that I often recur of it with something of the feeling which I suppose others experience when looking upon the pictures of dear departed ones." The ironies of this attribution are legion. In the first place, Prichard says that the picture is that of the "head of a statue supposed to be that of Rameses," which represents the ideal racial type he calls "the Indian." Prichard calls "the general expression" of the head "calm and dignified," which echoes Douglass's description of his mother as "remarkably sedate and dignified." Rather obviously, however, the figure is not, and could not be, "deep black" or "glossy." As Walker suggests, to find this figure in Prichard, Douglass had to pass over an abundant supply of illustrations that accompanied Prichard's description of several "African races." And, most ironically of all, the head is that of a man and not a woman at all.

If the picture of Douglass's black and glossy mother is that of an "Indian" male, Douglass's various versions of his mother also become progressively more articulate. Douglass ignored completely his mother's literacy in the 1845 *Narrative,* but by 1855 Harriet Bailey had become "the only one of all the slaves and colored people in Tuckahoe who enjoyed" the "advantage" of reading. What's more, Douglass "fondly and proudly ascribes to her an earnest love of knowledge." Accordingly, he now sees fit "to attribute any love of letters I possess, and for which I have got—despite of prejudices—only too much credit, not to my admitted Anglo-Saxon paternity, but to the native genius of my sable, unprotected, and uncultivated mother—a woman," he concludes, "who belonged to a race whose mental endowments it is, at present, fashionable to hold in disparagement and contempt."

Of these startling assertions and revisions, Walker's conclusion are most telling:

> With these changes Harriet Bailey's metamorphosis was completed. The dark woman who in the *Narrative* passed through Douglass' life almost literally a stranger in the night becomes the sable, tall fine-featured, impressive dignified mother. . . . She becomes a mother who made him feel like a prince, and who endowed him with the preeminent quality of language. It was she alone who enabled him to become a writer and speaker; she gave Douglass his "voice." No factitious reading of these passages is required to understand what Douglass was doing. Through the continued development and refinement of the autobiographical mother, Douglass was also developing and refining his own conception of self. He was driving self deeper and deeper into a proud identification with Harriet Bailey who above all else was a black slave.

Walker's close readings of Douglass, coupled with Preston's fact finding and Blassingame's detailed exposition of Douglass's rhetorical theory, comprise a major critique of that stolid black self which Douglass willed to history. Walker's scholarship especially unravels the historical Douglass, just as one stray thread, pulled properly, can unravel the weave of a whole cloth. With the publication of these volumes, we must now insist upon the recognition and identification of the black autobiographical tradition as the positing of fictive black selves in language, in a mode of discourse traditionally defined by rather large claims for the self. The self, in this sense, does not exist as an entity but as a coded system of signs, arbitrary in reference. This is not to argue against the existence of the self but only to argue that any attempt to recreate or represent a historical self in language is marked from the start by burdensome ironies.

There remains to be done a great work of scholarship, one that in full rhetorical power can create a life of Frederick Douglass that somehow gives us a sense of the complexities of the man and of the contradictions among the three public selves he recorded so eloquently in his autobiographies. Perhaps a great scholar can restore to the life of Douglass its decidedly human face. Perhaps our generation of scholars can eschew earlier needs to forge a distinctly Afro-American mythology, complete with our own mythic figures, and we can learn to love our heroes and antecedents with all of their weaknesses and foibles preserved intact. And perhaps Douglass's first great biographer will be the scholar who restored to Douglass his elusive date of birth, for all time henceforth a fact as verifiable as the time of day. For John Blassingame found, in a long-lost record that Captain Aaron Anthony maintained and in which he recorded only the barest details of "My Black People[s'] Ages," that Frederick Douglass was indeed born in February 1818. Just as Blassingame has given to Douglass that fact for which he searched to his death in vain, so perhaps will he give us the face of Douglass as resplendently as he has given us, through his speeches and writings, Douglass's great and terrible voice.

· 5 ·

Parallel Discursive Universes:
Fictions of the Self in
Harriet E. Wilson's *Our Nig*

> I sincerely appeal to my colored brethren universally for patronage, hoping that they will not condemn this attempt of their sister to be erudite, but rally around me a faithful band of supporters and defenders.
>
> Harriet E. Wilson, "Preface"

> No one has a kinder heart, one capable of loving more devotedly. But to think how prejudiced the world are towards her people; that she must be reared in such ignorance as to drown all the finer feelings. When I think of what she might be, of what she will be, I feel like grasping time till opinions change, and thousands like her rise to a noble freedom.
>
> Harriet E. Wilson, *Our Nig*

I picked up a copy of *Our Nig* while browsing at the University Place Bookshop in Manhattan in May 1981.[1] I was curious about the book's title. I am an avid collector of images of blacks in Western literature and art, and I had not before encountered the use of the word *nigger* in a title published before the end of the Civil War. I assumed that *Our Nig* was a book full of happy, shiny darkies, strumming banjos out in the field. Since I did not especially relish the notion of entering this fabricated never-neverland of racial fantasy, I put *Our Nig* on the shelf where it sat for about a year.

In May 1982, I finally read it. Immediately, I was convinced that *Our Nig* was the creation of a black novelist. There were several reasons for this, which I have outlined in my introduction to the second edition of *Our Nig*, published in March 1983 by

125

Random House. No reason was of more importance to my hypothesis, however, than the most obvious one: Mrs. H. E. Wilson *claimed* to be black. There was little to be gained by "passing" for black in 1859, either within the publishing world or without it. *Claim,* perhaps, is too strong a term, for the author of *Our Nig* does not make a case for her racial identity; rather, she presumes its self-evidence and treats the matter accordingly.

While some white authors such as Mattie Griffiths, who in 1857 published *The Autobiography of a Female Slave,* had adopted a black persona in their novels, few had pretended to be black. No black author became wealthy from writing a book, although Frederick Douglass, among others, did well as a writer. Harriet Beecher Stowe's artistic success was not hindered at all by her race. Presenting her race as black and not bothering to demonstrate or establish it, H. E. Wilson, it seemed to me, was quite probably a black woman. An interracial marriage, rendered with balance and a depiction of a dishonest black "fugitive slave" also were remarkably uncommon aspects of the received conventions of the sentimental novel, suggesting a curious rupture in this text's relation to that tradition, of which it so obviously was part but from which its structure departed dramatically. But how could I establish Mrs. H. E. Wilson's race and authorship? This essay recounts that curious tale, the resolution of which turned in large part upon the juxtaposition of two parallel discursive universes: the plot structure of a text claiming to be a "fiction" and the seemingly antithetical biographical documents published as the text's "Appendix," which claim to demonstrate that this fiction is indeed fact—"an Autobiography," as one dares to assert.

I

On the eighteenth day of August 1859, Mrs. Harriet E. Wilson entered at the clerk's office of the district court of Massachusetts the copyright of her novel, a fictional third-person autobiography, which she entitled *Our Nig; or, Sketches from the Life of a Free Black, in a Two Story White House, North. Showing That Slavery's Shadows Fall Even There.* The novel, printed for the author by the George C. Rand and Avery Company, was published by Wilson on September 5, 1859, under the pseudonym "By 'Our

Nig,' " the designation that forms the final line of the book's title. Wilson, in a disarmingly open preface to *Our Nig*, states her purpose for publishing her novel, a novel addressing a theme that, she confesses, could be misread:

> In offering to the public the following pages, the writer confesses her inability to minister to the refined and cultivated, the pleasure supplied by abler pens. It is not for such these crude narrations appear. Deserted by kindred, disabled by failing health, I am forced to some experiment which shall aid me in maintaining myself and child without extinguishing this feeble life.

Wilson explains that only an urgent need to support herself and her child has compelled her to publish this book, a book that takes as its central theme the nature of northern white racism as experienced by a free black indentured servant. We can begin to understand how controversial such a subject was if we remember that John Brown launched his aborted raid on Harper's Ferry in October 1859, just one month after Wilson published *Our Nig*. Despite the potential controversy, however, Harriet E. Adams Wilson asked her "colored brethren" to "rally around me a faithful band of supporters and defenders" and to purchase her book so that she might support herself and her child.

Just five months and twenty-four days later, the Amherst, New Hampshire, *Farmer's Cabinet* of February 29, 1860, included in its list of deaths the following item: "In Milford, 13th inst[ant], George Mason, only son of H. E. Wilson, aged 7 yrs. and 8 mos." George Mason Wilson, according to his death certificate, succumbed to "Fever" on February 15, 1860. The child quite probably received his name in honor of George Mason, the prominent Revolutionary era Virginia planter and statesman who opposed the institution of slavery. More relevant to our search for Harriet E. Wilson, however, George Mason Wilson, according to his death certificate, was the son of Thomas and Harriet E. Wilson. The "color" of the child is listed as "Black." This document alone confirms that "Mrs. H. S. Wilson," a designation echoed by the *Farmer's Cabinet* death notice, was a black woman, apparently the first to publish a novel in English.

The irony of George Mason Wilson's untimely death is that it confirms the racial identification of Harriet E. Wilson, his mother, who had published her first novel to raise funds to retrieve her son less than six months before. Had it not been for George's death and his death certificate, it would have proved remarkably difficult to confirm my strong suspicion that his mother was an Afro-American. His mother's concern for her only chlid's welfare is responsible for her retrieval from literary oblivion. The irony is profound.

George's death certificate made possible the confirmation of a number of details about Wilson, which parallel rather closely statements about her by three of her friends and printed as an "Appendix" to *Our Nig*. George's death serves as a convenient emblem of the tragic irony of his mother's life and subsequent literary reputation. His mother wrote a sentimental novel, of all things, so that she might become self-sufficient and regain the right to care for her only son; six months later, her son died of that standard disease of fever; the record of this death alone proved sufficient to demonstrate his mother's racial identity and authorship of *Our Nig*. These curious historical events could easily have formed part of a plot in sentimental fiction itself, if any author had been bold enough to venture into that shadowy realm of the highly improbable. Nevertheless, these are the facts, as unlikely as they may seem. That Wilson dared to name her text with the most feared and hated epithet under which the very humanity of black people had been demeaned both adds to the list of ironies in her endeavor and attests to an intelligence that turned racist epithet into irony, subverting a received definition by inverting its common usage.

With this audacious act of titling, Wilson became most probably the fifth Afro-American to publish fiction in English (after Frederick Douglass, William Wells Brown, Frank J. Webb, and Martin R. Delany), the third Afro-American to publish a novel, and (along with Maria F. dos Reis, who published a novel called *Ursula* in Brazil in 1859) one of the first two black women to publish a novel in any language. Despite these profound claims to a central place in the Afro-American literary tradition, however, Wilson and her text—for reasons as curious and as puzzling as they are elusive, reasons about which we can venture rather little more than informed speculation—seem to have been ignored or overlooked both by her "colored brethren universally" and by even the most scrupulous scholars during the next hundred and twenty-three years.

II

It is difficult to imagine how such a seminal contribution to black letters could have been ignored or lost precisely when both black and white abolitionists specifically and humanitarians generally, at least from the middle of the eighteenth century, seized upon the creative writings of the slave and ex-slave as crucial evidence of the fundamental unity of the human species and, therefore, of the urgent need to abolish human slavery by statute. I have traced the positing of this curious and arbitrary relation above. Suffice it to cite here only a few of Wilson's contemporaries who published   ·
their arguments about the nature and function of the literature of the black.

The New York *Colored American,* for example, in its editorial of May 6, 1837, addressed this matter of the "natural capacity" of the black by predicting the coming of a great black writer:

> [Afro-Americans] have all the natural requisites to them, in sci-
> ence and renown, what ancient Egypt once was. . . . What Han-
> nibal of old was, in honor and military prowess, some of our sons
> may be, and as Hanno and Terrence, excelled in the literary an-
> nals of the world, so may we, at least in our posterity. Take cour-
> age then brethren. The God of benevolence, the bountiful bene-
> factor of all mankind has given to us, as much physical strength
> and intellectual power as to any other men.

Sixteen years later, a black lawyer who published essays frequently in *Frederick Douglass' Paper* under the pseudonym "Dion," repeated the *Colored American*'s prediction of the importance of black authors "at least in our posterity." Decrying the number of black Miltons who were "mute and inglorious," Dion argued that black literature, despite noteworthy attempts, nevertheless "exists only . . . in the vast realm of probability," only one of the resonant phrases for which this perceptive critic shall be recalled. Wrote Dion on September 23, 1851:

> A [Phillis] *Wheatley,* indeed, may have sung in brief, yet admi-
> rable snatches, while in her chains; a [George Moses] *Horton* may

have caused the dark walls of his prison-house to echo to notes so sublime as almost to persuade surrounding lordlings to grant him freedom. . . . Still, colored American literature exists only, to too great an extent, in the vast realm of probability.

The ultimate political salvation of "the race," Dion continued, lay with a future generation of black authors, whose works would at last restore to African peoples their lost glory, precisely by disproving racist claims against their "capacities":

> The future may yet reveal to us—and in the feelings of hope, we dare predict, that the future *will* yet reveal to us the names of colored Americans so gloriously illustrated in the catalogue of literary excellence, as to remind the world of the days when dark-browed Egypt gave letters to Greece, and when the sons of Ethiopia "black skinned and wooly-haired," in despite of the archaeological researches of Glidden, and the flippant letters of modern tourists—were at once the originators and conservators of science. The lamp which then burned so brilliantly, has not yet entirely died out.

From David Hume and Thomas Jefferson on one side and from Jacobus Capitein and Wilhelm Amo on the other, racist detractors and black writers would see in the literary artifact a battleground of confrontation between those who thought the person of African descent to be innately inferior and those who thought him or her to be capable of the "liberation" of the race through the mere creation of a sublime art.

That Wilson's novel seems to have escaped the critical attention of her contemporaries is an anomaly worth pondering, for, despite her prefatory appeal to her brethren, that group of free northern blacks and abolitionists whom we readily characterize as her "natural" constituency apparently allowed her literary work to languish among the ranks of the unreviewed, failing by their collective silence to "rally around me a faithful band of supporters and defenders." The literacy of the black, long before Wilson published *Our Nig* in 1859, had even become a central, repeated theme of the slave narratives, black poems, and black fictions. The scenes of instruction of the slave, his or her initial encounter with formal, written language, recur as frequently in pre-Emancipation Afro-American literature as do the familiar rhetorical tirades against the heinous features of the tyrannical mask of enslavement itself. Thomas Smallwood, in his largely unknown slave narrative published at Toronto in 1851, describes the polemical role of literacy in his own development in terms remarkably suggestive of James Baldwin's poignant essay, published in *Harper's* in October 1953, entitled "Stranger in the Village." Smallwood writes:

> When that [ability to read and write] became known to his neighbours they were amazed at the fact that a black or coloured person could learn the alphabet, yea, learn to spell in two syllables. I appeared to be a walking curiosity in the village where I then lived, and when passing about the village I would be called into houses and the neighbours collected around me to hear me say the alphabet and to spell baker and cider, to their great surprise, (which were the first two words in the two syllables of Webster's Spelling Book).

Why should such a fuss be made about such a common phenomenon, Smallwood implicitly asked his readers?

> This may afford the reader a glimpse into the abyss of intellectual darkness into which the African race in America has been so long purposely confined, to serve the avarice and envies of their tyrannical oppressors, and to get out of which, by the aid of their friends, they are now struggling against many obstacles; prejudice on the part of the whites being among the most potent.

Antislavery novels are replete with direct statements of the intelligence of blacks. Harriett Beecher Stowe's *The Minister's Wooing,* published in the same year as *Our Nig,* contains a statement by Candace, "a powerfully built, majestic black woman, corpulent, heavy," which addresses this matter squarely: "I ain't a critter. I's neider huff nor horns. I's a reasonable being." Proslavery fiction, conversely, is replete with contrary notions, such as the following statement made by a black character, Tony, of "C. J. Peterson's" *The Cabin and the Parlor; or, Slaves and Masters* (1852):

> Whar's de nigger can play wid Tony? Whar's de artist dat knows de grand harmonics like me? Or can gib de last novelists of de fashionable world, from de gran' poke, to de tender delisuosities

of Lucy Neal. But yer don't comprehend dose tings 't all, niggers.
. . . De simplicities of yer degraded 'ditions allers forbids yer
risin' ter de soarin' heights of poetry and der spheres.

No matter how humorous we find such passages today, the intelligence of blacks was a salient, if often subtle, issue in the fight
against slavery. Needless to add, it was incumbent upon blacks
and their allies to demonstrate to the larger public through the
publication of books that nature had endowed the races equally,
even if the deleterious effects of human bondage relegated such
intelligence to dormancy. As the Rev. James W. C. Pennington
put the matter in his note "To the Reader," which prefaces Ann
Plato's *Essays* (the first book of essays published by a black
woman, in 1841):

> The fact is, this [publishing books] is the only way to show the
> fallacy of that stupid theory, that *nature has done nothing but fit
> us for slaves, and that art cannot unfit us for slavery!* . . . The
> history of the arts and sciences is the history of individuals, of in-
> dividual nations.

It was through such individual demonstrations of talent as Plato's,
Pennington argued, that the image of the black nation within a
nation could be restructured fundamentally.

While black writers maintained that the absence of an Afro-
American literature was merely one result of their subjugation,
they also knew that it was incumbent upon them to preserve those
few attainments, intellectual and practical, that, extraordinarily,
so many of them somehow managed to realize. By 1851, it was
apparent to the most sagacious that even these literary achievements were being lost and would continue to be lost in the absence of written records created and maintained by the blacks
themselves. James McCune Smith, the Edinburg-trained physician
and abolitionist, spoke for many when he wrote in 1851 in *Frederick Douglass's Paper* that

> the loss of the Alexandrian Library and its wealth of ancient lore
> is a deep grief to scholars, but I am convinced that there will be
> a profounder grief among thinkers, a century hence, that there is
> not now placed on record a succinct account of the true relation
> which the blacks now bear to this Republic—a concise statement
> of the facts embodied in their resistance and elevation herein

against odds sufficient to crush any ordinary variety of the human species.

Elevation, we know, was a key word within black discourse for demonstration of the race's capacity to produce literature. Despite McCune Smith's admonition, however, just eight years later Wilson's notable novel would be greeted by a critical silence oddly deafening in Boston, long identified as a major center of antislavery sentiment, epitomized by William Lloyd Garrison's weekly organ of the movement, *The Liberator,* which reviewed or reprinted reviews of hundreds of books by and about blacks. This silence is especially curious just eight years after Harriet Beecher Stowe had created a ready market for what came to be called negro fiction.

The popularity and favorable critical reception of Stowe's *Uncle Tom's Cabin,*[2] submitted in 1851 to the *National Era* with the subtitle "The Man that Was a Thing," created a genre that rather quickly came formally to be called Negro fiction, or the Negro novel. George Eliot's influential review of Stowe's *Dred; A Tale of the Great Dismal Swamp* (1856), printed in *The Westminster Review* in October 1856, defines the term:

> Looking at the matter simply from an artistic point of view, we see no reason to regret that Mrs. Stowe should keep to her original ground of negro and planter life, any more than that Scott should have introduced Highland life into "Rob Roy" and "The Fair Maid of Perth," when he had already written "Waverley." Mrs. Stowe has *invented* the negro novel, and it is a novel not only fresh in its scenery and its manners, but possessing that conflict of races which Augustin Thierry has pointed out as the great source of romantic interest—witness "Ivanhoe." Inventions in literature are not as plentiful as inventions in the paletot and waterproof department, and it is rather amusing that we reviewers, who have, for the most part, to read nothing but imitations of imitations, should put on airs of tolerance towards Mrs. Stowe because she has written a second negro novel, and make excuses for her on the ground that she perhaps would not succeed in any other kind of fiction. . . . But whatever else she may write, or may not write, "Uncle Tom" and "Dred" will assure her a place in that highest rank of novelists who can give us a national life in all its phases—popular and aristocratic, humorous and tragic, political and religious.

We may take Eliot at her word; despite the publication in 1851 of Emily Catherine Pierson's *Jamie, the Fugitive,* Stowe did indeed invent the Negro novel, especially since, among other descendants of its genre, it seems to have spawned almost immediately a rash of anti- and proslavery novels, with wonderful titles such as *Cousin Franck's Household, or Scenes in the Old Dominion* (1852); *The Planter's Victim* (1855), reprinted in 1860 as *Yankee Slave Driver; The Autobiography of a Female Slave* (1857); *Adela, the Octoroon* (1860); *The Unionist's Daughter* (1862); *Neighbor Jackwood* (1856); *Cudjo's Cave* (1863); and *Peculiar* (1864). All of these antislavery titles trace their literary heritage to *Uncle Tom,* while an equally marvelous assortment of proslavery titles were published as negations of *Uncle Tom,* including *Uncle Tom's Cabin Contrasted with Buckingham Hall* (1852); *Aunt Phillis' Cabin* (1852); *Uncle Robin in his Cabin in Virginia and Tom Without One in Boston* (1853); *The Lofty and the Lowly; or God in All and None All-Good* (1854); *The Planter's Northern Bride* (1854); *Frank Freeman's Barber Shop* (1851); *The Black Gauntlet* (1860); *The Ebony Idol* (1860); and *The Sable Cloud: A Southern Tale with Northern Comments* (1861).[3] Just as it is fair to say that Stowe invented the Negro novel, as defined by Eliot, it is also important to note, especially in an essay about Wilson and *Our Nig,* that Stowe "created" the novel written by Afro-Americans and that she provided a potent impetus to the publication of fiction by (white) women, two subgenres of fiction that met in 1859 in *Our Nig.*

Let us consider briefly the latter proposition. Of the eighteen titles published by 1861 as negative pastiches of *Uncle Tom's Cabin,* no less than nine, or fifty percent, were written by (white) women. One plausible explanation for the remarkably high percentage of women novelists who used the form to refute *Uncle Tom's Cabin* can be traced to William Gilmore Simms. Simms, editor of the Charleston *Southern Quarterly Review,* cited the "seemingly poetic justice of having the Northern woman answered by a Southern woman" and published Mrs. Louisa McCord's rather hysterical review, which reads in part:

To disprove slanders thus impudently uttered and obstinately persevered in is impossible unless those who are to judge the question had some little insight into the facts of the case, and could know something of our habits and our laws, thus being enabled to judge of the respective worth of the testimony brought before them. . . . To such as are willing to hear both sides we have endeavoured to invalidate Mrs. Stowe's testimony by proving that so far from being well acquainted with our habits and manners she has probably never set foot in our country, and is ignorant alike of our manners, feelings, and even habits of language.

Similarly, John R. Thompson, the editor of the *Southern Literary Messenger,* instructed his reviewer, George F. Holmes, to write a review "as hot as hell-fire, blasting and searing the reputation of the vile wretch in petticoats who could write such a volume."

But Stowe was to have other effects upon well-known women writers. Charlotte Brontë apologized to her publisher because *Villette,* she wrote, included "no matter of public interest. . . . I voluntarily and sincerely veil my face before such a mighty subject as that handled in Mrs. Beecher Stowe's work." George Eliot, on the other hand, was to attribute to Stowe the great theme of *Daniel Deronda.* While it is well known that Eliot's last novel, a bold study of Zionism, was written to attack English antisemitism, it is less well known that Eliot's statement about her intentions, frequently reprinted as a preface to the text, was made in a letter to Stowe. "As to the Jewish element in *Deronda,*" Eliot wrote Stowe,

I therefore felt urged to treat Jews with such sympathy and understanding as my nature and knowledge could attain to. . . . Towards the Jews . . . a spirit of arrogance and contemptuous dictatorialness is observable which has become a national disgrace to us. There is nothing I should care more to do, if it were possible, than to rouse the imagination of men and women to a vision of human claims in those races of their fellow-men who most differ from them in custom and belief.

Eliot echoes not only Stowe's sentiments, expressed in the latter's own preface to *Uncle Tom's Cabin,* but also some of her exact phrasing. Stowe's effect on other novelists, despite our contemporary readings of *Uncle Tom* and its limitations, must not be underestimated.

What may we deduce from these relations? The fact of Stowe's sex clearly neither hindered nor discouraged other women, mostly

Southern, from writing their first novels in response to *Uncle Tom's Cabin,* indeed primarily as negative pastiches of that immensely popular text. Similarly, if conversely, the fact of her sex seems to have encouraged other Northern women who held antislavery sentiments less than it did proslavery writers, perhaps because it was difficult to usurp or to rival Stowe's achievement. Almost overnight she became the veritable reigning monarch of women writers, as the reviews by George Eliot and one by George Sand, published in 1852 in *La Presse,* suggest. One woman author, Mattie Griffiths, attempted to step around Stowe by assuming a black woman's persona and writing in 1857 *The Autobiography of a Female Slave,* which was well reviewed. Indeed, so powerful was Stowe's position that even as early as 1852, Emily Catherine Pierson, whose *Jamie the Fugitive* (1851) was the first antislavery novel published by a woman, was moved sufficiently by a certain anxiety to print the following disclaimer in her second novel, *Cousin Franck's Household* (1852):

> Were we content to be an humble imitator, we know of no one whom we should be prouder to follow than the noble author of that wonderful work, "Uncle Tom's Cabin." But we owe it to ourselves to say that our little book was projected before the publication of the latter; and our Jamie Parker, we think, had only one predecessor—and that we had not seen—in this species of literature.

If Stowe's strength seems to have had a delimiting effect on other white women writers in the North, Caroline E. Rush's response was to attempt to enlist the new class of proslavery women writers to turn away from slavery as subject and begin to write about "white, wearied, wornout" women protagonists. Rush, prime propagandist for the peculiar institution, is a dubious source of proto-feminist urgings. Writing in her novel, *North and South, or Slavery and Its Contrasts* (1852), Rush first commands her readers to cease crying for Uncle Tom—"a hardy, strong and powerful Negro"—and start crying for pitiful, destitute children "of the same color as yourself." The freed blacks, of Philadephia for example, Rush continues, lack any "elegant degree of refinement and cultivation," thereby demonstrating implicitly that blacks are incapable of "elevation," enslaved or free. Eschew the profit motive, she concludes, and find a new subject:

Fine, profitable speculation may be made from negro fiction. Wrought up into touching pictures, they may, under the spell of genius, look like truth and have the semblance of reality, but where is the genius to paint the scenes that exist in our own cities?—to awaken a sympathy that shall give strength to the white, wearied, wornout daughters of toil?

It was to address this task, precisely seven years later, that Harriet E. Wilson published *Our Nig,* a novel written to demonstrate the suffering of a black, wearied wornout daughter of toil.

III

Harriet E. Wilson's rhetorical strategy does not seem to engage Harriet Beecher Stowe's at all; nor is her text directly related formally to the plots of her black precursors, William Wells Brown or Martin R. Delany. Rather, Wilson's tale is an original one in the tradition, related to Frank J Webb's only insofar as both texts unfold in the North. Wilson's compelling and relatively well-constructed novel, based as it is on her own autobiography, is a severe indictment of irresponsible black "abolitionists" but especially of the Northern white woman who beats her as regularly and as severely as Frederick Douglass's master whips the innocent slave, Aunt Hester. It is this use of these twin themes, published some two months before John Brown's aborted raid on Harper's Ferry, that helps us to understand why this major text of an Afro-American's antebellum experiences with a racism in the North as pernicious as that practiced in the South, was ignored by her contemporaries and had been lost to the Afro-American literary tradition until this time. It is rewarding to compare this text of a life to the plot structure of the fictional text itself, to demonstrate the curious manner in which the life and times of "Frado," the protagonist, and the life and times of Harriet E. Wilson, would-be author, dressmaker, and hairdresser, overlap as if in mirrored or repeated strategies of parallel self-presentation and representation. If, as Joan Rita Sherman has put the matter, by far the largest number of blacks remain "Invisible Poets," then it is also true that Harriet E. Wilson, Widow, is our tradition's Invisible Novelist.

Harriet E. Adams Wilson, at this stage in our research into the origins of the Afro-American literary tradition, is thought to be the very first Afro-American woman to publish a novel in English. In a tradition in which racial firsts have been heralded loudly and widely, as veritable talismans drawn out to counter racist aspersions cast upon Afro-American culture as a whole, the rediscovery of Harriet Wilson's text and the authentication of her sexual and racial identity have given to the Afro-American women's literary tradition a chronological extension of a full one-third, from 1892 to 1859. *Our Nig,* in addition, is a major example of generic fusion in which a woman writer appropriated black male (the slave narrative) and white female (the sentimental novel) forms and revised these into a synthesis at once peculiarly black and female. For Harriet Wilson is not only the first black woman novelist in the tradition, she is also the first major innovator of fictional narrative form.

What do we know of the biography of this newly emergent author whose text enjoyed its fullest readership a century and a quarter after its initial printing, in the same year in which Gloria Naylor received the American Book Award for *The Women of Brewster Place* and Alice Walker received both the American Book Award and the Pulitzer Prize for *The Color Purple?* What we know with certainty are a few elemental facts concerning her life between 1850 and 1860, the decade represented with little emendation in her autobiographical novel, *Our Nig.* It was the verification of these biographical details of her life that allowed for the positive identification of Wilson as both the text's thinly veiled subject and its author.

Harriet E. Adams was born in New Hampshire, in 1827 or 1828, according to the 1850 federal census, in which she is listed as being a twenty-two-year-old black female. Her marriage license of 1851 lists Milford, New Hampshire, as her birthplace. Not much else is known about her childhood or about her life between her birth and 1850. After 1850, however, various public documents reveal a number of details about her life which are depicted in *Our Nig.*

In 1850, Harriet Adams was living with a white family, the family of Samuel Boyles, in Milford. Boyles was a carpenter, who was married and the father of a seventeen-year-old son. It is possible that Adams was an indentured servant and that she based her account of Alfrado's barbarous treatment as a servant upon her experiences with Louisa Boyles, Samuel Boyles's wife.

Be that as it may, we know that shortly after the 1850 census was taken, Harriet Adams moved to "W_____, Massachusetts," taken there by "an itinerant colored lecturer." It was here that she went to live with a Mrs. Walker and became a "straw-sewer." Soon, however, because her "constitution was greatly impaired," Adams became Mrs. Walker's domestic servant and put aside her career as a milliner.

Early in the spring of 1851, the "itinerant colored lecturer" returned to town, accompanied by a fugitive slave. This slave, once a house servant, was named Thomas Wilson. Adams married Wilson on October 6, 1851, at Milford, then moved with him to New Hampshire.

George Mason Wilson, the only issue of this marriage, was born in late May or early June of 1852, approximately nine months after his parents' marriage. Shortly before the birth of this child, Thomas Wilson had run away to sea. George was born in the "County House" (Hillsborough County Farm) at Goffstown, New Hampshire, where the destitute of various sorts were herded.

Apparently, Thomas Wilson returned to his family as mysteriously as he had disappeared, only to desert them once again. Harriet was forced to return her son to the County Farm, where he eventually was to be rescued by "a kindly gentleman and lady" who took him as a foster child. Harriet Wilson's health had apparently deteriorated progressively, forcing her to relinquish her son because she could not "pay his board every week."

While George remained in a white foster home in New Hampshire, Harriet moved to Boston in 1855, where she was a dressmaker. She would remain at Boston until 1863, when she disappears from public documents. While at Boston, she wrote *Our Nig* and had it published on September 5, 1859. (The novel was copyrighted on August 18, 1859.) She wrote the novel, as she tells her readers in her Preface, so that she might retrieve her son from his foster home. Six months later, however, on February 15, 1860, George Mason Wilson died of "fever." After a final listing in the *Boston City Directory* of 1863, Harriet E. Adams Wilson disappears from public record.

If Wilson's life is obscure, the life of her text is equally so.

Printed by the George C. Rand and Avery Company in what must
have been a small run, the novel received almost no commentary
between 1859 and 1983. Nevertheless, it is a remarkable document of the consciousness of a black woman indentured in the
North, a consciousness shaped by a racist bondage as brutal psychologically as any rendered in the tradition.

Let me rehearse the signal elements of the plot. A white
orphan, Mag Smith, is seduced and abandoned by a wealthy gentleman, then scorned by her neighbors. She gives birth to a child
who dies within weeks of its birth. Ostracized, Mag Smith removes
herself to the margins of her society, living alone for years in her
hut. "A kind hearted African" named Jim is the only soul bold
enough to disturb Mag Smith's isolation. He proposes. She is
shocked and disgusted initially, but assesses the degree of her
desolation and decides that miscegenation is a better choice than
isolated poverty. Within a week, they marry.

"Two pretty mulatto" children and a few years later, Jim succumbs to consumption, leaving Mag in poverty once again. Jim's
partner, Seth Shipley, and Mag return to her previous home, "the
hut," determined to abandon her six-year-old daughter, Frado,
and to flee town. They leave the child at the home of a middle-class
white family, the Bellmonts, and depart, never to be heard from
again.

At age seven, Frado becomes an indentured servant, feeding
the hens, driving the cows, retrieving wood, washing dishes, clean-
ing the house, and suffering much abuse. She is beaten regularly
by the mistress of the house, the relentlessly evil Mrs. Bellmont.
For two years, she attends elementary school, only to be with-
drawn by her mistress who fears the effects that an education
might have upon her servant.

For years, Frado suffers at the hands of Mrs. Bellmont and her
miniature counterpart in evil, Mary. Her plight is relieved only by
her relationship with the male members of the Bellmont family,
particularly the older son, James, married and living in Baltimore.
James returns Frado's affection and plans to take her to Baltimore as his servant. Illness, however, forces him to return to
Massachusetts, to his parents' home, where both James's and
Frado's health declines.

At Chapter X, Frado reverses the action of the plot by preventing Mrs. Bellmont from beating her, threatening not to work if she is struck again. Frado, the narrator informs us, "stood like one who feels the stirring of free and independent thoughts." James dies, as does daughter Mary. Frado turns to books for relief and comfort.

In the spring of her eighteenth year, Frado at last is free, leaving her indenture with a lame leg, "one decent dress, and a Bible." She works as a servant until her ill health prevents physical labor. A series of generally horrendous working experiences ensue during the next few years, interrupted only by a warm relationship with an employer named Mrs. Moore. Frado's health deteriorates, waxing and waning, forcing her on and off public charity. Gradually, however, she perfects her talents at needlework. This mastery of a skill leads to one of her new forms of freedom. Frado soon leaves New Hampshire to move to Massachusetts to sew straw hats, living with a kind white woman who teaches her more about the art of sewing and gives her books to read.

Frado's brief but blissful period of freedom is interrupted, and eventually ended, by a black man who comes to town as part of the fugitive slave lecture circuit. He sees Frado, proposes, and marries her, all on one page of the text. The two move back to the New Hampshire town in which Frado was raised. Samuel, earning a living as a lecturer, leaves his wife for weeks on end, finally running away to the sea. Abandoned, Frado becomes ill, accepts public charity, and gives birth to a son. Samuel returns, rescues his family from the County Farm, only to abandon them once again. He dies of fever in New Orleans. Wilson, in this part of her text, writes close to her own experiences of love and betrayal.

The novel ends with a hurried and abbreviated account of Frado's adventures in New Hampshire and Massachusetts, fleeing slave catchers and "kidnappers," receiving abuse from "professed abolitionists" who "didn't want slaves at the South, nor niggers in their own houses, North." She learns, as did Harriet Wilson, how to dye gray hair back to its original color, and maintains herself in this way. The text concludes in Harriet Wilson's voice, a direct appeal to her readers to purchase her book so that she might retrieve her son. Six months later, we know, her son is dead.

Until the publication of the second edition of *Our Nig* in 1983, there existed almost no critical commentary on this novel, except for a brief mention by Herbert Ross Brown in *The Sentimental Novel in America* (1940), who marvels at Wilson's relatively balanced depiction of an interracial marriage. James Joseph Kinney's superb dissertation, "The Theme of Miscegenation in the American Novel to World War II" (1972), also analyzes the novel according to this theme, asserting along the way that the fiction is autobiographical.

The fullest contemporary reference to the novel is perhaps to be found in a letter that Lydia Maria Child sent on July 9, 1878, to Sarah Shaw. The relevant passage reads as follows:

> . . . Poor Mag! She was one of that host of forlorn beings, who go through life with souls gasping and perishing, for want of somebody to love them, and somebody to love. It is so hard to tell what to *do* with characters so blighted by neglect, and hardened by harshness! Every kind person is willing to make efforts to redeem them; but where to place them, after the process of redemption is begun,—that is the puzzling question. Compassion is not enough for them; they need the consciousness of being loved by somebody and of being essential to the comfort of some one. Dear Bessie Green's rule never to separate a mother from her illegitimate child was a wise provision for this craving of human nature. How to find a *home* for such outcasts as poor Mag is a very difficult problem. Public institutions are generally anything but healing to their wounded souls, and it is rare to find a family *all* the members of which are disposed to help them forget the past. In three cases, I tried the experiment of taking a cast-a-way into my own room for several months. While they were with me, all went well; but every case proved a failure after they went out into the world to earn their living; one after a probation of a few months, the other two after a term of years. I confess that if I had known human nature as well as I now know it, I never should have had courage to try such experiments. But is it not strange that some way cannot be discovered by which the elements of human society can be so harmonized as to prevent such frightful discords? Oh, Sarah, my heart is very weary striving to solve this strange problem of human life. If men only *could* be convinced that selfishness is very short-sighted *policy!* If they only *would* realize that to save another soul is the only way to save their own!

It seems likely that Child here refers to "lonely Mag Smith." Child is struck by Mag's seduction and subsequent abandonment, and the desperate behavior that this abandonment engenders. It seems curious that Mag Smith's condition assumes a precedent over Frado's, until we recall that the action of the plot is set in motion by Mag's unmarried pregnancy.

What does *Our Nig* teach us about the Afro-American tradition, beyond allowing us to chart beginnings of the black woman's tradition of the novel? As Martin Price argues, *Our Nig* recalls other sentimental novels, such as those of Defoe or Scott. It was not written in the first person, as Defoe's novels were, as the slave narratives were, but it cultivates a remarkable documentary authority—not least in that final appeal to the reader which can be read as an assertion of the tale's authentic subjectivity, of its "authenticity." But what recalls Defoe, apart from the strict attention to narrative, without description and evocation, is the openness of motives of various kinds. Frado acts out her dreams of independence or superiority, however unguardedly and humorously. She is not shorn of all aggression or self-esteem as is generally the case in the sentimental novel. The reader is drawn to her all the more because of this trait, and finds her more impressive as an individual for her capacity to resent, and especially to hate. Harriet Wilson's characterization of her protagonist in this way recalls the sort of complexity and abstention from moralistic simplification that makes a book such as *Moll Flanders* so attractive, and which is not to be found in any other black novel published before the turn of the century. Had Wilson lived, had she possessed, as Alice Walker has written of her, "a body of her own, a room of her own, and a love of her own," it is difficult to imagine the degree of artistic attainment that the black novel might have realized before the examples of Dunbar and Chesnutt. We can cogently argue, however, without strain that Wilson is the most accomplished and subtle black novelist of the nineteenth century.

IV

If Wilson chose to publish her novel under a pseudonym in order to protect her privacy or her identity, then we can admire the triumphant success of her attempt. For "Our Nig," that odd appella-

tion through which the black tradition's first female novelist chose
to name herself, never truly disappeared from the tradition, because she was never allowed to enter it. Unlike Harriet Jacobs,
whose identity as the pseudonymous "Linda Brent" was never in
question but whose capacity for full authorship of *Incidents in the
Life of a Slave Girl* (1861) remained in doubt until Jean Yellin
proved it in 1981, "Our Nig" has not been the subject of heated
debates among historians or literary critics, nor has her reputation
yet profited from either the black nationalist or the feminist movements, as have so many black and female figures. Rather, Wilson
exists for a new generation of readers, reading her well over a century after she published her tale of torture and abuse, in perhaps a
fuller form than she did for her contemporaries, even if the fragmented reconstruction that I venture is less than ideal or complete.
Indeed, I proffered less than complete results of six months' research into her life to generate more sustained studies of this enigmatic author whose life and times remain obscure.

As we have seen, the story of *Our Nig* turns on the life and
times of Frado, a mulatto child of six abandoned by her white,
widowed mother shortly after her black father's death. The child's
mother, Mag Smith, deceives a middle-class white family by ask-
ing if they would look after the child for her until her return from
"washing" at a neighbor's home. Frado, who never sees her mother
again, immediately becomes the indentured servant of this family.

Mrs. Bellmont, the tyrannical petite bourgeoisie who dominates
this household, overworks, insults, and beats Frado almost daily
for the next twelve years. At eighteen, exhausted and chronically
ill, Frado becomes a ward of the county, moving into and out of a
variety of accommodations and work experiences. One generous
woman with whom she lives teaches her to sew and to appreciate
"the value of useful books." The text reads:

> Expert with the needle, Frado soon equalled her instructress; and
> she sought also to teach her the value of useful books; and while
> one read aloud to the other of deeds historic and names re-
> nowned, Frado experienced a new impulse. She felt herself capa-
> ble of elevation; she felt that this book information supplied an
> undefined dissatisfaction she had long felt, but could not express.
> Every leisure moment was carefully applied to self-improvement.

Armed with this broadly conceived sort of literacy, Frado encounters a black man, a fugitive slave, falls in love, marries, and becomes pregnant. Her husband, who occasionally leaves her "to 'lecture'," turns out to be a fraud, a free black man who assumed the guise of a slave only to exploit the passions of the abolitionists. Frado bears her child in the "county farm"; her husband, away on a protracted business trip, succumbs to "Yellow Fever" in New Orleans. Frado has been betrayed once again.

The betrayal of good faith is, then, a repeated theme, a leitmotif, of *Our Nig*. Perhaps because the fiction represents so closely the apparent experiences of Wilson, *Our Nig* is not about anything more or less than the betrayal of certain forms of trust, of belief. *Our Nig* is not primarily a polemic against racism, and most certainly not a polemic against slavery. The betrayal of Frado by her mother is the crucial element that motivates Wilson's plot. This book is unique in American fiction in that an interracial marriage serves to generate and determine the ensuing events of the plot, as a structural element rather than as social commentary. Frado, the mulatto heroine, never truly belongs; she remains marginal, one who dwells at the margins of community, at the threshold of society, never part of a human institution. Just as her childhood was taken away from her, she must give up her child, whom she fosters to a decent white family. Frado is the nineteenth century's figure of alienation, the representation of the deleterious personal effects of prejudice. The plot of *Our Nig* has no parallel either in sentimental fiction generally or in Afro-American fiction until the next century. The narrator's direct plea, in the novel's ultimate chapter, both serves to reinforce this depiction of the alienated being and dispels the illusion of the fiction it has charted, by appealing to the reader to purchase this book so that "Our Nig" may retrieve her fostered son.

This blurring of fiction and fact is more fully explained by comparison of the novel's plot structure with the verifiable facts of its author's life.

What we know of Wilson has been pieced together from fragmented clues left painfully vague in the textual apparatus that frames her narrative, including her own "Preface" and a seven-page "Appendix," which consists of three letters written for the

occasion of publication by persons identifying themselves as "Allida," "Margaretta Thorn," and "C. D. S."

We may consider Wilson's "Preface" and the three appended
letters to comprise the documentary–biographical subsection of
the text, while the novel itself comprises the text's fictional representation of Wilson's experiences as an indentured servant in a
Northern white household before 1850. What is curious about the
relationship between these nonfictional and fictional discourses,
which together form the text of *Our Nig,* is this: the closer the
novel approaches the appended biographies, the less distance there
is between fact and romance, between (auto-) biography and fiction. This is one of the more curious aspects of this curious text:
the fiction, or the guise of her fictional account of her life, tends to
fall away the nearer her novel approaches its own ending and the
ending of her text, the composite biography written by Wilson's
friends. It is of considerable interest to outline the manner in
which one discursive field collapses into quite another, of a different status from the other, as outlined on the chart that follows this
chapter.

To be sure, there are tensions between biography and fiction
early in the novel. In chapter titles this tension first appears.
Chapter I, for example, Wilson calls "Mag Smith, My Mother."
The first-person pronoun would lead the reader to assume that the
novel is narrated in the first person; it is not. Rather, a third-
person narrator observes and interprets the thoughts and actions
of all concerned. Clearly, however, the narrator is telling Alfrado's
tale, a tale of abuse, neglect, betrayal, suffering, consciousness,
and certain death from that inevitable visitor of the sentimental
novel, the dreaded "fever." These stock devices, employed with
melodrama, direct appeal to the reader, and a certain florid, stilted
diction in speech and thought, nevertheless function to reveal Frado's saga to us. But Frado's drama, these lapses into first person
would suggest, is Wilson's tale as well. Chapter II, "My Father's
Death," and Chapter III, "A New Home For Me," afford other
instances of the first-person shift.

With Chapter IV and after, however, the chapter titles employ
the third person but are more often abstractions. These titles, in
order, follow: "A Friend For Nig," "Departures," "Varieties,"
"Spiritual Condition of Nig," "Visitor and Departure," "Death,"

"Perplexities—Another Death," "Marriage Again," and "The Winding Up of the Matter." What are we to make of the first-person lapses in the chapter titles? We can conclude, with Allida, that the novel is indeed "an Autobiography" of sorts, an autobiographical novel. Whether the lapses are the signs of an inexperienced authorship, struggling with or against the received conventions of her form, or whether we can attribute these to the intrusion of the rendering of a life upon the desires of a text to achieve the status of a fiction, these first-person traces point to the complexities and tensions of basing fictional events on the lived experiences of an author. As demonstrated in the comparative chart, later chapters contain events that parallel remarkably closely those experiences of Wilson's that we are able to document. Curiously enough, the first-person proprietary consciousness evinced in the titles of the early chapters does not parallel events that we have been able to document and shall probably not be able to document. Since these early chapters describe events far removed from the author's experiences closest in time to the period of writing, the first-person presences perhaps reveal the author's anxiety about identifying with events in the text that she cannot claim to recollect clearly and some of which she cannot recollect at all, such as the courtship and marriage of her mother and the protagonist's ultimate abandonment by her widowed parent. In later chapters, Wilson had no need to demonstrate or claim the direct relationship between author and protagonist since, as my research reveals, these two sets of events, the fictional and the biographical, overlap nicely.

The text's lacunae, its silences and reticences, Wilson explains away in her "Preface" as does the disembodied narrative voice in the novel's final chapter. In the "Preface," Wilson argues that she has remained silent about those events in her life that, if depicted, could well result in an adverse reaction against Northern whites and could thereby do harm to the antislavery movement:

> I do not pretend to divulge every transaction in my own life, which the unprejudiced would declare unfavorable in comparison with treatment of legal bondmen; I have purposely omitted what would most provoke shame in our good antislavery friends at home.

The novel's penultimate paragraph repeats that claim, but with a difference. This difference consists of a direct appeal to the reader to grant the author "your sympathy," rather than withholding it simply because more critical details are not depicted in the text:

> Still an invalid, she asks your sympathy, gentle reader. Refuse not, because some part of her history is unknown, save by the Omnipresent God. Enough has been unrolled to demand your sympathy and aid.

She has revealed quite enough, the narrator tells us, for her readers to be convinced of the author's merit of their "sympathy and aid." To ask of her even more would be to ask too much. While scholars wish for more details of the life to have been named in the novel, details ideally transpiring between 1850 and 1860 in the author's life (Chapter XII of the text), even they must remain content to grant the author her plea.

What do we find in this ultimate chapter in the very space where these absent details of the author's life should be? We read, instead, one of the novel's few direct attacks upon white Northern racism:

> She passed into the various towns of the State [New Hampshire] she lived in, then into Massachusetts. Watched by kidnappers, maltreated by professed abolitionists, who didn't want slaves at the South, nor niggers in their own houses, North. Faugh! to lodge one; to eat with one; to admit one through the front door; to sit next one; awful!

It is clear that Wilson's anxieties about offending her Northern readers were not the idle uneasiness most authors feel about their ideal constituencies.

We are free to speculate upon Wilson's myth of origins, a myth in which her protagonist, like so many of the slave narrators, figures as a mulatto. Mulattoes, most certainly, are terms of mediation, partaking of two fundamentally opposed forces. Her myth of origins, contained in the first half of *Our Nig,* attempts to reconcile two otherwise irreconcilable forces through the mythic structure itself. The social commentary explicit in the rendering of Mag Smith's marriage to Jim finds an implicit analogue in the text's subject, a mulatto woman who is the functional equivalent within myth of the trickster figure. The trickster, of course, is a mediator, but her mediation is only a trick, the trick of literary structure itself.

If *Our Nig's* early chapters truly are the stuff of fiction, her latter three chapters are the stuff of autobiography, following fairly closely the plot of her life, especially the life of the author posited in the text's "Appendix" by her friends. As these two texts—the text of the life of Frado the servant and the text of the life of Wilson the author—approach each other in Chapter XII of the novel, the effect is as if *Our Nig's* controlling consciousness succumbs under the strain of the conflict between the two discursive universes and speaks to the reader in Wilson's voice. For it is in the first sentence of this curious ultimate chapter that the narrator once again lapses into the first person, a shift of voice that functions to underscore the tension between the fictional and the autobiographical. This shift, coupled with the narrator's direct address, not only serves to dispel the spell of the fiction; it also constitutes a peculiar form of repetition of Wilson's prefatory appeal for patronage. Her concern to establish her veracity by printing three letters of sincerity and authenticity at the back of her book not only was a polemical gesture aimed at diffusing the intensity of her critics, but it also, one century and a quarter later, made it possible for this lost black and female author to be found.

Plot Summary of *Our Nig*	Biography of Harriet E. (Adams) Wilson
Chapter I	
1. Mag Smith was "early deprived of parental guardianship, far removed from relatives." (p. 5)	
2. As she "merged into womanhood," (p. 5) as an orphan, she was seduced and abandoned. (p. 6)	
3. Mag left her "few friends," sought "asylum among strangers," and gave birth to a child who died within a number of weeks. (p. 6)	
4. She "removed [herself] from the village" except when seen "returning her work to her employer." (p. 9)	
5. "Thus she lived [in her hut] for years." (p. 8)	
6. "A kind-hearted African" supplied her with fuel in exchange for her "mending or making garments." (p. 9)	
7. The fictional town is called "Singleton." (p. 10)	
8. The "African" "Jim" hits on the idea of marrying Mag. (p. 10)	
9. The "next Saturday" (p. 11), "he prevailed; they married" (p. 12), despite the "sermon on the evils of amalgamation." (p. 13)	
	Chapter II
10. "A comfortable winter passed after her marriage.	1. Born in Milford? New Hampshire, ca. 1828.
11. Within "time," they have "two pretty mulattos."	Birth of Harriet E. Wilson
	ca. 1828

2. Mrs. Wilson "was taken from home so young," according to Margaretta Thorn.

12. Within a "few years" (p. 14), "he became a victim of sumption" and died. (p. 15)

13. "She was now expelled from companionship with white people." (p. 15)

14. She returned to her "hovel" accompanied by Jim's business partner, Seth Shipley. (pp. 15-16)

15. Seth and Mag resolve to give away their "beautiful mulatto" six year old child, Alfrado, to the Bellmonts. (p. 17)

16. "One bright summer morning" (p. 20), the family departs leaving Frado at the Bellmonts' "large, old fashioned, two-story white house." (p. 31)

ca. 1834

Chapter III

17. The Bellmonts debate whether to keep the abandoned Frado, or send her to the "County Home." (pp. 24-6)

18. Frado is kept and put to work: feeding the hens; driving the cows; bringing in wood chips; dishwashing, etc. (p. 29)

19. Not doing her work exactly as commanded would be punished by a "whipping." (p. 29)

20. "Thus passed a year . . . Her labors were multiplied." (p. 30)

21. At age seven, she was "indispensible." (p. 30)

ca. 1835

22. On "opening day" at school, Frado is taunted by the other children as a "nigger." (p. 31)

151

Plot Summary of *Our Nig*	Biography of Harriet E. (Adams) Wilson

Plot Summary of *Our Nig*

23. Between terms of school, she was given more duties, including hay raking and guarding the grazing herd. (p. 39)

24. Frado is not allowed to shield her skin from the sun, since Mrs. Bellmont wants to make sure she is darker than daughter Mary Bellmont. (p. 39)

Chapter IV

25. Now nine years old, Mrs. Bellmont decided that Frado should quit school. "She felt that her time and person belonged solely to her." (p. 41)

26. At the end of the Spring, "absent son" James Bellmont comes to visit. (p. 42)

Chapter V

27. "James' visit concluded." (p. 52)

28. Frado hopes that he will take her away with him after his planned marriage. (p. 52)

29. She receives "additional burdens," including milking the cows, and tending the flocks of sheep (p. 52) and harnessing the horse. (p. 53) In short, to do the work of a boy." (p. 53)

30. James married Susan, a "Baltimorian lady of wealthy parentage." (p. 55)

Biography of Harriet E. (Adams) Wilson

ca. 1837

Chapter VI

Chapter VII

Chapter VIII

Plot Summary of *Our Nig*	Biography of Harriet E. (Adams) Wilson

Baltimore with his sister Mary accompanying him. (pp. 78–79)

38. Mrs. Bellmont, doubting that blacks have souls, prevents Frado from reading the Bible. Frado, however, continues to do so in her own room. (pp. 86–87)

39. Mrs. Bellmont claims that Frado "can't be spared" by letting her go to church any more. (p. 89)

40. Mr. and Mrs. Bellmont argue about the learning abilities of Frado and blacks in general. Also her monetary value and services are discussed. (pp. 89–90)

Chapter IX

41. "Frado was becoming seriously ill." (p. 94)

42. Frado "resolved to persevere" in prayer, despite Mrs. Bellmont's statement that "prayer was for whites, not for blacks.'" (p. 94)

Chapter X

43. Frado astonishes Mrs. Bellmont and prevents a beating by threatening not to work for her any longer if she is hit again. Frado "stood like one who feels the stirring of free and independent thoughts." (p. 105)

154

44. "Thus passed a year" (p. 105) where Frado received "the usual amount of scoldings, but fewer whippings." (pp. 105–106)

45. Daughter Mary Bellmont dies in Baltimore. (p. 106)

Chapter XI

46. "Frado had merged into womanhood." (p. 115) She spends her free time with her school books.

47. With the "approaching Spring," Frado is free to ca. 1846 leave and resolves to do so. Despite "delicate" health, and pleas from Mrs. B that she stay and be "grateful" for her situation, she leaves. (pp. 116–117).

48. "Frado was engaged to work for a family a mile distant." (p. 117)

49. Frado was given "a present of a silver half dollar," from Mrs. B. Frado was "alone in the world" with "one decent dress," a Bible from Susan, and a lame leg from a fall during *the past year.* (p. 117)

50. During a "pleasant" *"first summer,* Frado earned enough money to buy a small wardrobe." She also "prepared her own garments." (p. 117)

51. Mrs. Moore, her employer, was a "kind friend" (p. 117), but Frado's "failing health" hindered her work. (p. 118)

3. "Never enjoyed any degree of comfortable health since she was eighteen years of age," according to Margaretta Thorn.

Plot Summary of *Our Nig*	Biography of Harriet E. (Adams) Wilson
52. She moved to the house of a clergyman, and "her engagement with Mrs. Moore finished in the fall." (p. 118)	
53. By "*winter* she entirely gave up work" as she was "thoroughly sick." (p. 118)	
54. Frado again hopes she will die from her illness. She is removed to the Bellmonts' farm, in a drafty outbuilding.	
55. Frado "became reckless of her faith" (p. 119), but "slowly improved" her health under the care of Aunt Abby. (pp. 120–121)	ca. 1847
56. Frado returns to Mrs. Moore's house, but again her work proves to be too much for her. (p. 121)	
57. Mrs. B refuses to take her back.	
58. "Two maidens, (old,)" take Frado in for public charity, for *two years*. (p. 122)	ca. 1849
58. A greedy Mrs. Hoggs takes her in.	
60. When Frado learns to be "*very expert with a needle*" (p. 122) while recovering from her illness, Mrs. Hoggs reports her to the authorities as an "imposter." (p. 123)	
61. "This brought on a severe illness of *two weeks*, when Mrs. Moore again sought her." (p. 123)	
62. Mrs. Moore's husband deserts her and their four children (p. 123)	

156

63. Frado is pronounced ill again, and is allowed back on public charity at the Moore's house.

64. "Here she remained till sufficiently restored to sew again." (p. 124)

August 4, 1850

65. She moved to Massachusetts to *sew straw bonnets*. A "plain, poor, simple woman, who could see merit beneath a dark skin" (p. 124), heard her sorry story and took her in.

66. She soon became "expert with the needle" and "soon equalled her instructress." (p. 124).

67. Frado begins reading history and other "useful books." (p. 124) She continued her Christian experience.

Chapter XII

68. A fugitive slave arrives, and proposes marriage to Frado. (p. 126)

157

4. According to the 1850 federal census for Milford, New Hampshire, Harriet Adams was a 22 year old black woman born in New Hampshire, and living with the family of Samuel Boyles.

The W_____, Massachusetts, Period

5. "Allida" reports that Harriet Wilson was brought to W_____, Massachusetts by an "itinerant" colored lecturer.

6. W_____, Massachusetts was an "inclent town" with a straw hat industry.

7. According to "Allida," Harriet E. Wilson:
   A) Became an "inmate" of Mrs. Walker's household in W_____, Massachusetts.
   B) Began immediately as a "straw-sewer."
   C) Soon her "constitution was greatly impaired."
   D) Became at that point Mrs. Walker's domestic help.

8. The W_____, Massachusetts town is thought to be Westborough, Ware, Walpole, or Worcester.

9. "Allida" reports that "months passed." And then in the "early Spring of 1842,"
   A) The "lecturer" returns, this time with a fugitive slave.

Plot Summary of *Our Nig*	Biography of Harriet E. (Adams) Wilson
	B) The fugitive slave had been a house servant.
	C) "Suffice it to say," she says in a vague and discretely Victorian tone, "an acquaintance was formed, which, in due time, resulted in marriage."
	D) "In a few days, she left W———, . . . and took up her abode in New Hampshire."
	10. Given that "Allida" attests in 1859 to knowing Mrs. Wilson only about eight years (i.e., c. 1851–2), this date (of "1842") could not be a correct one from first hand knowledge. Most likely, this date is rather a typographical error for 1851 or 1852, considering that Thomas Wilson married Harriet Adams in Fall, 1851 (this marriage being reported in the Spring of 1852).

Marriage of Thomas Wilson
and Harriet Adams

October 6, 1851	11. Thomas Wilson is reported to have married a Harriet Adams on October 6, 1851 in Milford, New Hampshire.
	A) Thomas Wilson's residence is listed as "Virginia."
	B) Harriet Adams' residence is listed as "Milford."

69. They move back to Singleton and marry there. (p. 127)

C) The marriage record was "returned by Rev. E. N. Hidden" in April of the following year.

D) The 1850 federal census lists Rev. Ephraim N. Hidden as a Cong[regational] Clerg[yperson].

Birth of George Mason Wilson

12. George Mason Wilson was born in late May or early June of 1852.

A) His race is listed as "Black" on his death record.

B) His parents were Thomas and Harriet Wilson, of Virginia and Milford, New Hampshire respectively.

13. The birth occurred in Goffstown, New Hampshire—where the Hillsborough County Farm was located at the time.

14. "Allida" reports that "for a while" things went well for the new couple. But then the husband ran away to sea. "Days passed; weeks passed," and then Mrs. Wilson felt she had to go to the "County House," where she gave birth to her child.

70. Her new husband, Samuel, would leave frequently to "lecture," often for weeks. (p. 127)

71. Samuel runs away to sea. (p. 127)

72. It turns out he was not a fugitive slave, after all. (p. 128)

73. Left alone, she becomes ill, accepts public charity again, and gives birth to a child. (p. 128)

May or June 1852

159

Plot Summary of *Our Nig*	Biography of Harriet E. (Adams) Wilson
	New Hampshire Period After Birth of George Mason Wilson
74. "The *long absent* Samuel unexpectedly returned, and rescued her from charity." (p. 128)	15. "Allida" reports that "then" the husband returned. The family moves to "some town in New Hampshire, where, for a time, he supported her and his little son decently well."
75. Again, "after a long desertion . . . he had become a victim of yellow fever, in New Orleans." (p. 128)	16. "But again he left her as before," and this time for good, reports "Allida."
	17. Margaretta Thorn reports that the son was put on the "County Farm" while Mrs. Wilson was "in her sickness" and not able to "pay his board every week."
76. "She left ['her babe''] in charge of a Mrs. Capon, and procured an agency, hoping to recruit her health, and gain an easier livelihood for herself and child." (p. 129)	18. "At length," Ms. Thorn reports, "a kindly gentleman and lady took her little boy into their own family." Mrs. Wilson had taken him "from *that* place [the "County Farm"] and now he has a home."
	19. Mrs. Wilson, says Ms. Thorn, "wishes to educate her son." Ms. Thorn reports that as of her writing (1859), the child is accented, well-adjusted, and shows promise.
	Second Massachusetts Period
77. She "passed into the various towns of the State she lived in, then into Massachusetts."	20. The 1855 *Boston Directory* lists a Harriet Wilson as a "widow, house, 7 Robinson Alley."

21. The next year, 1856, a Harriet Wilson, "widow," is living in a "house, 1 Webster ave."

22. Also, a Harriet Wilson, "dressmaker," has a business (?) address at 19 Joy Street.

23. Harriet Wilson is listed as a "widow" living in a "house, 4 Webster ave." from 1856–63. After that year, she disappears from the Boston Directory.

24. Allida reports that "the heart of a stranger was moved with compassion, and bestowed a recipe upon her for restoring gray hair to its former color. She availed herself of this great help, and has been quite successful; but her health is again failing," and she has decided to write her "autobiography" as "another method of procuring her bread." No dates or places are given in this section of "Allida's" account of Mrs. Wilson's life after her husband left her.

Publication of *Our Nig*

August 18, 1859 25. *Our Nig* was copyrighted on August 18, 1859.

26. This novel was published by Mrs. Wilson on September 5, 1859.

78. She had various encounters with "Kidnappers," "Professed abolitionists" who "mistreated" her, "who didn't want slaves at the South, nor niggers in their own houses, North." (p. 129)

79. "A friend . . . provided her with a valuable recipe, from which she might herself manufacture a useful article for her maintenance." (p. 129)

80. "To the *present time*," she is employed in this type of manufacture. (pp. 129–30)

161

Plot Summary of *Our Nig*		Biography of Harriet E. (Adams) Wilson
		27. A copy was deposited at that time "by Mrs. H. E. Wilson, in the Clerk's office of the District Court of the District of Massachusetts."
		28. The novel *Our Nig* was printed for the author by George C. Rand & Avery printing company of Boston, Massachusetts. Rand & Avery were not known as regular publishers of novels.
		Death of George Mason Wilson
	February 13 or 15, 1860	29. George Mason Wilson, aged "7 years, 8 months," died in Milford, New Hampshire, on February 13 or 15, 1860.
		A) His race is listed as "Black."
		B) His parents were Thomas and Harriet E. Wilson.
		C) He died of the "fever."
		D) He was the "only son of H. E. Wilson."
		30. Mrs. Wilson's son, for whom she wrote *Our Nig,* hoping to realize enough money to be able to provide for him, died within six months after this book was published.
		Period After the Death of Mrs. Wilson's Son
		31. Mrs. Wilson was not living with the Boyles family

81. While "still an invalid," she remains religious and determined to "elevate" herself. (p. 130)

82. "*Only a few years* have elapsed since Mr. and Mrs. B passed into another world." Mrs. B's death

was "unspeakable." She died at Lewis' home. (p. 130)

83. "Only a few months since, Aunt Abby entered heaven." (p. 130).

84. "Jack and his wife rest in heaven." (p. 130).

85. "Susan and her child are yet with the living." (p. 130)

86. Jane "has never regretted her exchange of lovers." (pp. 130–131)

87. "Frado has passed from their memories," but she remembers them still. (p. 131)

* This useful chart was prepared by David A. Curtis, Director of Research for the Black Periodical Fiction Project.

according to the 1860 federal census for Milford, New Hampshire.

32. In the last chapter of the novel, the author, speaking in her own voice as she pleads for support for herself in her present destitute condition, tells how "Alfrado" "passed into the various towns of the State she lived in, then into Massachusetts."

33. No other information has been found concerning Mrs. Wilson for the period after the death of her son, except for the information contained in the *Boston Directories* for 1855–63.

Black Structures
of Feeling

It is one thing for a race to produce artistic material; it is quite another thing for it to produce the ability to interpret and criticize this material. This is especially true when the artistic gift is a matter of primitive development in the rich childhood of a people.

W. E. B. Du Bois

Ego turned angrily on him. "What are *you* getting out of it?"

"Knowledge of the new generation of interpreters."

Sagoe exploded. "You sound so fuckin' superior it would make a saint mad."

"Just be careful. When you create your own myth don't carelessly promote another's, and perhaps a more harmful one."

Wole Soyinka, *The Interpreters*

· 6 ·

Dis and Dat:
Dialect and the Descent

Singing a different stave, or closely hidden,
Oh there is precedent, legal tradition,
To sing one thing when your song means another.
                              Ezra Pound, *Near Perigord*

With torn and bleeding hearts we smile,
And mouth with myriad subtleties.
Nay, let them only see us, while we wear the mask.
                  Paul Laurence Dunbar, *We Wear the Mask*

I

Of all the artifacts out of Africa, it is indeed the mask that most
compels. The principal artistic attraction at the 1897 Exposition
in Brussels was a magnificent collection of African masks and
sculptures. Vlaminck, Matisse, Derain, Braque, and Picasso each
owned a number of African masks. The galleries of the old Troca-
dero and the studio of Paul Guillaume impressed French artists to
such an extent that the concepts of movement, rhythm, and self-
contained interiority that gave rise to cubism and dadaism arose
from a transformation of the African mask. Still, it is the mask
that attracts us to blackness, and rightly so. For therein is contained, as well as reflected, a coded, secret, hermetic world, a
world discovered only by the initiate.

Obatala, the Yoruba sculptural god, is not the artist of Apol-
lonian illusion; he is the artist of inner essence. The Yoruba mask
remains only a piece of carved wood, *Omolangidi ni i* ("He is
nothing but a doll in wood," as Denrele Obasa writes in *Awan
Akewi*), without *iwa* ("character")—in non-Yoruba terms, without the artist who bears it before his choral audience. In all Afri-

167

can art, the audience is the chorus, and the mask is wood until it becomes the mask-in-motion. The Western concept of mask is meaningless to, say, the Yoruba, precisely because the doll in wood cannot of itself signify. Once in motion, once the signification is effected, the misnomer "mask" becomes "mask-in-motion," or what "mask" itself implies to the Yoruba. Mask becomes functional—indeed, becomes—only in motion. (It is obvious that language fails us here, in part because our concepts presuppose the world in which we take them to apply. I am reminded here of Wittgenstein's latter doctrine of the inseparability of meaning and belief.)

Once effected, the mask is a vehicle for the primary evocation of a complete hermetic universe, one of force or being, an autonomous world, marked both by a demonstrably interior cohesion and by a complete neutrality to exterior mores or norms. This internal cogency makes it impervious to the accident of place or time. The mask, with its immobilized features all the while mobile, itself is a metaphor for dialectic—specifically, a dialectic or binary opposition embracing unresolved or potentially unresolvable social forms, notions of origins, or complex issues of value. Mask is the essence of immobility fused with the essence of mobility, fixity with transience, order with chaos, permanence with the transitory, the substantial with the evanescent. Through the mask, a code of meanings is established through the media of rhythm, movement, and tonal-specific harmonies that instantly, and in their turn, further create their own rhythm. In a collective as well as functional sense, the mask effects the "spiritual consolidation" of the race, in an especial universe governed only by laws of cohesive interiority. Mask enmeshes the day-to-day awareness of a people, surely a fundamental aesthetic value in all of African art.

Denrele Obasa's metaphor for mask—that it is nothing but a doll in wood—is, interestingly enough, etymologically sound in English.[1] As Theodore Thass-Thienemann argues, "The word *mask,* from Late Latin *masca,* has its origin in the Arabic *mas-chara,* denoting the masked person, like a clown or buffoon—thus a live doll. This Arabic loan word was not understood properly by the Roman people, who adopted it as *masca,* and we may surmise that they assimilated the foreign word to their own verbal resources. At least the first part of the compound sounded familiar to the Roman ear. The Latin *mās* or *mas, maris* properly denotes the 'little man'

. . . hence 'doll' and 'puppet.' " We see the literal correspondence.

And on another level—that is, the level of connotation—there is another correspondence that will come to bear on our notion of dialect as a verbal mask. Linguists also identify the Teutonic word *maskwo* as a progenitor of the English word *mask*. The word meant "net." And it is certain that as early as the ninth century, *max* was used in the sense of "mesh." And if the Late Latin *mascha* is indeed the modern word's antecedent, then our connotative connection is clearer still. For *mascha* was used as early as about 680 by Aldheim in association with *larva*, which had the senses "mask" and "specter," and *masca* occurs in the Lombard Laws, about 800, with the sense "witch." Already we begin to see a ritual connection. And as late as 1814, *mask* could be used to mean "to infuse." Surely these meanings lurk in our consciousness; certainly these resonances inform our usage. To net meanings not obvious; to enmesh a meaning somehow obscured; to remember, in this very act of decoding these subtle inferences now buried in artifice; to infuse with the newly translated or interpreted meaning—we imply all of these when we speak of "the mask." And we employ this analogue in English to describe an African concept we have come to call the mask, which in Yoruba ritual is essential to the art of recovering—that is, covering the human face with another, second surface—to re-cover, in an almost mystical sense, a self-contained, virtually autonomous world. It is a world not readily habitable—perhaps not even approachable—through any other means of transmission.

The African mask in the drama invokes and evokes a habit of mind, a state of being separate and distinct from the mundanity of everyday life. The mask—the mask-in-motion—transubstantiates the motley, disarrayed audience into the unified, homogeneous, choral community. The mask evokes a view of reality, of human experience, in the truest sense of a theatrical presence. With the mask, the choral world view is again organic, the creative act becomes collective, artistic expression becomes functional, and the scene is set for transition into the fourth stage, that nebulous, singular arena where God and human can interact to lament their primal severance—all this through the mask.

Dionysus, whom Wole Soyinka invokes as a quasi-counterpart to Ogun, was the god of masks and of theater as well. Our root words referring to mask indicate that "the holes of the mask . . . —

the openings of the mouth and the eyes—appear as the characteristic feature of the object mask." These holes, if you will, permit an insight into the true identity of the bearer. "Our languages distinguish two kinds of mask: the oral mask and the ocular mask. . . . On the oral level, the mouth is considered to be the aperture through which one can look behind the mask and gain an insight into" the hidden secrets of meanings. Since the word *persona* is of Latin origin, "it also refers to the oral mask which permits 'per-sound' to [the discovery of] the true identity of the actor hidden behind the mask."

Again, Thass-Thienemann is helpful here: "The ocular mask derives its name from the eyeholes. The Greek *opē* means 'opening, hole'; *omma,* from *op-ma,* means 'eye'; *pros-ōpon* means 'face, visage, countenance'; and *pros-ōpeion* means 'mask.' It is a conspicuous phenomenon of many languages that they denote the 'face' with reference to 'seeing' or 'eye.' So the Greek *ōps* means 'eye, face, countenance'; the same holds true for the German *Gesicht* or for the French *visage,* and so on. The psychological reason for this identification of 'face' and 'seeing,' however, is not, as generally supposed, that the 'look' is most characteristic of the 'face,' but that the face is considered to be a living ocular mask, as suggested also by the above Greek instances. Even the word *face,* from the Latin *faciēs,* refers to the artificial 'making up,' from the verb *faciō, -ere,* 'to make.' Much like the Greek *pros-ōpon* or the Latin *superficies,* 'surface,' it refers to the outer *sur-face* in contradistinction to the inside essence. Some people dream that they have lost their face. The 'loss of face' refers primarily to the loss of the hiding mask and being exposed, unmasked; it brings about the feeling of shame and the desire to hide in invisibility." Hence the genius of Ralph Ellison's archetypal confrontation between *Invisible Man*—who is faceless, who exists for us as a voice alone—and Rinehart, who dwells in that chaos of ever-shifting masks; thus the urge to disappear in invisibility once Rinehart's masks are discarded.

Ellison provided a metaphor for the very nature of language and for the confrontation between genius and *genius loci.* Derek Walcott argues that black language is metaphor, and hence words mask or stand between us and the thing language describes. We communicate through this peculiar sense of metaphoric transfer.

Yet, if to communicate is an essential and social function of all language, so is to conceal, to leave unspoken, to mask. As George Steiner argues, languages conceal and internalize more, perhaps, than they convey outwardly: "The element of privacy in language makes possible a crucial, though little understood, linguistic function."[2]

Let me paraphrase Steiner's argument. All reality is encoded in a distinctive idiom. Insofar as language is a mirror of or even a counterstatement to the world, it changes as rapidly and in as many ways as does reality or human experience itself. "A culture is imprisoned in a linguistic contour which no longer matches, or matches only at certain ritual, arbitrary points, the changing landscape of fact." Thus, there is the need for another poetic diction in that space between our debased dialect poetry at the turn of the century and the dialect of Langston Hughes and Sterling Brown; or there is that oddly short chronological space between the rhetorical stance of Booker T. Washington, who uses dependent clauses to qualify and hence whitewash the slave past, and the rhetorical stance of W. E. B. Du Bois, who somehow saw that without our own fiction of history, without "the unbroken animation of a chosen past," we become flat shadows.

Steiner's notion of privacy, as set forth in *After Babel,* is especially useful to the argument I wish to make about the masking function of dialect, of the self-conscious switch of linguistic codes from white to black or, more properly, from standard English to the black vernacular.

> No two historical epochs, no two social classes, no two localities use words and syntax to signify identical signals of value and inference. Neither do two human beings.

Rather, Steiner continues, "each living person draws . . . on two sources of linguistic supply": the current social usage that corresponds to his or her "level of literacy" and what Steiner calls "a private thesaurus." It is this private thesaurus that is "inextricably a part of [the] subconscious, of [our] memories so far as they may be verbalized." Accordingly, each speech-act can never escape "a private residue." Moreover, "the 'personal lexicon' in each of us inevitably qualifies the definitions, connotations, [and] semantic moves in public discourse." Even the idea of standard usage,

Steiner argues, is a fiction, a more or less statistical average, when in fact "the language of a community, however uniform its social contour, is an inexhaustible multiple aggregate . . . of finally irreducible personal meanings." This is what Steiner means by the privacy of language, which I would like to rename cultural or ethnic privacy. This element of privacy makes it possible for a culture to use language to mask its meanings from all but its own initiates. As Steiner concludes, "the human being performs an act of translation, in the full sense of the word, when receiving a speech-message from any other human being. Time, disparities in outlook, and distance make this translation even more difficult." So, too, does code-switching or linguistic masking. In literature, this same principle of individuation (at once cultural and temporal-specific as well as personal) requires that any thorough reading of a text out of the past of one's own language and literature is a manifold act of interpretation. That we do not usually realize this helps to explain how easily we can misread Phillis Wheatley's poetry or Frederick Douglass's narrative or, especially, dialect poetry.

The use of dialect in Afro-American poetry itself was a form of masking, a verbal descent underground to the Great Dis. In one sense, the poet makes a political act by sacrificing on the altar of his or her own muses, often sable as well as white. Each muse speaks one language and demands that the poet hold the nature of that language sacred. The poet, however, as Derek Walcott writes, "is the mulatto of style."[3] The poet has in this mutation—this dialect—an accessible linguistic system that turns the literate language upon itself, exploiting the metaphor against its master. Afro-American dialects exist between two poles, one English and one lost in some mythical linguistic kingdom now irrecoverable. Dialect is our only key to that unknown tongue, and in its obvious relation and reaction to English it contains, as does the Yoruban mask, a verbal dialectic, a dialectic between some form of an African *antithesis* all the while obviating the English *thesis*. This dialectic, in turn, establishes a new set of oppositions that plague the writer "dedicated to purifying the language of the tribe." That writer is the bastard rejected, it seems, by both parents; he or she is the *griot* accused, misused, and generally abused, "jumped on by both sides for pretentiousness or playing white," for pandering to humor and pathos. Yet in dialect this writer is able to contain a hermetic, closed world. As Walcott concludes:

> What would deliver [the New World Negro] from servitude was the forging of a language that went beyond mimicry, a dialect which had the force of a revelation as it invented names for things, one which finally settled on its own mode of inflection, and which began to create an oral culture of chants, jokes, fall-songs, and fables; this, not merely the debt of history was his proper claim to the New World. . . .
>
> So the people, like the actors, awaited a language. They confronted a variety of styles and masks, but because they were casual about commitment, ashamed of their speech, they were moved only by the tragic-comic and farcical. The tragic-comic was another form of contempt. They considered tragedy to be, like English, an attribute beyond them.

James A. Harrison, in *Anglia,* the German-English journal of philology, implied this potential of Negro speech as early as 1884. Harrison's essay, while extremely problematical as J. L. Dillard points out, is relevant here for its valorization of the figurative in black discourse, the spoken discourse that dialect poetry ostensibly imitates.[4] In an article called "Negro English," Harrison outlines specific characteristics of the independent language Negroes speak:

> Much of his talk is baby-talk, of an exceedingly attractive sort to those to the manner born; he deals in hyperbole, in rhythm, in picture-words, like the poet; the slang which is an ingrained part of his being as deep-dyed as his skin, is, with him, not mere word-distortion; it is his verbal breath of life caught from his surroundings and wrought up by him unto the wonderful figure-speech specimens of which will be given later under the head of Negroisms.

Harrison emphasizes the highly metaphorical nature of "Negro English," which makes it a ready conduit for figurative language or "picture-words." Further, Harrison suggests that what is considered generally to be slang or "mere word distortion" is in fact the hallmark of this new language, its capacity to create itself out of a standard English antecedent, which Harrison cannot name but the function of which he can describe in an uncharacteristically mystical manner:

> [The Negro] reproduces in words that imitate, often strikingly, the poetic and multiform messages which nature sends him through his auditory nerve. . . . Negro English is an ear-language altogether.

Negro English is, then, a mythopoeic language that is the product both of "a total abstraction of all means of self-cultivation from the field of negro life" and of a peculiar habit of mind that oddly insists on "mis-hearing":

> The humorous and proverbial character of many of these expressions shows a distinct feature of the Negro mind. The talk of the African abounds in metaphors, figures, similes, imaginative flights, humorous delineations and designations, saws and sayings. These have so interwoven themselves in his daily speech as to have become an unconscious and essential part of it.

Although he cites in detail the principles by which "Negro" language formation occurs, Harrison insists on an explanation that is essentially sociological rather than linguistic. Thus, even though he persists in identifying this speech with "the talk of the African," he also implies that "cultivation" would make this language a mere relic of the slave past. At the same time, he charts this mythopoeic quality of the Negro linguistic code and its cultural "correlatives" as features of a "black" habit of mind:

> The Negro passion for music and for rhythmic utterance has often been remarked; a Negro sermon nearly always rises to a pitch of exaltation at which ordinary prose accent, intonation, word-order are too tame to express the streaming emotion within; the sermon becomes a cry, a poem, an improvisation; it is intoned with melodious energy; it is full of scraps of Scripture in poem-form, and to say that it becomes an orgy of figures and metaphors sobbed or shouted out with the voice of Boanerges is hardly going at all too far.

This propensity for passionate rhythmic utterance has a secular dimension as well as the sacred one found in the sermon:

> The sermon style naturally exerts a powerful influence on the style of ordinary life; so that it is not remarkable if the utterance

and language of the household and the street are largely cast in a rhythmic mould. Nearly every Negro above the average is a hymn-maker. . . . He invents his own airs and tunes, which are often profoundly touching and musical.

Above all, it is the well-developed sense of visual imagery and concrete metaphor to which Harrison is drawn and which he sees as permeating almost the whole of Negro cultural expression because of the nature of Negro language. This precise feel for the apt metaphor, which virtually creates a thing through its naming but which equally allows a verbal image to stand for a thing, is a kind of verbal masking and is, Harrison concludes, the fundamental hallmark of the "Negro mind," a term replete with implications for a literary tradition. It is this capacity for metaphor that is contained so strikingly in the language of the spirituals but is most often strikingly absent from the body of dialect poetry.

The mask is a common motif in Afro-American poetry—common yet carefully veiled in the main. Of course, with slavery and the evolution of the slave songs into the spirituals, the mask was utilized in a political context—indeed, as a matter of personal safety—to say one thing, all the while meaning another, usually under the guise of religious expression. The spiritual "Go Down Moses" is a classic example. The hymn beseeches a prototypic Moses to seek out ole Pharaoh and demand of him with all the weight of the wrath of Jehovah himself "to let my people go." Anyone who has heard this sung with the force and command of, say, Paul Robeson, not only knows but feels the signification. The usage in this context is common; it is also obvious. That the mythical Pharaoh "way down in Egypt land" was no further divorced from the slave quarters than the distance from the big house to the field shanty is by now familiar.

> Go down, Moses,
> Way down to Egypt land,
> Tell ole Pharaoh,
> To let my people go.

The stanza itself became, as we shall see, a reference point for much of black poetry, as did nearly all of the spirituals. The spirituals are of such import to black poetic language that when they surface as referents in the poetry—spoken, sung, or danced speech—

they cannot but bear the full emotional and structural import of another lurking but not lost hermetic universe. Scores of reviews compared Paul Laurence Dunbar's "lyrics" with songs (as did Dunbar). Spirituals as referents give black poetry an opulence of meaning—one translated through time and space by an oral tradition of over three and a half centuries—not readily available to exterior exploration.

This assumption of especial meaning to the initiated becomes more than simply knowing the lines. An academic exercise of chasing down poetic allusions, while intellectually gratifying, cannot even begin to translate the organic world view that that allusion, that especial usage, suggests. That, of course, is our problem when reading, say, a poet in translation, since the best of poetic expression is essentially untranslatable; but it is also our problem when faced with understanding a poet in our own language whose universe underwent essential alterations in perception subsequent to his or her writing. In many instances, the gap is unbridgeable. This usage is, of course, obvious to us all, but there is another, far more subtle rendering.

It has been the traditional role of the black poet—again, given the nature of the oral tradition—to be the point of consciousness, or superconsciousness, of his or her people. It is the black poet who bridges the gap in tradition, who modifies tradition when experience demands it, who translates experience into meaning and meaning into belief. More often than not, however, this point of consciousness in Afro-American art has been the role of the musician rather than the writer. The reasons for this, I suspect, are not only socio-historical but also linguistic. The poet, and the musician-as-poet, through the process of translating meaning into belief, has had to serve a mythopoeic function, a function of incorporating experience into a people's pantheon of value, a process more integral to the stability of society than would be one of incorporating experience into belief. As Anthony Appiah notes, "the distinctively moral features of a way of life have to do with our relations to others, to the community. Ultimately in determining our goals we are faced simply with a decision. It is a matter of preference. The mistake that Kierkegaard made in presenting the issue was to see the choice as being about what one should believe. The real choice is about what one should value."[5] Unlike that of the

Western scientist, the black poet's mythopoeic function has never been to look plainly at the world through its veils; it has been to re-create in metaphor an outer world and in metonym an inner world in the image of a people, in terms where any opposition between the two is resolved. Thus, the black poet's primary task has been to create, by definition, reality for the members of his or her community, to allow them to perceive their universe in a distinctively new way. This new way is built on tradition, only now reformed to be valued anew. This is the black poet's mythopoeic role: to predict our future through his or her sensitivity to our past coupled with an acute, almost intuitive awareness of the present. "Present life for him," writes Wole Soyinka, "must contain within its manifestations of ancestor, the living, and the unborn."[6] By forging value, by solidifying meaning, the black poet, in his or her own way, forges myth. The importance of myth, of course, is not whether it is believed, or even verifiable; the importance of myth is whether or not it is valued. When no longer valued, myth is disposed of or modified into a new myth, often a mutation of that which it displaced. Through both nonverbal musical expression and verbal manifestations of mutated meaning, this step-by-step evolution is traceable structurally.

Why do I argue that the poet-musician has served this function more than the writer? It is primarily because the evocation of a theatrical or hermetic universe where only truth could be conveyed is for the black artisan bound to his or her language, a language inextricably interwoven with music. The medium of music itself carries its own value and its own tradition, again of a historically mutated meaning-into-value. It would be as idle to attempt to utter poetry without syllables as it is for a black poet, functioning mythopoeically, to utter poetry without music. Here again, language fails us. We must state this in a different manner: There can be no poetry in this context without music and myth. Indeed, "poetry" implies music and myth. The nature of black music is the nature of black speech, and vice versa. Not only is it unmusical to separate these, but it is simply not poetic. Nonverbal music itself contains the language, indeed the coded value, of hermetic tradition. To quote Soyinka from a slightly different context: "Only the battle of the will is thus primarily creative, from its spiritual stress springs the soul's despairing cry which proves its own solace, which alone reverberating within the cosmic vaults usurps (at least, and however briefly) the powers of the abyss. At the charged climax of the tragic rites we understand how music came to contain, the sole art form which does contain, tragic reality." This is certainly true for black poetry as well. Where language is not only another dimension of nonverbal music but also an elaborator on that medium and where "language still is the embryo of thought" and music a "daily companion," then "poetry"— again, poetry-music-myth—is by definition continuously mythopoeic. It can be nothing else.

Because of the nature of black poetic expression, then, the black poet is far more than a mere point of consciousness of the community. He or she is a point of consciousness of the language. In the former role—especially in black America—one is often bogged down by far too many political considerations. The latter role, however, though based in part on political reality, allows the poet to transcend his or her political reality and arrive at the core of the community's values and way of life. It is debilitating for a people's art to be tied merely to its immediate political reality. That which individuates a way of life is not only the set of principal goals a people hold but, more important, their central beliefs about human happiness and suffering (above all, about death), which play their part in determining choice and motivating action—indeed, in determining value. It seems an insufferable tense between the future perfect promise for dialect poetry that Harrison's essay holds and the still imperfect preserve of nineteenth-century dialect poetry. In most cases, efforts to employ a weak rhetorical art in acts of liberation from an oppressive political reality disrupt the poet's mythopoeic function. These disruptions— which usually result in the disintegration of the bond between black written art and music—debilitated the tradition of dialect poetry.

II

In 1931, James Weldon Johnson could assert assuredly that "the passing of traditional dialect as a medium for Negro poets is complete."[7] There is a ring of victory, both aesthetic and political, in Johnson's tone. In his first preface to *The Book of American Ne-*

gro Poetry (1922),[8] Johnson had described the necessarily urgent preoccupation of the emerging "New Negro" poet to be the "break away from, not Negro dialect itself, but the limitations on Negro dialect imposed by the fixing effects of long convention." And that convention, argued Johnson, was an unrealistic—indeed, insidious— archetypal portraiture of the black man as a head-scratching, foot-shuffling, happy-go-lucky fool. The use of dialect in black poetry, then, could only reinforce that convention; dialect, therefore, was a trap. *"Naturally* and by long association [dialect has been] the exact instrument for voicing this phase of Negro life; and by that very exactness it is an instrument with but two full stops, humor and pathos" (emphasis added). Form had come to determine sense, or worse, he implied, to delimit sense, to mold it into a too familiar stock response. Thus, because of the peculiar artistic treatment accorded "the black image" through the exploitation of black dialect, by both black and nonblack poets, Johnson argued, "there are phases of Negro life in the United States which cannot be treated in the dialect either adequately or artistically." This almost ideal, imposed limitation of the medium, continued Johnson, renders it useless to the new black poet, precisely because the would-be poet is almost psychologically bound to the weight of tradition and is thus unable to use dialect as effectively as, say, Claude McKay could do using the Jamaican patois. This is because of the entrapment of usage.

Although Johnson acknowledged that Dunbar used dialect "as a medium for the true interpretation of Negro character and psychology" and that the passage of "this quaint and musical folk speech as a medium of expression" would be a distinct loss, he mistakenly assumed that the poetic uses of dialect gave to it, "the humble speech of [the] people," an order and form beyond the potential of the dialect itself. "In it," wrote Johnson, Dunbar "wrought music." The distinction here, I would suggest, is crucial. Where Dunbar used dialect successfully, he managed to contain a musicality inherent in the form itself, significantly an oral form, in a stylized, literate, written form. It is not that Dunbar wrought music in dialect; dialect wrought music in Dunbar's best poetry. The distinction, again, is crucial, particularly when we compare Dunbar's "literate" verse with his dialect.

Himself a musician and a poet, Johnson knew that dialect it-

self—beyond convention, if such an aesthetic realm exists in a social context where every manifestation of poetic sensibility was by
definition a political act—could contain the sublime, especially in
the spirituals. "That this shortcoming [of the two full stops, humor and pathos] is not a shortcoming inherent in the dialect as
dialect," Johnson argued, "is demonstrated by the wide compass
it displays in its use in the folk creations." But because the use of
dialect in minstrelsy—a white parody of black sentiment—was firmly
rooted in the "slough of sentimentality" and because "these conventions were not broken for the simple reason that the individual
writer wrote chiefly to entertain an outside audience," the black
poet never managed to make the form his or her own, an especially odd anomaly considering that the form from the beginning
borrowed from the black person's verbal store. This line of thinking is even stranger when one considers that the black poet did not
have to retreat to some mythic Western Isles to experience the
poignancy of dialect; he or she had only to step out into the field,
or by this time into the street, and listen.

That dialect ceased to be a major form in the Harlem Renaissance (although Jean Toomer, Langston Hughes, and especially
Sterling Brown would most effectively move against the grain)
was of paramount importance to that literary movement's life-
blood, but not for the reasons Johnson so longingly wished. His
mistake, common among post-Renaissance writers, was to con-
fuse the absence of dialect poetry with a new and seminal relationship among poet and audience, possible subject matter, and
attitude. Much has been made of the notion that for the first time
in their aesthetic history the black poets of the Renaissance turned
to their own separate and unique experience as Afro-American
people to celebrate what was essentially and especially theirs. The
change, argued Alain Locke in *The New Negro,* heralded a new
era's racial consciousness of itself and of the artist's relationship
to his or her material and his or her medium. The artistic end of
this, Locke contended, would be art, the black person's entry into
the realm of the secret and the sublime. The result, of course,
would be a political liberation of the most subtle yet profound
sort.

Johnson was correct in asserting that the limitations of dialect
were brought about because "the individual writers wrote chiefly

to entertain an outside audience, and in accord with its stereotyped ideas about the Negro." But he failed to see the ramifications of his own contention that "herein lies the vital distinction between [the poets] and the folk creators, who wrote solely to please and express themselves." For with the passage of dialect went, in the main, the potential for the expression of that which was hermetic and singular about the black in America. With the passage of dialect went a peculiar sensitivity to black speech as music, poetry, and a distinct means of artistic discourse on the printed page.

This notion had been William Stanley Braithwaite's just four years before Johnson's first preface, in an essay called "Some Contemporary Poets of the Negro Race."[9] Dialect, Braithwaite argued strongly enough to force Johnson to address the matter in his preface,

> may be employed as the langue d'oc of Frederic Mistral's Provencal poems, as a preserved tongue, the only adequate medium of rendering the psychology of character, and of describing the background of the people whose lives and experience are kept within the environment where the dialect survives as the universal speech; or it may be employed as a special mark of emphasis upon the peculiar characteristic and temperamental traits of a people whose action and experiences are given in contact and relationship with a dominant language, and are set in a literary fabric of which they are but one strand of man in the weaving.

Dialect, Braithwaite continued, had been the language of the spirituals, the first black American poetry, at once "impassioned and symbolic," "the poetry of an ancient race passing through the throes of an enforced re-birth into the epoch of an alien and dominating civilization." Yet dialect as a written form of discourse had begun and culminated with the poetry of Dunbar: "It was a finale, in a rather conscious manner, of centuries of spiritual isolation, of a detached brooding and yearning for self-realization in the universal human scale, and in a childish gayety in eating the fruits of a freedom so suddenly possessed and difficult to realize." Dunbar, Braithwaite, admitted, wrestled the language from the exploitation of the minstrel parody. But he was "the end of a regime" as well as its beginning, because "he never ventured into the abstract intricacies and wrung from the elements of rhythmic principles the

subtle and most haunting forms of expression," and precisely because "he did not have the deep and indignant and impassioned
vision, or the subtle and enchanting art to sustain" the consciousness of the race.

With very few exceptions—notably Sterling Brown and Langston
Hughes, two examples to which we shall turn again and again—
poetic expression, and hence poetic image, became a stylized, literate experience for the printed page and the outside reader. And
because of this, black poetry—that is, the oral component of black
poetry, which even the formalized abuse of black language in its
parodies failed to smother completely—was sacrificed on the altar
of the universal to the spirit of Western art. Also, the triumph
over dialect drove these poets to the opposite extreme; they became self-conscious of displaying their experience, and hence their
art, as just another in the human community made distinct, where
distinct, by social context, by imposed forms.[10] Art for the black
poet was functional, but it could not remain collective.

Weldon Johnson concluded his section on dialect by saying that
"if he addressed himself to the task, the Aframerican poet might
in time break the old conventional mold; but I don't think he will
do it, because I don't think he considers it now worth the effort."
Because that task was not worth the effort, much of the poetry of
the Harlem Renaissance was destined to remain minor and was to
pale by comparison with the independent and collateral evolution
of black music.

Part of this confusion about the potential poetic uses of dialect
can be demonstrated to be rooted in the social role of the black
artist in the first quarter of this century. "The colored poet," Johnson lamented, "labors within limitations which he cannot easily
pass over. He is always on the defensive or the offensive. These
conditions are suffocating to breadth and to real art in poetry."
The question of just what Johnson implied by "real art in poetry"
notwithstanding, these political considerations of the black poet
made the value of dialect especially dubious to the "New Negro,"
for dialect was an oral remnant of slavery,[11] and it was that degradation to the dignity of a proud people that these artists, both con-
sciously and unconsciously, intended to abolish. Abolish dialect
they did, and with the bathwater went the baby.

There is nothing intrinsically limiting about the use of dialect in poetry, as Sterling Brown proved, as long as dialect is not seen to be mere misspellings of mispronounced words—in Johnson's words, "the mere mutilation of English spelling and pronunciation." True and dynamic dialect contains what Roman Jakobson calls "instances," the speech-segment of natural language. And that speech-segment must be seen to be, in Hugh Kenner's phrase, "a broken mirror of memory," be that race memory or linguistic memory, if not both. The form of dialect carried a distinct meaning, often independent from the language from which it arose. Because dialect was an independent form, it could carry independent meaning—a distinctively black meaning. Here, perhaps, Richard Ohmann's argument applies: "Each writer tends to exploit deep linguistic resources in characteristic ways—that is style, in other words, rests in syntactic options within sentences—and that these syntactic preferences correlate with habits of meaning that tell us something about this mode of conceiving experience."[12] Ohmann's argument is concerned with prose, but the relationship between form and meaning holds even more for poetry. Style and structure reflect understanding and meaning implicit in the use of language, in the very use of style and structure. One would be tempted to add that, if a meaning is in fact an independent one, then the form that contains it must be independent as well. Thus, when a people see their communal experience as a unique one, it is the poet who becomes the representative of the only vehicle they might have to convey this especial meaning or value in a verbal way. And that vehicle, of course, is their language.

If there was nothing intrinsically limiting about dialect in poetry, then why did most dialect poems fail, as Johnson, Braithwaite, and Countee Cullen[13] rightly observed? Johnson's own answer, again from his preface, given in an alarmingly offhanded manner, is "mere technique." This is an important statement, crucial to understanding the state of black poetry today. Black poetry during the Renaissance and the period surrounding it was marked by what Stephen Henderson calls urgency, a seemingly overwhelming sense of political purpose. Each poem penned during the Renaissance, jested Wallace Thurman, was "another bombshell fired at American Kulchur." And "political" in this sense must be seen as having at least two connotations. Claude McKay's *If We Must Die* (1919) is a political poem of the first order:

> If we must die—let it not be like hogs
> Hunted and penned in

Regardless of an evaluation of the sentiment, this sonnet could not help but be political, in a very obvious sense, in a postwar America. Yet there was still another sense of "political," one not so obvious at all.

For the Renaissance poets, the act of writing itself was an act of definition, not only of a personal, poetic sensibility but also of a people-hood through the exemplars of the race—Du Bois's "talented tenth," Braithwaite's "cultured few." Johnson himself saw this inherent intent of black poetics and said as much in his preface:

> A people may become great through many means, but there is only one measure by which its greatness is recognized and acknowledged. The final measure of the greatness of all peoples is the amount and standard of the literature and art they have produced. The world does not know that a people is great until that people produces great literature and art. No people that has produced great literature and art has ever been looked upon by the world as distinctly inferior.

The act of poetic creation was both collective and functional, but collective and functional as defined by the larger, largely white outside world. True, these are two canons of African poetics, as old as Kilimanjaro and just as enduring. But the sense of function here implied by the Victorian deans of the Renaissance—Johnson, Locke, Braithwaite, Du Bois—was to "elevate the race"[14] in the eyes of an incredulous white world; internal function could be only secondary. Here is to be found the distinction between African poetics and the poetics espoused during the Renaissance: the overriding requisite of black art was that it ennoble the race's image-qua-culture bearers in the pantheon of Western people's art. This was the first and foremost function; it was a trap.

This sense of urgency had many ramifications for the poetry of the Renaissance, none of which proved productive. Although this is not a popular view, many of these writers were not primarily poets, either in the traditional West African sense of the *griot* or in the Western sense. They were polemicists, concerned with making an almost literal statement.[15] Their concern was with the basic "what" and not the basic "how." Also, many of these poets borrowed with very little modification the forms of white poetry. Far too often, their models were not of the first order; these black mockingbirds did not supersede the creations of their borrowed forms. Nor, upon reflection, could they have been expected to, considering their conception of poetic priority. They produced second-rate poetry, and the result was self-defeating: mediocre poetry, it was said, from a mediocre intellect.[16]

Johnson knew this: "The pressure upon [the black poet] to be propagandic [sic] is well-nigh irresistible. . . . These conditions are suffocating to breadth and to real art in poetry." And yet, he argued elsewhere in his preface, the best of black poetry dealt thematically with race. "I have," he declared, "no intention of depreciating the poetry not stimulated by a sense of race that Af-ramerican poets have written; much of it is as high as the average standard of American poetry and some of it higher; but not in all of it do I find a single poem possessing the power and artistic final-ity found in the best of the poems rising out of racial conflict and contact." "Race" contained and sustained a dynamic and a sense of the language not otherwise found in "nonracial" poetry. "All of which," Johnson concluded, "is merely a confirmation of the ax-iom that an artist accomplishes his best when working at his best with materials he knows best."

Aesthetic theories of the period were punctuated by this term "race." In fact, for Johnson and his contemporaries, race was used as a blanket concept to denote two very divergent significations; rarely, though, is the distinction drawn in Johnson's argument. "Race" to Johnson meant the political oppression of Negro Amer-icans vis-à-vis white Americans. Yet the notion of race as descrip-tive of a sensibility outside a political context, beyond time and space, escaped Johnson, as it did most of his contemporary poets. It was an oversight. Johnson said of race that "up to this time, at least, [it] is perforce the thing the American Negro knows best. Assuredly, the time will come when he will know other things as well as he now knows 'race,' and will, perhaps, feel them as deeply; or, to state this another way, the time should come when he will not have to know 'race' so well and feel it so deeply." There is something fundamentally wrong with this notion of the poet turning outside of himself or herself for meaning and for value. While we can understand Johnson's anxiety and desire to see the black artist escape the confinements of protest—to escape, in effect, from "the race problem"—there is in his argument a not-so-latent urge to the universal, which universal, in practice at least, tended to demand the sacrifice of all that was not somehow Judeo-Christian. This is why dialect had to be abandoned and why Johnson himself translated his own *God's Trombones* from dialect into standard English: dialect was a form apart, its meaning lurking beneath the surface of meaning, its meanings implicit in the forms it took in poetry—meanings ultimately derived, as we shall see below, from black mythology and black music. Not only in his language but also in the racial experience of Africans in the New World was to be found the poetic art for which Johnson so longingly searched, but, because of the prescriptions he placed on art, he would search in vain. Johnson was forced to conclude that "even now [the black poet] can escape the sense of being hampered if, standing on his racial foundation, he strives to fashion something that rises above mere race and reaches out to the universal in truth and beauty."

No poet, ultimately, knows more than race. "Mere race" was not to be risen above but to be plunged into. While Johnson could demand the avoidance of the minstrel-vaudeville use of mispronunciation and while he could suggest that "what the colored poet in the United States needs to do is something like what Synge did for the Irish; he needs to find a form that will express the racial spirit by symbols from within rather than symbols from without, such as the mere mutilation of English spelling and pronunciation," he did not recognize that that form, especially poetic form, had to be constructed in a language that reflected and was capable of containing the symbols from within. That language, of course, was black speech, a coded, danced speech which carried its own significations. It reflected implicitly a world view set apart from that contained in the languages from which it arose, be they Romantic or Bantu. Dialect contained its own hermetic, autonomous universe, to be invoked only through the spoken word. One did not believe one's eyes, if one were black; one believed, said Sterling Brown, one's ears.

By the time Johnson's second preface appeared in 1931, the abandonment of dialect was indeed complete. And with the dynamic and distinctive form of mask went the potential to express "the peculiar turn of thought" that sustains a literary movement. The black poetry of the Renaissance, without dialect, strayed further and further from black music, from the music necessary to keep verse itself the essentially untranslatable medium it is. Because the black poets saw their obligation to something called art, they abnegated their responsibility to their language. Most were destined to remain secondary poets because they could not master their own distinctive poetic diction. Only Jean Toomer's *Cane,* Langston Hughes's first two volumes of poetry, and Sterling Brown's *Southern Road* demonstrated the use of this black poetic diction, precisely because these poets were the point of consciousness of their language.

III

Ultimately, it must be to the poetry that we turn. The problem with any close reading of black poetry, particularly in dialect, is that of translation of the music itself into meaningful language. This music is the poetry of the rhythmic word; the printed word cannot be fully understood as "meaning" if treated alone—there is no escape from this. Syntax itself, in these forms, becomes music. The use of dialect in poetry, for instance, must be seen in the context of the music from which it springs—black speech and black music (especially the spirituals), which is the final referent. For all its technical failings, dialect poetry at its best was an attempt to capture the movement and signification of the music that conveyed the words. It failed where it did primarily for two reasons: the poetry became a stilted literary form, devoid of the metaphorical character of the language of the spirituals, proverbs, secular songs, and folklore from which it sought to divorce itself and hence lost its capacity to be a verbal mirror; and, out of aesthetic decision, a technical failing, or the very limitation of literary form, the poetry echoed the minstrel or plantation traditions of dialect usage rather than its vital origins.

Ray Garfield Dandridge's "Sprin Fevah" is a classic example. From the first pair of lines,

> Dar's a lazy, sortah hazy,
> Feelin' grips me, thoo and thoo;

one feels the movement of the poem bounding into triteness, a triteness of sentiment and expression. The speech sounds forced, of the sort written but never spoken or sung. It reflects not the speech patterns of the countryman whose sentiment this is intended to be but the poet's desire to entertain through novelty. It is the poem's rhyme scheme that is off; breath—the soft "a," the extended "ah's," the "oo's" in "thoo"—is constricted by a racy rhythm that any blues singer worth the weight of a steel banjo would not dare inflict upon his or her audience. The brisk movement, where effective in black music and good dialect, is dependent on the concrete imagery the lines can carry. Indeed, even the spirituals' detractors readily admitted the vividness and specificity of the imagery, a sort of conjure-into-being with the musical word.

> An' I feels lak doin' less dan enythin';

"Less dan enythin'," obviously, is meant here to carry the line, to convince us that the break in movement is justified by the powerful image at the end. But again, the image fails, because "less dan enythin' " can entail meanings so numerous as to border on the ridiculous in ways that, say, "less dan nuffin' " could not. Less than nothing is not very much; it is specific. This line has more problems. The poet is arbitrary in his "mere mispronunciation." If "an" and "dan," for example, are visual representations of the actual sounds produced by black speech, "doin' " must certainly fail. If one pronounced "doing" as "doin' " is intended to suggest, its spelling would be closer to "duen." "Doin' " is a poor literate translation, meant for the eye of the uninitiate, not meant to suggest a sound.

This same limitation of the visual suggestion plagues the "dough" in the first two lines of the following; but, again, there are more problems:

> Dough de saw is sharp an' greasy,
> Dough de task et ha'd is easy,
> An' de day am fair an' breezy,
> Dar's a thief dat steals embition in de win'.

"Is" in the first two lines here is out of place. The most assaulting aspect of black dialect is the unique use of the verb "to be." No one who could have uttered this would have said "is sharp" or "is easy." He or she would have said "be shahp" or "be eezy." Nor would the inflection of "easy" allow it to be presented so. "There would be a heavy "z" sound, and the apparent ease with which "easy" and "greasy" rhyme would have jarred. "Fair" would have been pronounced "faer." One also wonders strongly if "am" would be allowed to express what "be's" in this sense, "am" seems to be used most effectively to create a musical effect to emphasize, as in "shoo am," its "a" being a diphthong.

The one line in the first stanza with some potential to be interesting is the final one:

> Dar's a thief dat steals embition in de win'.

This line is an attempt to capture the imagery of the wind so common in the spirituals, such as

> Sometimes I feel like an eagle in de air

or, more appropriately, the common use of wind as a fulfiller of destiny, which if it could be restrained would restrain time and fate:

> Hol' de win'! Hol' de win'!
> Hol' de win', don't let it blow.

And:

> If yer wanter dream dem heavenly dreams,
> 'Way in de middle of de air;
> Lay yo' head on Jord'n's stream,
> 'Way in de middle of de air.

But, once again, the imagery of *Sprin Fevah* is vague; one is not certain if "embition" performs its stealing "in de win' " or if our thief is out and about, preying "in de win'." The image fails, as does the language meant to contain it.

One could find much more to criticize in the final stanza, but the point has been made. The poem fails in its use of the language to destroy, more visually than orally, standard English pronunciation. And to what end? one may ask. The heightened imagery so common to the spirituals—in fact, the primary poetic capacity of the language—is nowhere to be found. If dialect has one overwhelming feature, it is its capacity to carry imagery compactly, its separate language not only conveying the image but focusing it, strengthening it by contrast with its standard English reflection.[17]

The poem's most damning flaw by far may be its use of the form to entertain without thought, to convey an ill-considered humor unworthy of the form, in words vapid, empty of imagery, and marred by the failure to conjure the specific (such as "easy," "breezy," "greasy," "neutrolize," "analyze," and "pursistin' "). The poem is a poor one; the poet has mistaken simplicity for simplemindedness. (One is reminded of Dante Gabriel Rossetti's parody of dialect found in Stowe's *Uncle Tom's Cabin,* entitled *Uncle Ned:* "Him tale dribble on and on widout a break, / Till you hab no eyes for to see; / When I reach Chapter 4 I had got a headache; / So I had to let Chapter 4 be.") This poem is typical of much that was wrong with dialect poetry. Only rarely did its lines assume their full rhythmic burden, laden with allusion, rich in reference, connoting the unique turn of mind of the black; never did dialect poetry approximate the almost inexplicable modulations of the spirituals. Dialect poetry failed, too, when it tried to cram a live, spoken form into a rigid, written one, oblivious to its internal logic, unaware of its linguistic possibilities, technically inadequate to preserve the poetry as spirit. The spirituals never made these errors. Dialect poetry choked and wasted a spirit and produced a mediocre body of trivia.

It is right that the spirituals should be our reference point for dialect poetry, since the spirituals—"as anonymous as earth" succeeded so well exactly where dialect was to fail: in using a new form to convey a new meaning, a meaning inseparable from belief, both of which gave rise to that form. The lines from this standard European hymn, for example—

> At this table we'll sit down,
> Christ will gird himself and serve us sweet manna all around

—were translated into the lines

> Gwine to sit down at the welcome table,
> Gwine to feast off milk and honey.

This transformation is a significant one, not because it has taken a tame sentiment and made of it an assertive one but because it teaches us something about the nature of the interrelationship of sense and sound. "Gwine," for instance, is still commonly found in black speech. It is basically untranslatable, yet, with a little reflection, we must see that the full import of the word goes tar beyond its referent, "I am going to," and implies far more. "Gwine" implies not only a filial devotion to a moral order but also the completion, the restoration, of harmony in what had heretofore been a universe out of step somehow. "Gwine" asserts a reordering, again this restoration rhythmic, its diphthong heightening its force on the heels of the breathily spoken "gw" sound, the "w" tempering the hard "g." "Gwine" connotes unshakeable determination, the act to come now made certain to come by the act of speech. "Gwine" leaves no room for doubt, for question, for vacillation. In part, this use of "gwine" is similar to the premise of Yoruba tragedy that through ritual a synthesis is effected to lament the primal severance of people from God. A sensitive reading of "gwine" alerts one to the fact that some essentially different thing is about to happen here, beyond the use of the normal meaning of "I am going to." "Gwine" contains a concept, a way of looking at the world, not fully translated by "I am going to." With "gwine," people accept their primal place in the bosom of God; people relieve God's grief at the severance, again interacting with God—an interaction mistakenly said to be absent from the spirituals.

When using a word, we wake into resonance its entire previous history. A text is embedded in specific historical time; it has what linguists call a diachronic structure. To read fully is to restore all that one can of the immediacies of value and intent in which speech actually occurs.

But there are other meanings here as well, lurking somewhere between Timbuktu and the Old City of Jerusalem. "Down," for instance, carries with it the import of its usage in the spiritual "Go Down Moses." Our poet is not "gwine to sit down," but is going to sit, down at the welcome table. The distinction, again, is crucial, for "down" in the latter sense leads from the same place appointed by God for the enactment of primal tragic action, where fate and will can meet. "Down" is the Afro-American "Fourth Stage," that place where Yahweh told Moses exactly what to say to ole Pharaoh, "way down in Egypt land," to "let my people go." Almost as strongly, "down" also implies the not-so-mythic (but mythically recalled) land from which black people were severed, the Africa of their fathers where people were people and people were free. Here, "down" implies more than a place distinct, a place set apart, the place of fulfillment; it implies the return not only to the native land but also to the native order, an inevitable order, which only God's will coupled with all the acts of assertion contained in "gwine" can conjure. Thomas Wentworth Higginson, in a largely overlooked passage from his article "Negro Spirituals" in *Atlantic Monthly* (1867), offhandedly makes a remarkably similar observation about the spiritual "Down in the Valley."[18] The lines of the hymn are as follows:

> Way down in de valley,
>   Who will rise and go with me?
> You've heern talk of Jesus,
>   Who set poor sinners free.

Higginson thought that

> de valley and de lonesome valley were familiar words in [the Negro's] religious experience. To descend into that region implied the same process with the "anxious-seat" of the camp-meeting. When a young girl was supposed to enter it, she bound a handkerchief by a peculiar knot over her head, and made it a point of honor not to change a single garment till the day of her baptism, so that she was sure of being in physical readiness for the cleansing rite, whatever her spiritual mood might be. More than once, in noticing a damsel thus mystically kerchiefed, I have asked some dusky attendant its meaning, and have received the unfailing answer,—framed with their usual indifference to the genders of pronouns,—'He in de lonesome valley, sa.

Higginson did not realize, of course, that the key place was not "the valley" but "down in de valley" or, more correct, "down de valley," as the form survives today. "Table," to return to the line "down at the welcome table," by virtue of its position at the end of the line, is also crucial here; its connotations of fulfillment of the Holy Word, the full rotation along the circumference of time, supplemented by the celebration of this completion with the feast of milk and honey, complete the strength of the signification. The line is a noble one, its magic created through concrete images, its associative properties both subtle and strong.

Let us examine two other examples briefly, for the sake of clarity. There is a particular density to black sacred language that is rooted in an almost separate mythology and ontology melded together from African and European strains. The lines from a standard European hymn, for example, were translated from

> To hide yourself in the mountains,
> To hide yourself from God

to

> Went down to the rocks to hide my face,
> The rocks cried out no hiding place.

These lines work only because the poet found not just *a* different way of saying, but *the* different way of saying and thus captured the specialness of that which was to be conveyed. The meaning has changed in the translation. Matters of origin, genesis, and priority, therefore, become secondary concerns in literary analysis. The spirituals make the language contain a turn of mind, subtle and sublime, poignant and compact, concrete—"the poetry of an ancient race passing through the throes of an enforced rebirth into the epoch of an alien and dominating civilization"—yet transcendent. Again, we have the oppositions between will and fate, choice and destiny. The movement occurs through rhythm: the prodigal fleeing the wrath of God faces the unbearable sight of that wrath—the unchanging face of the rocks, daring not to utter the unspeakable name of Yahweh, answers "no hiding place" . . . "no hiding place." It is the spoken word that is holy; the prodigal must unavoidably believe his ears, not his eyes. Again, "down" is the place of confrontation, within the spirit of the soul, of the poet with the ineffable. In this instance, the ineffable terror of God's judgment leads to the hiding of the face; this action is related not only to the Hebrew notion of the unbearability of the countenance of Yahweh but also to the notion of the unbearability and even the unspeakableness of the name of God. It is also derived from the mode of the mask the slaves used to adapt to their new world, a world they could only partially know, seen from a perspective buried in their lost world, a world they could only fragmentarily recall. The flight to the rocks, repeated to invoke the futility of the attempt to hide, suggests human attempts to flee the inexorable by seeking refuge in natural elements. Yet the rocks themselves yield to the omniscience of God: "no hiding place." To hide one's face was not enough; one thinks of the Yoruba aesthetic value of character (*iwa*) and composure. The rhythm in these lines affects a presence removed from the terror of their import and thus supports a counterpoint between that which is described and the feelings this internal movement effects. These lines suggest joy; they cannot be sung, paradoxically, without suggesting a certain joy, a resignation to the absurd. The music and intonation, therefore, are not somehow neutral conduits; they carry the meaning that makes the difference in the transformation. The context is a joyous one, tragic yet sustaining to the human dimension by the process of delineation.

A final example, given without exegesis, is the transformation of John's vision in Revelation 6:12-13:

> And I beheld when he had opened the sixth seal, and lo, there was a great earthquake; and the sun became black as sackcloth of hair, and the moon became as blood;
>
> And the stars of heaven fell unto the earth, even as a fig tree casteth her untimely figs, when she is shaken of a mighty wind.

In a remarkable translation, this awesome rendition of judgment became:

> Moon went into de poplar tree,
> An' star went into blood.

Or still another, yet less resourceful:

> My Lord, what a morning when de stars begin to fall,
> You'll see de worl' on fire,
> You'll see de moon a bleedin' an'
> De moon will turn to blood.[19]

Star into blood; moon into poplar tree; the candor of the moon, dripping of blood—the full knowledge of time, when the elemental is seen to be internal, when the permanency of nature is seen to be but an extension of the essential in humanity, when the unity of all created things becomes manifestly fundamental—this the message of the slave, contained in a language here, as Braithwaite noted, like "wood notes wild that have scarcely yet been heard beyond the forest of their own dreams." In these images, dialect is at its most effective, and the poet not only has accepted his or her role as the point of consciousness of the language but has pushed that language to express that which is untranslatable.

· 7 ·

The Same Difference:
Reading Jean Toomer, 1923-1982

The Negro's curious position in this western civilization forces him into one or the other of two extremes: either he denies the Negro entirely (as much as he can) and seeks approximation to an Anglo-Saxon (white) ideal, or, as in the case of your London acquaintance, he overemphasizes what is Negro. Both of these attitudes have in their source a feeling of (a desire not to feel) inferiority. I refer here, of course, to those whose consciousness and condition make them keenly aware of white dominance. The mass of Negroes, the peasants, like the mass of Russians or Jews or Irish or what not, are too instinctive to be anything but themselves. Here and there one finds a high type Negro who shares this virtue with his more primitive brothers. As you can imagine, the resistance against my stuff is marked, excessive. But I feel that in time, in its social phase, my art will aid in giving the Negro to himself.

Jean Toomer, 1922

> Oh, black skinned epic, epic with the black spear,
> I cannot sing you, having too white a heart,
> And yet, some day, a poet will rise to sing you
> And sing you with such truth and mellowness, . . .
> That you will be a match for any song
> Sung by old, populous nations in the past.

Stephen Vincent Benet, 1927
"John Brown's Body"

We are hypnotized by literacy.

Jean Toomer, 1931

I wrote and wrote and put each thing aside, regarding it as simply one of the experiences of my apprenticeship. Often I would be depressed and almost desperate over the written thing. But, on the other hand, I became more and more convinced that I had the real stuff in me. And, the "feeling" of my medium, a sense of form, of words, of sentences, of rhythms, cadences, and rhythmic patterns. And then, after several years' work, suddenly, it was as if a door opened and I knew without doubt that I was *inside*. I knew literature. And *what* was my joy!

Jean Toomer, 1934

Perhaps . . . our lot on the earth is to seek and to search. Now and again we find just enough to enable us to carry on. I now doubt that any of us will completely find and be found in this life.

Jean Toomer, 1951

I

Let me rehearse the skeletal facts of Jean Toomer's life. On March 29, 1894, Nina Elizabeth Pinchback, aged twenty-six, married Nathan Toomer, aged fifty-three. Nine months later, shy three days, Nathan Eugene Toomer was born, on December 26, 1894. Within a year of his birth, his father would leave his mother, ostensibly for financial reasons; by 1899, their divorce would become final.

Toomer's first two decades read like the diary of a transient. In 1910, the child moved to Washington to live with his grandparents, the P. B. S. Pinchbacks, one year after his mother's death. Eugene attended the University of Wisconsin in 1914 and the Massachusetts College of Agriculture in 1915, then moved to Chicago in 1916. By 1919, he had moved back East to New York, where he met Waldo Frank. In 1920, he returned to Washington; one year later, he sojourned to Sparta, Georgia, where he taught school for two months, an experience, Toomer admits, that served as the basis of *Cane*. Within the two years after he left Georgia, Toomer met Gorham Munson and Mae Wright, had an affair with Margaret Naumberg (Waldo Frank's wife), published *Cane,* and encountered the teachings of George Ivanovich Gurdjieff. In 1924, he took his first trip to Fontainbleau to study with Gurdjieff, a pilgrimage he would make again in 1926, 1927, and 1929. Between 1925 and 1929, Toomer would write several works that he would not see published, including *Values and Fictions* (1925), *The Gallonwerps* (1927), and *Mr. Limp Krok's Famous Ride* and *Transatlantic* (1929). In 1931, Toomer privately published

Essentials: Definitions and Aphorisms and married Margery Lati-
mer, who would die in 1932 giving birth to a daughter, Margery,
in the same year that he copyrighted "Portage Potential" and
wrote "Caromb." In 1933, he wrote "Eight-Day World" and met
Georgia O'Keefe. One year later, he married Marjorie Content in
Taos, then moved to New York. In 1935, the couple settled at
Doylestown, Pennsylvania. For the next thirty years, with the major
exception of a 1939 pilgrimage to India and then to New Mexico,
Toomer spent his days exploring, through the written word, his
apparently unfulfilled quest for a philosophy of mystical transcen-
dence, which after 1940 he was able to do to some institutional
extent through the Society of Friends. Just two years after his
death in 1967, the *New York Times Book Review* featured prominently Robert Bone's essay on the major import of Toomer's
Cane. The irony is not merely that Toomer would be rediscovered
in the midst of the Black Power and Black Arts movements; the
irony is that his death saved him from what for forty years it had
been important for this writer to deny: that he was a black writer,
resurrected by one of the blackest African political ideologies
of all.

Few writers have ever enjoyed such a critical reception in their
lifetimes, from such a politically and aesthetically motley assortment of reviewers. Not only did Max Eastman and Claude McKay
publish his work in *The Liberator,* but Alan Tate and William
Stanley Braithwaite thought that *Cane* was a seminal modernist
text. Tate, writing in the Nashville *Tennessean,* said that sections
of *Cane* "challenged some of the best modern writing" and that
the book was "highly important for literature." Braithwaite, in an
essay entitled "The Negro in Literature" published in the *Crisis* in
September 1924, could barely restrain his enthusiasm:

> These rambling remarks on the Negro in literature I may well
> bring to a close with this public confession that I believe that of
> all the writers I have mentioned, the one who is most surely
> touched with genius is Jean Toomer the author of "Cane." I
> believe this, not only on account of what he has actually accom-
> plished in "Cane," but for something which is partly in the ac-
> complishment and partly in the half articulate sense and impres-
> sion of his powers. This young man is an artist; the very first
> artist in his Race who, with all an artist's passion and sympathy

for life, its hurts, its sympathies, its desires, its joys, its defeats, and strange yearnings, can write about the Negro without the surrender or compromise of the artist's vision. It's a mere accident that birth or association has thrown him into contact with the life that he has written about. He would write just as well, just as poignantly, just as transmutingly, about the peasants of Russia, or the peasants of Ireland, had experience but given him the knowledge of their existence. "Cane" is a book of ecstasy and bronze, of dusk and flame, of ecstasy and pain, and Jean Toomer is a bright morning star of a new day of the Race in literature![1]

Even Wallace Thurman, in his bitter satire of the Harlem Renaissance, *Infants of the Spring* (1932), spared Toomer's reputation when he spared little else. One of his characters says:

I don't expect to be a great writer. I don't think the Negro race can produce one now, any more than can America. I know of only one Negro who has the elements of greatness, and that's Jean Toomer. The rest of us are merely journeymen, planting seed for someone else to harvest.[2]

Such open and honest admiration, it is reasonable to assume, would virtually force an imitation of the first work in a second work of a similar sort. For Toomer, however, *Cane* would apparently satisfy this mode of representation, which he willfully eschewed for what he thought to be more universal, more daring subjects and mimetic principles.

Eugene Pinchback Toomer, 1894–1967, the grandson of P. B. S. Pinchback who on December 11, 1872, had begun a forty-three-day term as governor of Louisiana, published two books, well over one dozen short stories and poems not collected in *Cane,* six "dialogues," six critical reviews, one play, and almost twenty discrete pieces of nonfiction. Although his second book, *Essentials: Definitions and Aphorisms,* was printed privately in 1931, his first book, *Cane,* has been printed five times, in 1923, 1927, 1967, 1969, and 1975, and has been discussed critically by such an unlikely array of writers and critics as W. E. B. Du Bois and Alain Locke, Granville Hicks and Gorham Munson, Sterling Brown and Langston Hughes, Allen Tate and Sherwood Anderson, Darwin Turner and J. Saunders Redding, Houston Baker and Robert Stepto, Alice Walker and Toni Morrison, John Hope

Franklin and Nathan Ruggins. When added to the critical commentary upon the splendid collection of his writings, edited by Darwin Turner and entitled *The Wayward and the Seeking,* the criticism of Toomer's works amounts to a remarkable record of criticism of American literature since 1923.

Despite the remarkably extensive body of critical writings about Toomer and his works, neither Toomer nor his texts afford simple or straightforward readings. For Toomer's biographical facts, like his origins and antecedents and most of his post-*Cane* writings, remain in shadow and indeterminate. Even the generic status of *Cane,* composed as it is of multiple forms and shifting points of consciousness, remains a matter of considerable scholarly dispute. Few texts in the Afro-American tradition, nevertheless, have compelled such generous attention from critics whose presuppositions are fundamentally antithetical. It is *Cane*'s very ambiguity, of structure and of densely metaphorical lyricism, that continues to compel such a diversity of discursive responses, as do few texts in the American canon. Although several aspects of his life and works command the scholar's attention, it is through his lyrical fiction, *Cane,* that Toomer is best known.

If the trope of blackness in Western discourse has signified an absence, the sheer absence of invisibility, the "already-read text"[3] of blackness itself, then Jean Toomer's *Cane,* and Jean Toomer himself, site themselves ironically in the tradition as perhaps the "blackest" text and author of all. Toomer, consummate craftsman of the writerly text, signifies the ultimate of the black and chiasmatic rhetorical gesture: Toomer and text, less than a decade after *Cane*'s first printing in 1923, literally and figuratively crossed over. The double signification of the figure of crossing over in black discourse is apt here: the trope as used in the nineteenth-century mythic discourse of the spirituals and tales figures death, or more literally a passage through that threshold or limen that marks the troubled terrain between the "quick" and the dead; in secular discourse, crossing over signifies, either as a lament or as an accusation, he or she who abandons the race once and for all, to become "the completely other," to become white, to transmute one's racial self alchemically, completely, totally, without leaving a trace, through the incantation of the written word.

Without leaving a trace? Toomer, much to the chagrin of the

black writers and critics who in the late sixties traced him to *Cane,* decided for complex reasons, which he repeatedly revised, agonized over, or erased in the fragmented versions of an *Autobiography* he never published, to become "just American" and, concomitantly, not to become or remain "a negro." Toomer's gesture was complex: he apparently believed that he must displace the absence of being called "a negro" for a desired presence he would realize by calling himself "The First American," the title of a poem Toomer wrote during what Darwin Turner calls "The *Cane* Years" and which, Toomer tells us, "could grow and ripen and be embodied in 'The Blue Meridian.' "

Significantly, it was through a growing self-confidence with his ability to name things with words that Toomer, in part, felt free to redefine himself, to cross over. Robert Frost, Sherwood Anderson, and the Imagists, Toomer writes, gave him the mastery to make his ultimate rhetorical claim: "I began feeling that I had in my hands the tools for my own creation." "In America," he continues about the intention of "The First American," "we are in the process of forming a new race, that I was one of the first conscious members of this race." Toomer's account of a colored friend's reading of "The First American" bears citation:

> Soon after I had written it I read it to a friend of that time, a colored fellow of more than ordinary mental grasp. I considered him a sort of prodigy. I read the poem, and he looked blank. I explained it, and he looked puzzled. So I plunged in and gave him my position and my experiences at some length. At the end he said three words, "You're white."
>
> "What are you?" I asked.
>
> "Colored."
>
> I threw up my hands. "After all I've said you still don't get the point. I am not talking about whites or blacks, I am talking about Americans. I am an American. You are an American. Everyone is an American. Don't you see what I mean?"
>
> He shook his head then, he shook it ever afterwards. My reality was but words to him, words quite unrelated to what was real for him.[4]

Toomer's colored fellow of more than ordinary mental grasp responded as would a host of colored fellows of more than ordinary mental grasp. Toomer's "tools for my own creation," paradoxically, were "but words," yet words with which he put his Negro ancestry under erasure: his grandfather, P. B. S. Pinchback, Toomer rewrites, "passed" or crossed over to being a Negro only to seek and gain political office during the Reconstruction; Toomer simply reversed the chiasmus. If Grandfather Pinchback was white, then Grandson Jean was Negro. This mode of erasure, commonly thought to be the Heideggerian or Derridian, James Weldon Johnson introduced into the formal tradition in 1912 in his nameless protagonist's narrative, *The Autobiography of an Ex-Coloured Man*. Johnson's phrase "ex-coloured" is simply another form of "colored." (Perhaps the most famous x of all in the tradition is Malcolm's X.) Toomer's *Cane* revises key tropes found in Johnson's novel, just as Toomer's biographical details parallel uncannily those of Johnson's protagonist.

To be a human being, an "Earth-Being" in Toomer's phrase, Toomer felt that he had to efface his mask of blackness, the cultural or racial trace of difference, and embrace the utter invisibility of being an American. Jacques Derrida, in one of those curious intersections of parallel discursive universes, describes this gesture in another text milieu: "The 'matinal trace' of difference is lost in an irretrievable invisibility, and yet even its loss is covered, preserved, regarded, and retarded. This happens in a text, in the form of presence."[5] Toomer's "trace," in the sense that I am defining it, is *Cane*, that tell-tale trace of blackness that is textual and rhetorical and for which he has been recalled, then resurrected, by three generations of critics of Afro-American literature. Toomer's crossing over, in that ironic double sense of "passing" and "dying," then, his critics have erased in our own stubborn ways. For it is the repeated, reread text of *Cane* that proved to be a seminal text for the New Negro Renaissance of the twenties and for the New Black Poetry movement of the sixties, two movements for which the bold quest for the new proved to be so ironically belated, so fraught with nostalgia for an Africa that never was. Where, other than in a "Renaissance," could a "new" Black-Negro be contained?

I do not mean to belittle or underestimate the import of Toomer's gesture of reappellation by calling it a rhetorical gesture. On the contrary, Toomer's stance as the invisible American, or Milton's oxymoron "darkness visible," critics often adjudge by his own difference. "He never wrote another *Cane*," is the recurring refrain of Toomer criticism, "after he passed." Robert Hayden, the poet for whom Toomer stood as precursor, rendered this judgment in 1967 on the poet he so admired:

> Toomer published relatively little after *Cane* and nothing which equalled that work. Eventually he gave up writing altogether, having beforehand turned away from Negro material. In fact, he ceased to identify himself as a Negro and "crossed the color line."[6]

There is something about the structure of Hayden's paragraph that is progressively damning: the association between loss of subject, the black subject, and silence; loss of self and loss of the racial presence of the lyrical voice of *Cane*. Toomer's poem, "And Pass," is relevant to cite here:

> When the sun leaves dusk
> On far horizons,
> And night envelopes
> Empty seas
> And fading dream-ships;
> When the stars have eyes,
> And their light blends
> With darkness—
> I stand alone,
> Salute and pass
> Proud shadows[7]

"And Pass" Mr. Toomer did, from a central position in the tradition to a silent, netherworld of would-be transcendental mysticism.

Toomer's opinions about the matter are curious. Darwin Turner, in a most sensitive account of this complex matter published in *In a Minor Chord*, enables us to begin to understand both the subtlety of the idea of race in Toomer's discourse and the patterns of assertion and denial that Toomer knitted as an act of will. In June 1922, in a letter to John McClure, Toomer seems to revel in this complexity and its concomitant fluidity:

> As near as I can tell, there are seven race bloods within this body of mine. French, Dutch, Welsh, Negro, German, Jewish, and Indian. . . . One half of my family is definitely colored. For my

own part, I have lived equally amid the two groups. And, I alone, as far as I know, have striven for a spiritual fusion analogous to the fact of racial intermingling. . . . Viewed from the world of race distinctions, I take the color of whatever group I at the time am sojourning in. As I become known, I shall doubtless be classed as a Negro. I shall neither fight nor resent it. There will be more truth than they know in what they say, for my writing takes much of its worth from that source.[8]

In August 1922, Toomer wrote to *The Liberator* about his attitude toward "the Negro group":

Within the last two or three years, however, my growing need for artistic expression has pulled me deeper and deeper into the Negro group. And as my powers of receptivity increased, I found myself loving it in a way that I could never love the other. It has stimulated and fertilized everything of worth that I have done.[9]

Less than one year later, however, Toomer demanded that his publisher, Boni and Liveright, not define him to be a Negro writer in *Cane*'s publicity:

If my relationship with you is to be what I'd like it to be, I must insist that you never use such a word, such a thought again.[10]

Yet, just a few months earlier, Toomer had rendered a more complex response. In April 1923, Claude Barnett of the Associated Negro Press wrote directly to Toomer to ask if he were or were not "negroid":

For sometime we, and by we I mean a group of three friends, the other two whom are literary men, one colored and one white, have wondered who and what you are. There have been several arguments, the literary men contending that your style and finish are not negroid, while I, who am but the business manager of a news service, felt certain that you were—for how else could you interpret "us" as you do unless you had peeked behind the veil?[11]

Toomer's response, dated six days later, reads in part:

The true and complete answer is one of some complexity, and for this reason perhaps it will not be seen and accepted until after I am dead. . . . Let me state then, simply, that I am the grandson of the late P. B. S. Pinchback. From this fact, it is clear that your contention is sustained. I have "peeped behind the veil."

And my deepest impulse to literature (on the side of material) is
the direct result of what I saw.[12]

Toomer continues, but in an attempt to define literary influence
more broadly than through a supposed mystical relation between
sensibility and race:

Insofar as the old folk-songs, syncopated rhythms, the rich sweet
taste of dark-skinned life, insofar as these are Negro, I am, body
and soul, negroid. My style, my esthetic, is nothing more or less
than my attempt to fashion my substance into works of art. For
it, I am indebted to my inherent gifts, and to the entire body of
contemporary literature. I see no reason why my style and finish
could not have come from an American with Negro blood in his
veins. The pure fact is that they have so come, and hence your
friends' contentions are thrown out of court.[13]

It would not be until Ralph Ellison paused to reflect upon that
complex relationship between "experience" and the experience
of literary influence that a black writer would put the matter so
suggestively.

It was in 1930 that Toomer officially passed from the literary
black race, since in that year he denied James Weldon Johnson
reprint rights to publish his works in the *Book of American Negro
Poetry;* such a gesture, made to Johnson, a dean of black arts
and letters, most certainly constituted a rite of passage from
within to without. In February 1932, he wrote the following lines
to Nancy Cunard, who was then editing her monumental collection of Africana called *Negro:*

Though I am interested in and deeply value the Negro, I am not
a Negro.[14]

He had, at last, inscribed his denial.

Even more curious is a diary entry of 1930, which Turner cites
in a footnote:

I do not *know* I possess it; . . . it is a carrying on of my grandfather's statement that he had negro blood.[15]

The fact of race, Toomer here characterizes as his grandfather's
statement, a mere rhetorical gesture that he wishes to erase rhetorically. It was not his grandfather's statement that Toomer found

so very difficult to erase, however; it was rather the blackness of
Cane. As Toomer writes in one of his autobiographical manu-
scripts:

> The folk-spirit was walking in to die on the modern desert. That
> spirit was beautiful. Its death was so tragic. Just this seemed to
> sum life for me. And this was the feeling I put into "Cane."
> "Cane" was a swan-song. It was a song of an end. And why no
> one has seen and felt that, why people have expected me to write
> a second and a third and a fourth book like "Cane," is one of
> the queer misunderstandings of my life.[16]

Toomer's remarkably fluid notion of race is of less importance
to the critics than is the place of *Cane* in the Afro-American
canon, a place the critic can determine only formally. Not only
are tropes such as repetition, catechesis, parataxis, and chiasmus
and modes of mimesis from *Cane* refigured in Sterling Brown's
Southern Road (1932) and Zora Neale Hurston's *Their Eyes
Were Watching God* (1937), but also in Ralph Ellison's *Invisible
Man* (1952) and Toni Morrison's *Sula,* to list only a few such
intertextual relationships. Toomer forces us to abandon any definition of Afro-American literature that would posit the racial
identity of an author as its principal criterion. For if it were possible to convene all of the authors in the tradition at a New
Orleans bag party at Mardi Gras, and if we reversed the rule to
exclude those authors lighter than the paper bag hanging over the
doorway, then Toomer would not be the only one who would not
make the cut. Toomer teaches us the limitations of biographical
criticism and also its implicit fascination as a text of its own, as a
parallel text, as it were, to literary structures such as *Cane:*

> *Oracular.*
> *Redolent of fermenting syrup,*
> *Purple of the dusk.*
> *Deep-rooted cane.*[17]

Perhaps Toomer did pass; yet, perhaps once the definitive edition of the *Complete Works* is published, we shall be able to begin
to consider that received, wishful opinion. We seem to want this
to be true, given what appears to be at issue here. Toomer's so-
called loss of voice we too easily attribute to his loss of face, to
his self-willed effacement of his "dark" past. Not only did he

revise the contours of his family tree; he also prevented the excerption of segments of *Cane* in an anthology of Negro literature. What could stand as a more apt or more eloquent judgment of Toomer than the deafening silence that he appears to have suffered through than this? What is the difference, the "critical difference" in Johnson's words, between the black Toomer and the white? Johnson here is helpful:

> If human beings were not divided into two biological sexes, there would probably be no need for literature. And if literature could truly say what the relations between the sexes are, we would doubtless not need much of it then, either. Somehow, however, it is not simply a question of literature's ability to say or not to say the truth of sexuality. For from the moment literature begins to try to set things straight on that score, literature itself becomes inextricable from the sexuality it seeks to comprehend. It is not the life of sexuality that literature cannot capture; it is literature that inhabits the very heart of what makes sexuality problematic for us speaking animals. Literature is not only a thwarted investigator but also an incorrigible perpetrator of the problem of sexuality.[18]

Johnson's provocative assessment of the interpretation of sexuality and textuality would seem to be of relevance here. Toomer would probably agree with the critic, glossing the passage with that wonderfully black oxymoron, "It's the same difference," meaning thereby that if we substitute "race" for "sex" the utterance holds true—as true as Johnson's provocative claim can be. The notion of difference, of the same difference, we glean from the Afro-American proverb generally known as "The Same Difference": "Tain't much difference 'twist a hornit an 'a yaller-jacket when dey bofe git under your clo'es." The difference between "difference" and "diffunce" notwithstanding, the implied sexuality of racism, sexuality as trace of racism, "bofe . . . under your clo'es," reinforces the urge toward substitution. The conflation of sex and race is part of (racist) Western anthropological discourse: as early as the eighteenth century blacks were known as "the lady of the races," and Freud called woman "the dark continent of man."

In its own curious manner, in a mode of fiction that one commentator called "Negroid Lyricism,"[19] Toomer thematizes this matter of the same difference of sex and race, of both their mutual metaphorical substitution and their essential interrelationships:

> Dark swaying forms of Negroes are streetsongs that woo virginal houses. . . .
>
> Dan Moore walks southward on Thirteenth Street . . . girl eyes within him widen upward to promised faces . . . negroes open gates and go indoors, perfectly.[20]

It is in this substitution that Toomer, boldly suggests this conflation. Toomer, rhetorically at least, obliterated the "diffunce" between white and black, married two white women, then agonizingly proceeded not to create "literature," systematically producing draft after draft of "Aphorisms" and an *Autobiography* whose intent, by definition, was to posit a self-sufficient and plentiful self before he wrote *Cane.* In a curious and perhaps perverse sense, Toomer's was a gesture of racial castration, which, if not silencing his voice literally, then at least transformed his deep black bass into a false soprano. Toomer did not want so much to be white as most of us, like his "colored fellow of more than ordinary mental grasp," would have it; rather, he sought to be racially indeterminate, which Johnson suggests to be the nature of the castrato. Toomer's curiously nationalistic gesture toward indeterminacy, to be "just American," certainly helps to explain the shared reaction of (male) critics to the false soprano of his racially neutered and mystical works, such as *Essentials: Definitions and Aphorisms* (1931), which was the second book he published.

Essentials, Darwin Turner tells us, Ogden Nash thought was "interesting" but felt that "the Depression was not a time in which to expect financial profit from it." *Remember and Return,* a revised, expanded manuscript of the same order as *Essentials,* Toomer could not publish. In this text, Toomer speaks directly to those critics for whom his soprano rings false, compared to the lyrical bass of *Cane:*

> Since then I have become psychological, to include even more of that labyrinth—and this is the simplest explanation I can give to those who expect poetry from me, get psychology, morality, and something of religion, and are puzzled.
>
> I am not less poet; I am more conscious of all that I am, am not, and might become. . . .

> I count it good that any poet stops writing his own small verse, that any man stops doing his own small work, and becomes a student of the Great Work.[21]

The critical difference for Toomer was not so much his race, it seems to me, as what he sought to represent and how he represented it. Toomer sought to displace the lyrical particularity of *Cane* with a novel mode of mimesis, for which even the modernist fragmented structure of *Cane* was inadequate. The critical difference to Toomer, between his black and his erased black self, was a problem with which he wrestled in language; his was not the problem as much of the subject as of the representation of the subject:

> The reality of man's life, as I perceive and understand it, is complex beyond the possibility of formulation. How represent in sequence that which exists simultaneously? Where begin, where end? Yet a book about man must be written in sequence, and it must begin and end. Thus a book about human life, in its very structure, is a first-class misrepresentation, no matter what facts and truths it may contain.[22]

The problem of simultaneity of representation, which Toomer solved in *Cane* by his masterful use of the trope of repetition, no longer sufficed. Toomer longed for a difference of immediacy, one that repetition only mimicked or imitated, falsely, rhetorically, tropologically; he sought a language radical in implication, one that conveyed the transcendental, colorless, signified paradoxically in a medium through which writer, text, and reader produced meaning, but *a* meaning, that very meaning intended by the author and the text:

> If it is to approach true representation it must be made to do so by a dynamic, creative and critical relationship established between the words and he who writes them and he who reads them. As such relationships are as rare in literature as they are in life, it follows that even the excellent books, due both to their defects and to man's negligence, tend to become agents of error and arrestation.
> My realization of this "inadequacy" has not deterred me from writing, but it has kept me from attempting to construct a mental "system" under the illusion that such a system would be an accurate and complete representation of man's reality.[23]

Perhaps we are only just learning to read Jean Toomer, the Jean Toomer who wrote after *Cane*. His concerns as a writer are post-modern, as a critic post-structural, anticipatory. Toomer sought to save his texts from a critical discourse that would delimit them, that would read them as part of the racial problem. Like Dr. Johnson, he found literature as such, the literature of *Cane,* to be obsolete, redundant, false, once he obliterated "the two biological" races, and hence their differences. He seems to have feared repetition—the repetition of repeating himself. Rather, he sought to realize, to occupy, for the erased Negro, that privileged space in which reader, writer, and word are one each time they confront one another.

Toomer, in this sense, became less concerned with representing the race and thereby "liberating" it—an impossibility—than with inventing an entirely new discourse, an almost mythic discourse in a strict sense of that term, in which irreconcilable opposites, sexual and racial differences were not so much reconciled as absent, unutterable, unthinkable, and hence unrepresentable. To encounter nine years of interpretations of Toomer's place as a writer in the tradition is to come to understand, through one particular example, both the modern history of American criticism and the painful search of one sensitive writer to be understood. If it is true, as Toomer wrote in *Essentials,* that "we are hypnotized by literacy," then it is also true, as the instance of Toomer demonstrates so precisely, that only certain sorts of literacy hypnotize certain sorts of readers. The full sweep of Toomer's literary works remains to be assessed until a complete edition, carefully edited with variants preserved, restores his post-modern texts to what may well prove to be his fullest readership.

II

These all-too-familiar facts of Jean Toomer's biological and metaphorical crossings and reversals enjoy the status of mythologies, naming as they do unreconciled tensions in the dialogical structure of Afro-American discourse and, perhaps as some psychiatrists theorize, in Afro-American psychology. Toomer, we say, literally wrote himself out of the canon and out of the race. Critics invoke this aspect of Jean Toomer, or more properly of what we could well label the fiction of Jean Toomer, as a rite of exorcism, of purgation, of the heinous, unspeakable crime of the betrayer. To cross over and not to subvert the foe from within cannot, the tradition holds, be condoned. The Jean Toomer of *Cane* largely ceases to exist in Afro-American literary history by 1930, except through that blackest of black traces he imprinted on the New Negro Renaissance, which of course was *Cane* itself.

It should not prove surprising, therefore, that much of the published Toomer criticism is, in some sense or other, biographical or pseudo-psychological. Another recurring aspect of Toomer criticism, however, is more or less formal, or textual. The reasons for this fairly anomalous concern for the text, in a critical tradition that has privileged both content and a theory of realistic mimesis, are of necessity ironic and somewhat paradoxical. Toomer's book elicited from critics an attention to literary language unprecedented, it is fair to say, in the Afro-American tradition before 1923. The ostensibly fragmented, discontinuous, oracular "negroid lyricism" of *Cane* directed attention to itself as much as did Toomer's concern to represent the oral black culture as a counterpoint to the controlling consciousness of each discrete section of his carefully crafted book. *Cane,* in this sense, is doubled-voiced, not so much privileging a somehow pure black traditional voice as drawing upon its traces to suggest from within truly multiple points of view. What so many critics took to be glimpses of negro psychology, "psychology" standing as a key word of the twenties, Toomer effected by this tension among conflicting and conflicted points of view. From the beginning, then, Toomer's writing, for several reasons, enjoyed a scrutiny of its uses of language that many black authors have never enjoyed.

After he passed from the race, however, and at least once decided to prevent his work from being anthologized in a collection of black literature, critics had little choice but to explicate the text, or else to ignore Toomer altogether, because of his heresy and perhaps the unavailability of *Cane.* An example at midcentury is apt here.

In a summary of a special issue of *Phylon,* edited by Mozell C. Hill and M. Carl Homan and devoted to "The Negro in Literature: The Current Scene," Alain Locke, in "Self-Criticism: The Third Dimension in Culture," wondered aloud at the conspicuous absence of *Cane* from critical attention:

> I am personally surprised that no one referred to the phenomenal early appearance of such "universal particularity" in Jean Too-mer's *Cane* in 1923. Here was something admirably removed from what Mr. [G. Lewis] Chandler [in "A Major Problem of Negro Authors in Their March Toward Belles-Lettres," printed in the same number of *Phylon*] calls very aptly "promotional literature," but it is Negro through and through as well as deeply and movingly human. It was also exempt from any limitation of provincialism although it gave local color convincingly.[24]

Moreover, Locke continues, it is precisely *Cane*'s combination of craft and matter with which Afro-American literature can at last realize its "great era," precisely as had Russian literature:

> To wish for more of this is to ask for the transmuting quality of expert craftsmanship combined with broad perspective or intui-tive insight, one or the other. For we must remember the two ways in which Russian literature achieved its great era; through the cosmopolitan way of Turgenev, Tolstoi and Chekov and the nativist way of Dostoievski, Gogol and Gorghi, each of which produced great writing and universal understanding for Russian experience.[25]

Locke's equation of the necessity for great writing and the uni-versal representation of experience is of signal import in the his-tory of Afro-American literary criticism; for the history of the critical reevaluations of *Cane,* his reference to Toomer signifies Toomer's absence from the canonical authors that a younger generation of critics were forging. Locke was not only attempting to rebut J. Saunders Redding's comments about *Cane* printed in the *American Scholar* just a year before (that it was "extremely arty, self-conscious and experimental"), but also he was con-cerned to keep the memory of *Cane* alive as a text still resonant in the tradition. Three years later, in a major essay entitled "From *Native Son* to *Invisible Man,*" Locke argues perceptively that *Cane,* with *Native Son* and *Invisible Man,* is one of the three historical moments in Afro-American fiction.

Although at midcentury Jean Toomer and *Cane* were conspicuously absent from most black criticism (Hugh Gloster in *Negro Voices in American Fiction* had in 1948 argued for *Cane*'s seminal formal importance in defining new modes of representation in fiction, especially of realistic modes), such had most certainly not always been Toomer's fate. Just as *Cane* had been reviewed in the first decade of its publication generally in the most favorable terms, so too would it be resurrected in the mid-sixties as a cardinal text of both the New Negro Renaissance and the Black Arts movement, resurrected paradoxically precisely when Negroes became newly black, as the blackest text of all. Let us consider how *Cane* was reviewed in its first incarnation.[26]

John Armstrong, writing in the *New York Tribune* less than a month after *Cane* appeared, defined the grid with which *Cane* would be decoded for the next decade. Toomer has depicted "real negroes," "negroes altogether removed from the Octavus Roy Cohen and Irvin Cobb sort of inadequate caricatures." Already *Cane* is being read against the mimetic principles implicit in representations of Afro-American speech in the dialect verse made so popular by Joel Chandler Harris and Uncle Remus. Toomer, unlike Cohen, Cobb, and even his black precursors, has found a language through which "to recognize the authenticity of the race negroes delineated."

Experience, certainly, is privileged here. But so too is Toomer's lyricism, "an authentic lyric voice," a manner of manipulating language that has enabled Toomer to transcend received figurations of the black, such as the caricatures peculiar to musical comedy, burlesque, and Broadway, but also to black fiction. As Armstrong writes:

> It has always been felt that there are negroes in America with genuine poetic feeling, intellect and discrimination approximating the standards of the more civilized whites. One has always known this and wondered, likewise, why they were never presented in our fiction. Seemingly until this book was written no one has had the courage or perhaps the inclination to seek out these real negroes and hold them up to view honestly.

Honesty in depiction notwithstanding, the problem with representation of this "authentic negro" has been and remains a prob-

lem of language: "to paint the emotional color and vivacity of the
negro requires a resource of sensibility whose ultimate dimensions
often escape rather than are captured by the pursuing word."
Toomer's mastery of the lyrical, pursuing word is the achievement
of *Cane*.

Matthew Josephson, writing in the same month in *Broom,* reviewed *Cane* and William Carlos Williams's *The Great American
Novel* together. Josephson echoes Armstrong's opinions about
Cane's lyricism, but also its authenticity, which he thinks akin to
"Dostoyevski and his possessed Russian characters." Josephson,
however, is the first critic to write that the remarkable aspects of
Toomer's representation of black oral forms is that he manages
to depict the "superb folk-music and folk-poetry" of "this unconsciously gifted race" in the "literary medium, young, headstrong,
unreserved, but ultimately faithful." Few subsequent critics have
recognized the artistry of this tension of the privileged oral voice
counterpointed antiphonally against the written voice of *Cane*'s
controlling center of consciousness.

Bruno Lasker, in a review of *Cane* and Waldo Frank's *Holiday,*
observes that *Cane* is a significant rupture from "social fiction"
because it has concerned itself with psychological, rather than
documentary, realism. Lasker, however, raises a question about
Toomer's identity, but not in those terms that we might expect.
Rather, Lasker accuses Toomer of being Frank: "Is not 'Jean
Toomer' a polite fiction?" Here the critic erases Toomer and sup-
plants Frank, who wrote the first introduction to *Cane,* because
he says the styles of writing are so similar between the texts.
"What does it matter whether Rembrandt painted those pictures
or Bols," he asks, "so long as they are genuine Rembrandts!"
Lasker's review defines a problem of identity broader than that
of the willed racial self; it was this matter of language, of mimesis
and subject, that seems to have haunted Toomer, or at least that
he felt compelled to address in his diaries and autobiographies.

The *Boston Transcript* review declares Toomer's more lyrical
flourishes to be not "articulate" yet finds the book to be important
because of the rather new fiction of the Negro it contains: "Probably this book is a daring overflow, for it presents the black race
as we seldom dare represent it, mournful, loving beauty, ignorant,
and full of passion untutored and entirely unconnected with the

brain." Stylistically, *Cane* is "impressionistic," "something akin to drama," and "unusual in its method." The *Springfield Republican,* similarly, found *Cane* to be a difficult text precisely because of this unusual method of narration: "The reader not possessed of the key to ejaculatory expressionism and impressionism will find some of this vaudeville hard to follow. He may think that in some of it there is more of the showman than of the actor and his part." The review claims the reference to vaudeville to have been made by Toomer's publishers, Boni and Liveright. "Fond of vaudeville? Vaudeville is what Jean Toomer's "Cane" . . . is called by its publishers."

Robert Littell's *New Republic* review repeats the similarity between the styles of Toomer and Frank, seeming "curiously to coincide at their weakest points," by which Littell seems to mean what he calls "lyric expressionism." An example of the problematic of lyric expressionism Littell humorously describes as sentences that "pass from poetry into prose, and from there into Western Union." Littell's review, however, is most noteworthy because he addresses the import of *Cane* both through its mimetic principles and through the relation of the figures depicted to those received figures of blacks against which Toomer is reacting. Citing Frank's arresting image of Toomer's transformation of a black South "heretofore sunk in the mists of muteness," now finding its voice in "the eminence of song," Littell reads *Cane*'s world of the South in this way:

> Not the South of the chivalrous gentleman, the fair lady, the friendly, decaying mansion, of mammies, cotton and pickaninnies. Nor yet the South of lynchings and hatreds, of the bitter, rebellious young negro, and of his emigration to the North. *Cane* does not remotely resemble any of the familiar, superficial views of the South on which we have been brought up. On the contrary, Mr. Toomer's view is unfamiliar and bafflingly subterranean, the vision of a poet far more than the account of things seen by a novelist—lyric, symbolic, oblique, seldom actual.

It is this suggested interruption of a supposed one-to-one relationship between reality and its representation that Littell signifies to be the major rhetorical innovation of *Cane*. It is a gesture that links *Cane,* ironically, to *Native Son* and directly to *Invisible Man.*

As Littell concludes, Toomer has depicted "old country" through "new ways of writing."

Montgomery Gregory, writing in *Opportunity* in December 1923, is concerned to demonstrate the irony that in *Cane* "southern life should be given its most notable artistic expression by the pen of a native son of negro descent." Citing, as his contemporaries did frequently, H. L. Mencken's description of the South as a "cultural Sahara," Gregory argues that "the white South, with few exceptions, has sacrificed art for propaganda." "Great art," he concludes, like great deeds, cannot flourish in a land of bigotry and oppression." Black art, he continues, has suffered from essentially middle-class notions of propriety and their concomitant strictures upon the use of Afro-American mythic discourse as the stuff of literature. The resultant void of representation, therefore, has made it possible for "caricatures of the race" to stand in the stead of "bona fide portraits."

The publication of *Cane,* however, has redressed these imbalances, for Toomer "combines the inheritance of the Old Negro and the spirit of the New Negro." As had Rene Maran, whose *Batouala* won the Prix Goncourt in 1921, Toomer's *Cane* "avoid[ed] the pitfalls of propaganda and moralizing on the one hand and the snares of a false and hollow race pride on the other hand." *Cane* was, in short, an " 'aesthetic equivalent' of the Southland." To counter attacks upon Toomer's willingness to depice black characters who are, to say the least, less than middle-class, Gregory carefully maintains that Toomer's is a psychological, not a reportorial, realism, "a realism of the emotions." Toomer is not attempting, moreover, a sociological study of the race; rather, "no effort is made to create ideal characters or to make them conform to any particular standard." It is in the strength of his "portraitures" of the several sorts of Negro, Gregory concludes, that Toomer's genius lies. "Kabnis," accordingly, he sees as the book's most stellar part.

Whereas Gregory's major *Opportunity* review attempts to show the import of Toomer's novel to the language of black fiction, W. E. B. Du Bois's *Crisis* review heralds the book because of one of its repeating themes, that same theme that Gregory mentions only implicitly and the criticism for the use of which he seems intent upon protecting Toomer from. Du Bois puts it bluntly,

"The world of black folk will some day arise and point to Jean
Toomer as a writer who first dared to emancipate the colored
world from the conventions of sex. . . . [He] is the first of our
writers to hurl his pen across the very face of our sex convention-
ality." As Gregory had suggested, Du Bois admits that this openness to such themes "is going to make his black readers shrink and
criticize; and yet they are done with a certain splendid, careless
truth." Though thematically bold and daring, however, Toomer's
style, Du Bois seems to think, is marred by "his apparently undue
striving for effect":

> His art carries much that is difficult or even impossible to under-
> stand. The artist, of course, has a right deliberately to make his
> art a puzzle to the interpreter (the whole world is a puzzle) but
> on the other hand I am myself unduly irritated by this sort of
> thing.

Nevertheless, the sections of this book do "have their strange
flashes of power, their numerous messages and numberless reasons for being." Just as Du Bois praised the book for a certain
sort of realism, a realism of sexual depiction in a body of fiction
prudish even by standards of the twenties, so did he feel free to
damn it for its failure to name its subjects boldly, to strip them
bare of illusion. Du Bois, the great realist, would countenance
none of *Cane*'s lyricism and ambiguities of language, yet he would
praise its lyrical subject matter, as if the two were distinct.

In February 1924, Allen Tate reviewed *Cane* for the Nashville
Tennessean. Tate's review, entitled "Negro Poet Depicts Simple
Life of Race," is concerned to show that Toomer has displaced
Paul Laurence Dunbar, "that poet who was a bit too inured to our
civilization and its supposed superiority ever to get quite into the
soul of his own race, and expressed [sic] it in an authentic idiom."
Unlike Dunbar's work, Tate continues, Toomer's book "has its
origins in the consciousness of the race itself." Toomer, Tate concludes, is a "true artist" unlike other black writers, because he assumes his propositions rather than claiming them:

> I suppose it is characteristic of most oppressed races that when
> they do find a speaking voice, they utter an accent of resentment
> usually divided between sentimental self-pity and a propaganda
> for complete liberation.

Toomer, by contrast, eschews the need to declaim; instead, he renders "the beauty of life which he is enabled to see in the simple lives and tragedies of his people." Toomer, finally, is not a protest writer: "He leaves the problems of his race aside; he speaks as a poet."

Alice Beale Parsons, like Du Bois, is concerned to direct attention to Toomer's prose; unlike Du Bois, however, Parsons finds in Toomer's prose a remarkably new element in American fiction: "Just as the white has imitated negro music with its plaintive melodies and fascinating syncopation, so too will white writers imitate this subtly melodic, syncopated prose, which, strangely enough, gets many of its characteristics from [Waldo] Frank, an innovator who has had a wide and on the whole disastrous effect upon writers of the youngest generation." Perhaps of even more significance, Parsons discusses the place of Toomer in the history of Afro-American creative writing. Curiously, Parsons, after much wavering, decides that perhaps Toomer is not the long-awaited black-creative savior-in-letters for whom the Harlem Renaissance searched in vain; rather, he was a conduit between the tradition and a nameless successor, a crucial antecedent of a writer yet to come, such as Ralph Ellison:

> To be wholly Toomer is not an easy undertaking. To be it consciously, articulately, for the first time in the history of one's race, would be a gigantic feat. Perhaps no man can finally accomplish it until the way has been smoothed for him by many sensitive artists, like Du Bois, like McKay and like Toomer, of whom we can say for the present that he is the lucky guardian of something that is more than talent, and that to read him is pure joy.

Other critics, however, thought that this great black genius had arrived. As Robert T. Kerlin concludes in a 1926 *Opportunity* review,

> *Cane* is written partly in verse form, partly in prose: all of it has the spirit of poetry. It is, in respect to content and form, an audacious book, stamped all over with genius.

Kerlin argues implicitly that *Cane*'s import derives from its existence as a text of two literary traditions, the Anglo-American and the Afro-American, a bold—and accurate—claim to make, the first such claim made by a critic:

Who does not know that the Negroes have an understanding of *our* Scriptures—which of course are ours only by imperfect adoption—which leaves us wondering, and ought to leave us humiliated? But I am now speaking about poetry, not religion, though the two are not far asunder.

He continues:

When 'an atom of dust in agony on a Georgia hillside' hears in the winds through the cracks of his cabin the whisperings of vagrant poets, what may not be expected of that same 'atom' when the agony, intensified, understood, has at command the language of Shakespeare, Shelley, Sandburg?

It is Kerlin, alone of *Cane*'s reviewers, who clearly recognizes the text's significance to be its gesture toward bridging two traditions of influence, two text milieux, as a truly double-voiced discourse.

Three years later, Toomer received another enthusiastic review for a short story he published in *The Dial* in December 1928, called "Mr. Costyve Duditch." Granville Hicks isolates another story, "York Beach," printed in *The New American Caravan* in 1929, for a severe, if thematic, critique in a *Hound and Horn* review printed in 1930. And, although Gorham Munson would praise Toomer's second book, *Essentials: Definitions and Aphorisms,* in a 1931 note to the New York *World Telegram,* the New Orleans *Times Picayune*'s anonymous review not only is more typical of that book's critical reception but also helps us to understand why Toomer's readership would seem to have deserted him for almost two full decades.

In a sensitive review of *Essentials,* the *Times Picayune* reviewer aptly summarizes the fate of Toomer's readers since *Cane* appeared eight years before:

Those who . . . felt that the publication of *Cane* a few years ago signalized the appearance of a remarkable creative genius in prose, one who might 'create a new form,' have been a little dismayed by the philosophical evolution of Jean Toomer, author of that promising collection of sketches. One felt that the best of the pieces contained a strength of imagination and emotion and above all, of rhythm, that portended rare and beautiful things. It seemed that blending of blood and spiirt, Caucasian and African, in Jean Toomer would produce a haunting and powerful blend in art.

Despite such brilliant beginnings, the reviewer continues, Toomer's writings have not "followed the simple course of a literary artist, creating merely literary works." Rather, "an obsession with spiritual values has appeared in his fiction," resulting in fictions that approach the discourses of philosophy and religion, "tales and sketches that are muddled." Indeed, "the fine clarity of his early sketches has vanished; their soft, vigorous rhythms have grown confused. Jean Toomer has emerged as a thinker, as a seeker after truth, a philosopher, perhaps a messiah," rather than as a poet. "One is not quick," the reviewer concludes, "to admit that the change has been for the best." After discussing the themes Toomer developed in *Essentials,* the reviewer makes a bold prediction which other reviewers would not share, that is, until *Cane* would be rediscovered and reprinted in the 1960s:

> In *Essentials* Jean Toomer commands high respect. Some of his aphorisms compare with those of Novalis, and the reviewer can think of no higher praise. Perhaps the author's progress from *Cane* toward his philosophical revelation will result in finer literary creations, eventually, than *Cane* itself promised. Certainly, Jean Toomer's work is valuable, whatever form it takes.

Three of the four final essays that I analyze respond to the volume of Toomer's uncollected writings edited by Darwin Turner and published in 1980. The other essay, published by Robert Bone in 1969, reviews the 1969 edition of *Cane,* which Arna Bontemps edited. Bone's essay is a major reevaluation of *Cane;* perhaps *reclamation* more appropriately describes the import of Bone's review, for he was the first critic to employ a central journalistic medium to announce the canonization of a black text, or, as Bone concludes, "the canon of American Negro letters."

Bone not only makes *Cane*'s thematic unity apparent, but he also shows the text's structural unity, culminating in "Part III, Kabnis," which "is concerned with the black writer's quest for a usable past." Bone's is a sensitive reading; although dated somewhat by reference to such code words as "authentic [black] self" and "soul," it nevertheless suggests an underlying unity of this text which had long fascinated, yet often confused, its readers. Bone argues of its form:

The form of *Cane* is a function of the author's universal vision. The book is a miscellany of stories and sketches, interspersed with poems, and culminating in a one-act play. Like its author, *Cane* defies classification, flying in the face of a priori judgments. It belongs to no genre; it simply *is*. Yet the book displays both a structural and a stylistic unity. The style, which is modernist and highly metaphorical, supports the author's philosophical intentions. For metaphor destroys perceptual categories, demanding of the reader a fresh and individual response. It was in this fashion that Jean Toomer intended to confront the world.

Bone also maintains that race, in *Cane,* is a metaphor for such oppositions as spirit and flesh, intellect and feeling, female and male. It is this gesture of metaphorical substitution of sex for race that characterizes *Cane* as the first modernist text in the tradition.

Toomer's resurrection in the sixties, of course, turned largely on *Cane*'s themes of the return. As Bone put it in 1969, "*Cane* represents a pilgrimage to the soil of one's ancestors. It is a spiritual journey that every black American must undertake if he hopes to discover his authentic self." The curious matter of "authenticity of self notwithstanding, it was this thematization of the myth of the return that made *Cane* readable as a "nationalist" text. Within one decade, however, a second group of polemical interpreters would find in *Cane* a salient text for their own purposes. As Du Bois noted in 1924, *Cane* contains bold and original representations of women unlike much of the fiction written by Afro-American males. Drawing upon tropes introduced into the tradition by Toomer, then revised by Zora Neale Hurston in *Their Eyes Were Watching God,* a generation of black women writers, including Toni Morrison, Toni Cade Bambara, Alice Walker, and Gayl Jones, among others, would assume central places in the Afro-American canon. Two of these writers, Morrison and Walker, reviewed Darwin T. Turner's edition of Toomer's uncollected writings on the same day, July 13, 1980, for two major book reviews, the *New York Times Book Review* and the *Washington Post Book World.*

Morrison's review amounts to a major meditation on the poet and his obsession with transcending the social or racial category of "Negro." Morrison writes, "race is unequivocally the overriding preoccupation of Jean Toomer's life: not Blackness or even

being a Negro, but having (or having to have) a race at all." His
black ancestry, she concludes correctly, albeit a small part of a
complex racial whole, "bedevils his days and his intellect." Morrison singles out the fragments of Toomer's autobiographies, in
which he goes to marvelous lengths to demonstrate how un-black
he is, and his story, "Withered Skin of Berries," which she says
"is quite the best, rivaling easily the heights achieved in *Cane*." It
was, in short, "Toomer's artistic and racial sensitivity that made
him so expert in rendering the machinations of race and color-
as-class." Race was Toomer's great and terrible subject, a subject
he loved to hate. Was it, Morrison asks rhetorically, "a seal both
of approbation and closure" that forced or enabled him conveniently to discard his subject as dead, as "a swan song," in favor
of his bloodless and vapid prose of "racelessness and universal
harmony"? We do not yet know; we do know, however, that
Toomer was most eloquent, most the poet, when he addressed the
matter. Morrison concludes:

> In spite of Jean Toomer's yearning for racelessness, his horror
> of "dark blood," what is astonishing is how eloquent he was
> about the drop that bedeviled him; how moving he was about
> those who shared it. What would have been no more than an
> after dinner story in France or Russia became an opus in this
> country where, racially speaking, the difference between one
> snowflake and an avalanche does not exist.

It was, as Morrison implies, in the charting of differences that
Toomer made poetic discourse uniquely his own yet Western and
Afro-American at the same time.

Walker's reading of Toomer is remarkable for its concern to
demonstrate the considerable textual influence that *Cane* had upon
the writing of the Harlem Renaissance, especially upon Langston
Hughes and Zora Neale Hurston. *Cane*'s effect was telling:

> Hughes was moved to explore the dramatic possibilities of inter-
> racial, intrafamilial relationships in the South in his plays and
> poems. Hurston was encouraged, in her own work, to portray the
> culture of rural black Southerners as generative, vibrant, and
> destined for a useful, if vastly changed future in the modern
> world, though Toomer himself had considered Cane the "swan
> song" of that culture.

Few texts in any tradition inform the direction of subsequent texts in such dramatic terms.

But Walker's essay is also remarkable for the assessment she makes of the tropes of sex and race, so central to *Cane,* and their relation to the facts of Toomer's life. Behind the text of *Cane,* she argues, lies Toomer's grandmother:

> Feminists will be intrigued by what Toomer writes about his mother and grandmother. His mother was an intelligent woman, utterly dominated by her father, whom she spent her whole, relatively short life trying to defy. . . . His grandmother was also dominated by her husband until his health began to decline in old age. Then she, old and ill herself, blossomed magnificently from a sweet, silent shadow of her husband into a woman of high humor, memorable tales, satiric jibes at any and everything. She is reported to have had 'some dark blood.'

The language of *Cane,* Walker concludes, is informed by this woman, to whom he dedicates the book, and he models the female figures in *Cane* after "the tragic indecisiveness and weakness of his mother's life." Rather than standing as the swan song of traditional black oral culture, Walker concludes, *Cane* was Toomer's swan song "to the 'Negro' he felt dying in himself." *Cane* was Toomer's "parting gift," a gift the tradition should retain, Walker writes, yet let its creator go.

Darryl Pinckney's review of Toomer's collected works, published in *The New York Review of Books* fifty-eight years after the first review of *Cane,* is in my opinion the most balanced account of Toomer's life and works. Pinckney is appropriately dialectical in that he critiques the idea, the "tainting wish for retribution, a neurotic alertness to the wages of treason among black artists," that sees Toomer's uncertain and unfulfilled quest as treasonous; but Pinckney also renders a sensitive, if telling, assessment of the curious man whose works are collected in the book:

> Handsome, curious, variously talented—Toomer did not lead a life true to his own nature. For all the promise of his early years, he seems to have suffered profoundly from a collapse of will. The problem Toomer's work presents is not so much his attitude toward race—his ideas came from improvisation, the accommodation a passionately private person tried to make with the world.

The problem, the sadness of Toomer, was that his lyrical gift could not hold his free-fall into philosophy.

This, too, is my judgment of a writer the bulk of whose works remains unpublished. Toomer would have us treat all differences as of the same order, and yet only in denying the racial difference—especially his own—did passion and lyricism inform his use of language.

· 8 ·

Songs of a Racial Self:
On Sterling A. Brown

"Nigger, your breed ain't metaphysical."
                    Robert Penn Warren, "Pondy Woods," 1928

"Cracker, your breed ain't exegetical."
                    Sterling Brown, interview, 1973

By 1932, when Sterling Brown published *Southern Road,* his first book of poems, the use of black vernacular structures in Afro-American poetry was controversial indeed. Of all the arts, it was only through music that blacks had invented and fully defined a tradition both widely regarded and acknowledged to be uniquely their own. Black folktales, while roundly popular, were commonly thought to be the amusing fantasies of a childlike people, whose sagas and anecdotes about rabbits and bears held nothing deeper than the attention span of a child, à la Uncle Remus or even *Green Pastures.* And what was generally called dialect, the unique form of English that Afro-Americans spoke, was thought by whites to reinforce received assumptions about the Negro's mental inferiority.

Dorothy Van Doren simply said out loud what so many other white critics thought privately. "It may be that [the Negro] can express himself only by music and rhythm," she wrote in 1931, "and not by words."

Middle-class blacks, despite the notoriety his dialect verse had garnered for Paul Laurence Dunbar and the Negro, thought that dialect was an embarrassment, the linguistic remnant of an enslavement they all longed to forget. The example of Dunbar's popular and widely reviewed "jingles in a broken tongue," coinciding with the conservatism of Booker T. Washington, was an episode best not repeated. Blacks stood in line to attack dialect poetry.

William Stanley Braithwaite, Countee Cullen, and especially James
Weldon Johnson argued fervently that dialect stood in the shadow
of the plantation tradition of Joel Chandler Harris, James Whit-
comb Riley, and Thomas Nelson Page. Dialect poetry, Johnson
continued, possessed "but two full stops, humor and pathos." By
1931, Johnson, whose own "Jingles and Croons" (1917) embodied the worst in this tradition, could assert assuredly that "the
passing of traditional dialect as a medium for Negro poets is complete."

As if these matters of sensibility were not barrier enough, Johnson believed, somehow that until a black person ("full-blooded"
at that) created a written masterpiece of art, black Americans
would remain substandard citizens.

Johnson here echoed William Dean Howells's sentiments. Howells wrote that Paul Laurence Dunbar's dialect verse "makes a
stronger claim for the negro than the negro yet has done. Here in
the artistic effect at least is white thinking and white feeling in a
black man. . . . Perhaps the proof [of human unity] is to appear
in the arts, and our hostilities and prejudices are to vanish in
them." Even as late as 1925, Heywood Broun could reiterate this
curious idea: "A supremely great negro artist who could catch the
imagination of the world, would do more than any other agency
to remove the disabilities against which the negro now labors."
Broun concluded that this black redeemer with a pen could come
at any time, and asked his audience to remain silent for ten seconds to imagine such a miracle! In short, the Black Christ would
be a poet. If no one quite knew the precise form this Black Christ
would assume, at least they all agreed on three things he could
not possibly be: he would not be a woman like feminist Zora
Neale Hurston; he would not be gay like Countee Cullen or Alain
Locke; and he would most definitely not write dialect poetry.
Given all this, it is ironic that Brown used dialect at all. For a
"New Negro" generation too conscious of character and class as
color (and vice versa), Brown had all the signs of the good life:
he was a mulatto with "good hair" whose father was a well-known
author, professor at Howard, pastor of the Lincoln Temple Con-
gregational Church, and member of the D.C. Board of Education
who had numbered among his closest friends both Frederick Douglass and Paul Laurence Dunbar. Brown, moreover, had received

a classically liberated education at Dunbar High School, Williams College, and Harvard, where he took an M.A. in English in 1923. Indeed, perhaps it was just this remarkably secure black aristocratic heritage that motivated Brown to turn to the folk.

Just one year after he had performed the postmortem on dialect poetry, James Weldon Johnson, in the preface to Brown's *Southern Road,* reluctantly admitted that he had been wrong about dialect. Brown's book of poetry, even more profoundly than the market crash of 1929, truly ended the Harlem Renaissance, primarily because it contained a new and distinctly black poetic diction and not merely the vapid and pathetic claim for one.

To the surprise of the Harlem Renaissance's "New Negroes," the reviews were of the sort one imagines Heywood Broun's redeemer–poet was to have gotten. The *New York Times Book Review* said that *Southern Road* is a book whose importance is considerable: "It not only indicates how far the Negro artist has progressed since the years when he began to find his voice, but it proves that the Negro artist is abundantly capable of making an original and genuine contribution to American literature." Brown's work was marked by a "dignity that respects itself. . . . There is everywhere art." Louis Untermeyer agreed: "He does not paint himself blacker than he is." Even Alain Locke, two years later, called it "a new era in Negro poetry." *Southern Road*'s artistic achievement ended the Harlem Renaissance, for that slim book undermined all of the New Negro's assumptions about the nature of the black tradition and its relation to individual talent. Not only were most of Brown's poems composed in dialect, but they also had as their subjects distinctively black archetypal mythic characters, as well as the black common man whose roots were rural and Southern. Brown called his poetry "portraitures," close and vivid detailings of an action of a carefully delineated subject to suggest a sense of place, in much the same way as Toulouse-Lautrec's works continue to do. These portraitures, drawn "in a manner constant with them," Brown renders in a style that emerged from several forms of folk discourse, a black vernacular matrix that includes the blues and ballads, the spirituals and worksongs. Indeed, Brown's ultimate referents are black music and mythology. His language, densely symbolic, ironical, and naturally indirect, draws upon the idioms, figures, and tones of both the sacred and the profane vernacular traditions, mediating between these in a manner unmatched before or since. Although Langston Hughes had attempted to do roughly the same, Hughes seemed content to transcribe the popular structures he received, rather than to transcend or elaborate upon them, as in "To Midnight Man at LeRoy's": "Hear dat music . . . / Jungle music / Hear dat music . . . / And the moon was white."

But it is not merely the translation of the vernacular that makes Brown's work major, informed by these forms as his best work is; it is rather the deft manner in which he created his own poetic diction by fusing several black traditions with various models provided by Anglo-American poets to form a unified and complex structure of feeling, a sort of song of a racial self. Above all else, Brown is a regionalist whose poems embody William Carlos Williams's notion that the classic is the local, fully realized. Yet Brown's region is not so much the South or Spoon River, Tilbury or Yoknapatawpha as it is "the private Negro mind," as Alain Locke put it, "this private thought and speech," or, as Zora Neale Hurston put it, "how it feels to be colored me," the very textual milieu of blackness itself. Boldly, Brown merged the Afro-American vernacular traditions of dialect and myth with the Anglo-American poetic tradition and, drawing upon the example of Jean Toomer, introduced the Afro-American modernist lyrical mode into black literature. Indeed, Brown, Toomer, and Hurston comprise three cardinal points on a triangle of influence out of which emerged, among others, Ralph Ellison, Toni Morrison, Alice Walker, and Leon Forrest.

Brown's poetic influences are various. From Walt Whitman, Brown took the oracular, demotic voice of the "I" and the racial "eye," as well as his notion that "new words, new potentialities of speech" were to be had in the use of popular forms such as the ballad. From Edward Arlington Robinson, Brown took the use of the dramatic situation and the ballad, as well as what Brown calls the subject of "the undistinguished, the extraordinary in the ordinary." Certainly Brown's poems "Maumee Ruth," "Southern Cop," "Georgie Grimes," and "Sam Smiley" suggest the same art that created Miniver Cheevy and Richard Cory. From A. E. Housman, Brown borrowed the dramatic voice and tone, as well as key figures: Housman's blackbird in "When Smoke Stood Up from Lud-

low" Brown refigures as a buzzard in "Old Man Buzzard." Both
Housman's "When I Was One and Twenty" and Brown's "Telling
Fortunes" use the figure of "women with dark eyes," just as
Brown's "Mill Mountain" echoes Housman's "Terence, This Is
Stupid Stuff." Housman, Heinrich Heine, and Thomas Hardy seem
to be Brown's central influence of tone. Robert Burns's Scottish
dialect and John Millington Synge's mythical dialect of the Aran
Islander in part inform Brown's use of black dialect, just as Rob-
ert Frost's realism, stoicism, and sparseness, as in "Out, Out—,"
"Death of the Hired Man," "Birches," "Mending Wall," and "In
Dives' Dive" inform "Southern Road," "Memphis Blues," and
"Strange Legacies." Brown's choice of subject matter and everyday speech are fundamentally related to the New Poetry and the
work of Amy Lowell, Vachel Lindsay, Edgar Lee Masters, and
Carl Sandburg, as well as to the common language emphasis of
the Imagists. In lines such as "bits of cloud-filled sky . . . framed
in bracken pools" and "vagrant flowers that fleck unkempt mead-
ows," William Wordsworth's *Lyrical Ballads* resound. Brown rejected the "puzzle poetry" of Ezra Pound and T. S. Eliot and severely reviewed the Southern Agrarians' "I'll Take My Stand" as
politically dishonest, saccharine nostalgia for a medieval never-
neverland that never was. Brown never merely borrows from any
of these poets; he transforms their influence by grafting them onto
black poetic roots. These transplants are splendid creations indeed.

Michael Harper has collected nearly the whole of Brown's body
of poetry, including *Southern Road, The Last Ride of Wild Bill*
(1975), and the previously unpublished *No Hiding Place,* Brown's
second book of poems which was rejected for publication in the
late thirties because of its political subjects and which seems to
have discouraged Brown from attempting another volume until
1975. Inexplicably, two poems of the five-part "Slim Greer" cycle, "Slim in Hell" and "Slim Hears 'The Call,' " are missing, as is
the major part of "Cloteel" and the final stanza of "Bitter Fruit of
the Tree," oversights that a second edition should correct. Nevertheless, this splendid collection at last makes it possible to review the whole of Brown's works after years when his work remained out of print or difficult to get. Forty-two years separated
the first and second editions of *Southern Road.*

Rereading Brown, I was struck by how consistently he shapes the tone of his poems by the meticulous selection of the right word to suggest succinctly complex images and feelings "stripped to form," in Frost's phrase. Unlike so many of his contemporaries, Brown never lapses into pathos or sentimentality. Brown renders the oppressive relation of self to natural and (black and white) man-made environment in the broadest terms, as does the blues. Yet Brown's characters confront catastrophe with all of the irony and stoicism of the blues and black folklore. Brown's protagonists laugh and cry, fall in and out of love, and muse about death in ways not often explored in black literature. Finally, his great theme seems to be the relation of being to the individual will, rendered always in a sensuous diction, echoing what critic Joanne Gabbin calls "touchstones" of the blues lyric, such as "Don't your bed look lonesome / When your babe packs up to leave," "I'm gonna leave heah dis mawnin' ef I have to ride de blind," "Did you ever wake up in de mo'nin', yo' mind rollin' two different ways— / One mind to leave your baby, and one mind to stay?" or "De quagmire don't hang out no signs." What's more, he is able to realize such splendid results in a variety of forms, including the classic and standard blues, the ballad, a new form that Stephen Henderson calls the blues-ballad, the sonnet, and free verse. For the first time, we can appreciate Brown's full range, his mastery of so many traditions.

In the five-poem ballad cycle "Slim Greer," Brown has created the most memorable character in black literature, the trickster. In "Slim in Atlanta," segregation is so bad that blacks are allowed to laugh only in a phone booth:

> Hope to Gawd I may die
> If I ain't speakin' truth
> Make de niggers do their laughin'
> In a telefoam booth.

In "Slim Greer," the wily Greer in "Arkansaw" "Passed for white, / An' he no lighter / Than a dark midnight / Found a nice white woman / At a dance, / Thought he was from Spain / Or else from France." Finally, it is Slim's uncontainable rhythm that betrays:

An' he started a-tinklin'
Some mo'nful blues,
An' a-pattin' the time
With No. Fourteen shoes.

The cracker listened
An' then he spat
An' said, "No white man
Could play like that. . . .

Heard Slim's music
An' then, hot damn!
Shouted sharp—"Nigger!"
An' Slim said, "Ma'am?"

Brown balances this sort of humor against a sort of "literate" blues, such as "Tornado Blues," not meant to be sung:

Destruction was a-drivin' it and close behind was Fear,
Destruction was a-drivin' it hand in hand with Fear,
Grinnin' Death and skinny Sorrow was a-bringin' up de Rear.

Dey got some ofays, but dey mostly got de Jews an' us,
Got some ofays, but mostly got de Jews an' us,
Many po' boys castle done settled to a heap o'dus'.

Contrast with this stanza the meter of "Long Track Blues," a poem Brown recorded with piano accompaniment:

Heard a train callin'
Blowin' long ways down the track;
Ain't no train due here,
Baby, what can bring you back?

Dog in the freight room
Howlin' like he los' his mind;
Might howl myself,
If I was the howlin' kind.

In "Southern Road," Brown uses the structure of the worksong, modified by the call-and-response pattern of a traditional blues stanza:

Doubleshackled—hunh—
Guard behin';

Doubleshackled—hunh—
Guard behin';
Ball an' chain, bebby,
On my min'.

White man tells me—hunh—
Damn yo' soul;
White man tells me—hunh—
Damn yo' soul;
Get no need, bebby,
To be tole.

Brown is a versatile craftsman, capable of representing even destruction and death in impressively various ways. In "Sam Smiley," for example, he describes a lynching in the most detached manner: "The mob was in fine fettle, yet / The dogs were stupid-nosed; and day / Was far spent when the men drew round / The scrawny wood where Smiley lay. / The oaken leaves drowsed prettily, / The moon shone benignly there; / And big Sam Smiley, King Buckdancer, / Buckdanced on the midnight air." On the other hand, there is a certain irony in "Children of the Mississippi": "De Lord tole Norah / Dat de flood was due / Norah listened to de Lord / An' got his stock on board, / Wish dat de Lord / Had tole us too."

Brown also uses the folk-rhyme form, the sort of chant to which children skip rope: "Women as purty / As Kingdom Come / Ain't got no woman / Cause I'm black and dumb." He also combines sources as unlike as Scott's "Lady of the Lake" and the black folk ballad "Wild Negro Bill" in his most extended ballad, "The Last Ride of Wild Bill." Often, he takes lines directly from the classic blues, as in "Ma Rainey," where three lines of Bessie Smith's "Backwater Blues" appear. Perhaps Brown is at his best when he writes of death, a subject he treats with a haunting lyricism, as in "Odyssey of Big Boy":

Lemme be wid Casey Jones,
Lemme be wid Stagolee,
Lemme be wid such like men
When Death takes hol' on me,
When Death takes hol' on me. . . .

> Done took my livin' as it came,
>   Done grabbed my joy, done risked my life;
> Train done caught me on de trestle,
> Man done caught me wid his wife,
>   His doggone purty wife.

He achieves a similar effect in "After Winter," with lines such as "He snuggles his fingers / In the blacker loam" and "Ten acres unplanted / To raise dreams on / Butterbeans fo' Clara / Sugar corn fo' Grace / An' fo' de little feller / Runnin' space."

When I asked why he chose the black folk as his subject, Brown replied:

> Where Sandburg said, "The people, yes," and Frost, "The people, yes, maybe," I said, "The people, maybe, I hope!" I didn't want to attack a stereotype by idealizing. I wanted to deepen it. I wanted to understand my people. I wanted to understand what it meant to be a Negro, what the qualities of life were. With their imagination, they combine two great loves: the love of words and the love of life. Poetry results.

Just as Brown's importance as a teacher can be measured through his students (such as LeRoi Jones, Kenneth Clarke, Ossie Davis, and many more), so too can his place as a poet be measured by his influence on other poets, such as Leopold Senghor, Aimé Césaire, Nicolas Guillen, and Michael Harper, to list only a few. Out of Brown's realism, further, came Richard Wright's naturalism; out of his lyricism came Hurston's *Their Eyes Were Watching God;* his implicit notion that "De eye dat sees / Is de I dat be's" forms the underlying structure of *Invisible Man.* In his poetry, several somehow black structures of meaning have converged to form a unified and complex structure of feeling, a poetry as black as it is Brown's. This volume of poems, some of which are recorded on two Folkways albums, along with his collected prose (three major books of criticism, dozens of essays, reviews, and a still unsurpassed anthology of black literature) being edited by Robert O'Meally and a splendid literary biography by Joanne Gabbin, all guarantee Brown's place in literary history. Brown's prolific output coupled with a life that spans the Age of Booker T. Washington through the era of Black Power, makes him not only

the bridge between nineteenth- and twentieth-century black literature but also the last of the great "race men," the Afro-American
men of letters, a tradition best epitomized by W. E. B. Du Bois.
Indeed, such a life demands an autobiography. A self-styled "Old
Negro," Sterling Brown is not only the Afro-American poet laure-
ate; he is a great poet.

· 9 ·

The Blackness of Blackness:
A Critique on the Sign
and the Signifying Monkey

Signification is the Nigger's occupation.

Traditional[1]

Be careful what you do,
Or Mumbo-Jumbo, God of the Congo,
And all of the other
Gods of the Congo,
Mumbo-Jumbo will hoo-doo you,
Mumbo-Jumbo will hoo-doo you,
Mumbo-Jumbo will hoo-doo you.

Vachel Lindsay, *The Congo*

I need not trace in these pages the history of the concept of signification. Since Ferdinand de Saussure at least, signification has
become a crucial aspect of much of contemporary theory. It is
curious to me that this neologism in the Western tradition cuts
across a term in the black vernacular tradition that is approximately two centuries old. Tales of the Signifying Monkey had
their origins in slavery. Hundreds of these have been recorded
since the nineteenth century. In black music, Jazz Gillum, Count
Basie, Oscar Peterson, Oscar Browne, Jr., Little Willie Dixon,
Nat "King" Cole, Otis Redding, Wilson Picket, and Johnny Otis—
at least—have recorded songs called either "The Signifying Monkey" or simply "Signifyin(g)." My theory of interpretation, arrived at from within the black cultural matrix, is a theory of
formal revisionism, it is tropological, it is often characterized by
pastiche, and, most crucially, it turns on repetition of formal
structures and their differences. Signification is a theory of read-

235

ing that arises from Afro-American culture; learning how to signify is often part of our adolescent education. That it has not been
drawn upon before as a theory of criticism attests to its sheer familiarity in the idiom. I had to step outside my culture, to defamiliarize the concept by translating it into a new mode of discourse,
before I could see its potential in critical theory. My work with
signification has now led me to undertake the analysis of the principles of interpretation implicit in the decoding of the signs used
in the Ifá oracle, still very much alive among the Yoruba in Nigeria, in a manner only roughly related to Harold Bloom's use of
the Kabbalah.

I

Signifyin(g): Definitions

Perhaps only Tar Baby is as enigmatic and compelling a figure
from Afro-American mythic discourse as is that oxymoron, the
Signifying Monkey.[2] The ironic reversal of a received racist image
in the Western imagination of the black as simianlike, the Signifying Monkey—he who dwells at the margins of discourse, ever pun-
ning, ever troping, ever embodying the ambiguities of language—is
our trope for repetition and revision, indeed our trope of chiasmus
itself, repeating and reversing simultaneously as he does in one
deft discursive act. If Vico and Burke or Nietzsche, de Man, and
Bloom, are correct in identifying four and six master tropes, then
we might think of these as the master's tropes and of signifying as
the slave's trope, the trope of tropes, as Bloom characterizes metalepsis, "a trope-reversing trope, a figure of a figure." Signifying
is a trope in which are subsumed several other rhetorical tropes,
including metaphor, metonymy, synecdoche, and irony (the master tropes), and also hyperbole and litotes, and metalepsis (Bloom's
supplement to Burke). To this list we could easily add aporia,
chiasmus, and catechesis, all of which are used in the ritual of
signifying.
    Signifying, it is clear, in black discourse means modes of figura-
tion itself. When one signifies, as Kimberly W. Benston puns, one
"tropes-a-dope." Indeed, the black tradition itself has its own subdivisions of signifying, which we could readily identify with the

typology of figures received from classical and medieval rhetoric, as Bloom has done with his "map of misprision." The black rhetorical tropes, subsumed under signifying, would include marking, loud-talking, testifying, calling out (of one's name), sounding, rapping, playing the dozens, and so on.[3]

Let us consider received definitions of the act of signifying and of black mythology's archetypal signifier, the Signifying Monkey. The Signifying Monkey is a trickster figure, of the order of the trickster figure of Yoruba mythology (*Esu-Elegbara* in Nigeria and *Legba* among the Fon in Dahomey), whose New World figurations (*Exu* in Brazil, *Echu-Elegua* in Cuba, *Papa Legba* in the pantheon of the *loa* of *Vaudou* in Haiti, and *Papa La Bas* in the *loa* of *Hoodoo* in the United States) speak eloquently of the unbroken arc of metaphysical presupposition and patterns of figuration shared through space and time among black cultures in West Africa, South America, the Caribbean, and in the United States. These trickster figures, aspects of *Esu,* are primarily mediators: as tricksters they are mediators, and their mediations are tricks.[4]

The versions of *Esu* are all messengers of the gods: he who interprets the will of god to people, he who carries the desires of people to the gods. *Esu* is guardian of the crossroads, master of style and the stylus, phallic god of generation and fecundity, master of the mystical barrier that separates the divine from the profane worlds. He is known as the divine linguist, the keeper of *ase* (*logos*) with which Olodumare created the universe.

Yoruba mythology, *Esu* always limps because his legs are of different lengths: one is anchored in the realm of the gods, and the other rests in this human world. The closest Western relative of *Esu,* of course, is Hermes; and, just as Hermes's role as interpreter lent his name readily to "hermeneutics," our metaphor for the study of the process of interpretation, so too can the figure of *Esu* stand as our metaphor for the act of interpretation itself for the critic of comparative black literature. In African and Latin American mythology, *Esu* is said to have taught *Ifa* how to read the signs formed by the sixteen sacred palmnuts which, when manipulated, configure into what is known as the signature of an *Odu,* two hundred and fifty-six of which comprise the corpus of *Ifa Divination.* The *Opon Ifa,* the carved wooden divination tray used in the art of interpretation, is said to contain at the center of

its upper perimeter a carved image of *Esu,* meant to signify his relation to the act of interpretation, which we can translate either as
itumo ("to unite or unknot knowledge") or as *yipada* ("to turn
around or translate"). That which we now call close reading, the
Yoruba call *Oda fa* ("reading the signs"). Above all else, *Esu* is
the Black Interpreter, the Yoruba god of indeterminacy or *ariye-
muye* (that which no sooner is held than it slips through one's
fingers).[5] As Hermes is to hermeneutics, *Esu* is to *Esu tufunaalo*
(bringing out the interstices of the riddle).

The *Esu* figures, among the Yoruba systems of thought in Dahomey and Nigeria, in Brazil and Cuba, in Haiti and at New Orleans, are divine; they are gods who function in sacred myths, as
do characters in a narrative. *Esu's* functional equivalent in Afro-
American profane discourse is the Signifying Monkey, a figure
who would seem to be distinctly Afro-American, probably derived
from Cuban mythology, which generally depicts *Echu-Elegua* with
a monkey at his side,[6] and who, unlike his Pan-African *Esu* cous-
ins, exists in the discourse of mythology not primarily as a character in a narrative but rather as a vehicle for narration itself. It is
from this corpus of narratives that signifying derives. The Afro-
American rhetorical strategy of signifying is a rhetorical act that
is not engaged in the game of information giving. Signifying turns
on the play and chain of signifiers, and not on some supposedly
transcendent signified. Alan Dundes suggests that the origins of
signifying could "lie in African rhetoric." As anthropologists demonstrate, the Signifying Monkey is often called the Signifier, he
who wreaks havoc upon the Signified. One is signified upon by
the signifier. He is indeed the "signifer as such," in Julie Kristeva's
phrase, "a presence that precedes the signification of object or
emotion."[7]

Scholars have for some time commented upon the peculiar use
of the word "signifying" in black discourse. Though sharing some
connotations with the standard English-language word, "signifying" has rather unique definitions in black discourse. Roger D.
Abrahams defines it as follows:

> Signifying seems to be a Negro term, in use if not in origin. It
> can mean any of a number of things; in the case of the toast
> about the signifying monkey, it certainly refers to the trickster's
> ability to talk with great innuendo, to carp, cajole, needle, and

lie. It can mean in other instances the propensity to talk around
a subject, never quite coming to the point. It can mean making
fun of a person or situation. Also it can denote speaking with the
hands and eyes, and in this respect encompasses a whole complex
of expressions and gestures. Thus it is signifying to stir up a fight
between neighbors by telling stories; it is signifying to make fun
of a policeman by parodying his motions behind his back; it is
signifying to ask for a piece of cake by saying, "my brother needs
a piece of cake."[8]

Essentially, Abrahams concludes, signifying is a *"technique* of indirect argument or persuasion," "a language of implication," "to
imply, goad, beg, boast, by *indirect* verbal or gestural means."
"The name 'signifying,' " he concludes, "shows the monkey to be
a trickster, signifying being the language of trickery, that set of
words or gestures achieving Hamlet's 'direction through indirection.' " The monkey, in short, is not only a master of technique,
as Abrahams concludes; he *is* technique, or style, or the literari-
ness of literary language; he is the great Signifier. In this sense,
one does not signify something; rather, one signifies in some way.[9]

There are thousands of "toasts" of the Signifying Monkey, most
of which commence with a variant of the following formulaic
lines:

> Deep down in the jungle so they say
> There's a signifying monkey down the way
> There hadn't been no disturbin' in the jungle for quite a bit,
> For up jumped the monkey in the tree one day and laughed,
> "I guess I'll start some shit."[10]

Endings, too, tend toward the formulaic, as in the following:

> "Monkey," said the Lion,
> Beat to his unbooted knees,
> "You and your signifying children
> Better stay up in the trees."
> Which is why today
> Monkey does his signifying
> A-way-up out of the way."[11]

In the narrative poems, the Signifying Monkey invariably repeats
to his friend, the Lion, some insult purportedly generated by their
mutual friend, the Elephant. The Lion, indignant and outraged,

demands an apology of the Elephant, who refuses and then trounces the Lion. The Lion, realizing that his mistake was to take the monkey literally, returns to trounce the monkey. Although anthropologists and sociolinguists have succeeded in establishing a fair sample of texts of the Signifying Monkey, they have been less successful at establishing a consensus of definitions of black signifying.

In addition to Abraham's definitions, definitions of signifying by Zora Neale Hurston, Thomas Kochman, Claudia Mitchell-Kernan, Geneva Smitherman, and Ralph Ellison are of interest here for what they reveal about the nature of Afro-American narrative parody, which I shall attempt first to define and then to employ in a reading of Ishmael Reed's *Mumbo Jumbo* as a pastiche of the Afro-American narrative tradition itself. Kochman argues that signifying depends upon the signifier *repeating* what someone else has said about a third person, in order to *reverse* the status of a relationship heretofore harmonious; signifying can also be employed to *reverse* or *undermine* pretense or even one's opinion about one's own status.[12] This use of repetition and reversal (chiasmus) constitutes an implicit parody of a subject's own complicity in illusion. Claudia Mitchell-Kernan, in perhaps the most thorough study of the concept, compares the etymology of "signifying" in black usage with usages from standard English:

> What is unique in Black English usage is the way in which signifying is extended to cover a range of meanings and events which are not covered in its Standard English usage. In the Black community it is possible to say, "He is signifying" and "Stop signifying"—sentences which would be anomalous elsewhere.[13]

Mitchell-Kernan points to the ironic, or dialectic, relationship between identical terms in standard and black English, which have vastly different meanings:

> The Black concept of *signifying* incorporates essentially a folk notion that dictionary entries for words are not always sufficient for interpreting meanings or messages, or that meaning goes beyond such interpretations. Complimentary remarks may be delivered in a left-handed fashion. A particular utterance may be an insult in one context and not another. What pretends to be informative may intend to be persuasive. The hearer is thus constrained to attend to all potential meaning carrying symbolic systems in speech events—the total universe of discourse.[14]

This is an excellent instance of the nature of signifying itself. Mitchell-Kernan refines these definitions somewhat by suggesting that the Signifying Monkey is able to signify upon the Lion only because the Lion does not understand the nature of the monkey's discourse: "There seems something of symbolic relevance from the perspective of language in this poem. The monkey and the lion do not speak the same language; the lion is not able to interpret the monkey's use of language." The monkey speaks figuratively, in a symbolic code; the lion interprets or reads literally and suffers the consequences of his folly, which is a reversal of his status as King of the Jungle. The monkey rarely acts in these narrative poems; he simply speaks. As the Signifier, he determines the actions of the Signified, the hapless Lion and the puzzled Elephant.[15]

As Mitchell-Kernan and Zora Neale Hurston attest, signifying is a sexless rhetorical game, despite the frequent use in the "masculine" versions of expletives that connote intimate relations with one's mother. Hurston, in *Mules and Men,* and Mitchell-Kernan, in her perceptive "Signifying, Loud-talking, and Marking," are the first scholars to record and explicate female signifying rituals.[16] Zora Neale Hurston is the first author of the tradition to represent signifying itself as a vehicle of liberation for an oppressed woman, and as a rhetorical strategy in the narration of fiction.

Hurston, whose definition of the term in *Mules and Men* (1935) is one of the earliest in the linguistic literature, has made *Their Eyes Were Watching God* into a paradigmatic signifying text, for this novel resolves that implicit tension between the literal and the figurative contained in standard English usages of the term "signifying." *Their Eyes* represents the black trope of signifying both as thematic matter and as a rhetorical strategy of the novel itself. Janie, the protagonist, gains her voice on the porch of her husband's store, not only by engaging with the assembled men in the ritual of signifying (which her husband had expressly forbidden her to do) but also by openly signifying upon her husband's impotency. His image wounded fatally, her husband soon dies of a displaced "kidney" failure. Janie "kills" her husband rhetorically. Moreover, Hurston's masterful use of the indirect discourse allows her to signify upon the tension between the two voices of Jean Toomer's *Cane* by adding to direct and indirect speech a strategy through which she can privilege the black oral tradition, which Toomer found to be problematical and dying. Hurston's is the "speakerly text."

The text of *Their Eyes,* moreover, is itself a signifying structure, a structure of intertextual revision, because it revises key tropes and rhetorical strategies received from precursory texts, such as W. E. B. Du Bois's *A Quest of the Silver Fleece* and Jean Toomer's *Cane.* Afro-American literary history is characterized by tertiary formal revision: Hurston's text (1937) revises Du Bois's novel (1911), and Toni Morrison in several texts revises Ellison and Hurston; similarly, Ellison (1951) revises Wright (1940, 1945), and Ishmael Reed (1972), among others, revises both. It is clear that black writers read and critique other black texts as an act of rhetorical self-definition. Our literary tradition exists because of these precisely chartable formal literary relationships.

The key aspect of signifying for Mitchell-Kernan is "its indirect intent or metaphorical reference," a rhetorical indirection which she says is "almost purely stylistic." Its art characteristics remain foregrounded. By "indirection," Mitchell-Kernan means that

> the correct semantic (referential interpretation) or signification of the utterance cannot be arrived at by a consideration of the dictionary meaning of the lexical items involved and the syntactic rules for their combination alone. The apparent significance of the message differs from its real significance. The apparent meaning of the sentence signifies its actual meaning.[17]

This rhetorical naming by indirection is, of course, central to our notions of figuration, troping, and of the parody of forms, or pastiche, in evidence when one writer repeats another's structure by one of several means, including a fairly exact repetition of a given narrative or rhetorical structure, filled incongruously with a ludicrous or incongruent content. T. Thomas Fortune's "The Black Man's Burden" is an excellent example of this form of pastiche, signifying as it does upon Kipling's "White Man's Burden":

> What is the Black Man's Burden,
> Ye hypocrites and vile,
> Ye whited sepulchres
> From th' Amazon to the Nile?
> What is the Black Man's Burden,

> Ye Gentile parasites,
> Who crush and rob your brother
> Of his manhood and his rights?

Dante Gabriel Rossetti's "Uncle Ned," a dialect verse parody of Stowe's *Uncle Tom's Cabin*, is a second example:

> Him tale dribble on and on widout a break,
> Till you hab no eyes for to see;
> When I reach Chapter 4 I had got a headache;
> So I had to let Chapter 4 be.

Another example of formal parody is to suggest a given structure precisely by failing to coincide with it—that is, to suggest it by dissemblance. Repetition of a form and then inversion of the same through a process of variation is central to jazz. A stellar example is John Coltrane's rendition of "My Favorite Things" compared to Julie Andrews's vapid original. Resemblance, then, can be evoked cleverly by dissemblance. Aristophanes's *The Frogs*, which parodies the styles of both Aeschylus and Euripides; Cervantes's relationship to the fiction of knight-errantry; Henry Fielding's parody of the Richardsonian novel of sentiment in *Joseph Andrews*, and Lewis Carroll's double parody in *Hiawatha's Photographing* (which draws upon Longfellow's rhythms to parody the convention of the family photograph) all come readily to mind. Ralph Ellison defines the parody aspect of signifying in several ways relevant to our discussion below of the formal parody strategies at work in Ishmael Reed's *Mumbo Jumbo*.

In his complex short story "And Hickman Arrives" (1960), Ellison's narrator defines signifying in this way:

> And the two men [Daddy Hickman and Deacon Wilhite] standing side by side, the one large and dark, the other slim and light brown, the other reverends rowed behind them, their faces staring grim with engrossed attention to the reading of the Word, like judges in their carved, high-backed chairs. And the two voices beginning their call and countercall as Daddy Hickman began spelling out the text which Deacon Wilhite read, playing variations on the verses just as he did with his trombone when he really felt like signifying on a tune the choir was singing.[18]

Following this introduction, the two ministers demonstrate the definition of signification, which in turn is a signification upon the antiphonal structure of the Afro-American sermon. This parody of form is of the same order as Richard Pryor's parody of both the same sermonic structure and Stevie Wonder's "Living for the City," which he effects by speaking the lyrics of Wonder's song in the form of and with the intonation peculiar to the Afro-American sermon in his "reading" of "The Book of Wonder." Pryor's parody is a signification of the second order, revealing simultaneously the received structure of the sermon (by its presence, demystified here by its incongruous content), the structure of Wonder's music (by the absence of his form and the presence of his lyrics), and the complex yet direct formal relationship between the black sermon and Wonder's music specifically, as well as that between black sacred and secular narrative forms generally.

Ellison defines signifying in other ways as well. In his essay on Charlie Parker, entitled "On Bird, Bird-Watching, and Jazz" (1962), Ellison defines the satirical aspect of signifying as one aspect of riffing in jazz:

> But what kind of bird was Parker? Back during the thirties members of the old Blue Devils Orchestra celebrated a certain robin by playing a lugubrious little tune called "They Picked Poor Robin." It was a jazz community joke, musically an extended signifying riff" or melodic naming of a recurrent human situation, and was played to satirize some betrayal of faith or loss of love observed from the bandstand.[19]

Here again, the parody is twofold, involving a formal parody of the melody of "They Picked Poor Robin" as well as a ritual naming, and therefore a troping, of an action observed from the bandstand.

Ellison, of course, is our Great Signifier himself, naming things by indirection and troping throughout his works. In his well-known review of LeRoi Jones's *Blues People,* Ellison defines signifying in yet a third sense, then signifies upon Jones's reading of Afro-American cultural history, which he argues is misdirected and wrongheaded. "The tremendous burden of sociology which Jones would place upon this body of music," writes Ellison, "is enough to give even the blues the blues." Ellison writes that Lydia Maria Child's title, *An Appeal in Favor of That Class of Americans called Africans,* sounds like a fine bit of contemporary ironic signifying—*"signifying"* here meaning, in the unwritten dictionary of American Negro usage, "rhetorical understatements." It tells us much of the thinking of her opposition, and it reminds us that as late as the 1890s, a time when Negro composers, singers, dancers and comedians dominated the American musical stage, popular Negro songs (including James Weldon Johnson's "Under the Bamboo Tree," now immortalized by T. S. Eliot) were commonly referred to as "Ethiopian Airs."[20]

Ellison's stress upon "the unwritten dictionary of American Negro usage" reminds us of the problem of definitions, of signification itself, when one is translating between two languages. The Signifying Monkey, perhaps appropriately, seems to dwell at this space between two linguistic domains. One wonders, incidentally, about this Afro-American figure and a possible French connection between *signe* ("sign") and *singe* ("monkey").

Ellison's definition of the relation his works bear to those of Richard Wright constitutes our definition of narrative signification, pastiche, or critical parody, although he employs none of these terms. His explanation of what we might call implicit formal criticism, however, comprises what we have sometimes called troping, after Geoffrey Hartman, and which we might take to be a profound definition of critical signification itself. Writes Ellison:

> I felt no need to attack what I considered the limitations of [Wright's] vision because I was quite impressed by what he had achieved. And in this, although I saw with the black vision of Ham, I was, I suppose, as pious as Shem and Japheth. Still I would write my own books and they would be in themselves, implicitly, criticisms of Wright's; just as all novels of a given historical moment form an argument over the nature of reality and are, to an extent, criticisms each of the other.[21]

Ellison in his fictions signifies upon Wright by parodying Wright's literary structures through repetition and difference. Although this is not the place for a close reading of this formal relationship, the complexities of the parodying can be readily suggested. The play of language, the signifying, starts with the titles. *Native Son* and *Black Boy*—both titles connoting race, self, and presence—Ellison tropes with *Invisible Man,* invisibility an ironic response of absence to the would-be presence of "blacks" and "natives," while "man" suggests a more mature, stronger status than either "sons" or "boy." Ellison signifies upon Wright's distinctive version of naturalism with a complex rendering of modernism; Wright's reacting protagonist, voiceless to the last, Ellison signifies upon with a nameless protagonist who is nothing but voice, since it is he who shapes, edits, and narrates his own tale, thereby combining action with the representation of action, thereby defining reality by its representation. This unity of presence and representation is perhaps Ellison's most subtle reversal of Wright's theory of the novel as exemplified in *Native Son,* since Bigger's voicelessness and powerlessness to act (as opposed to react) signify an absence, despite the metaphor of presence found in the novel's title; the reverse obtains in *Invisible Man,* where the absence implied by invisibility is undermined by the presence of the narrator as the narrator of his own text.

There are other aspects of critical parody at play here, too, one of the funniest being Jack's glass eye plopping into his water glass before him, which is functionally equivalent to the action of Wright's protagonist in "The Man Who Lived Underground," as he stumbles over the body of a dead baby, deep down in the sewer. It is precisely at this point in the narrative that we know Fred Daniels to be "dead, baby," in the heavy-handed way that Wright's naturalism was self-consciously symbolic. If Daniels's fate is signified by the objects over which he stumbles in the darkness of the sewer, Ellison signifies upon Wright's novella by repeating this underground scene of discovery but having his protagonist burn the bits of paper through which he has allowed himself to be defined by others. By explicitly repeating and reversing key figures of Wright's fictions, and by defining implicitly in the process of narration a sophisticated form more akin to Hurston's *Their Eyes Were Watching God,* Ellison exposes naturalism to be merely a hardened convention of representation of "the Negro problem" and perhaps part of the problem itself. I cannot emphasize enough the major import of this narrative gesture to the subsequent development of black narrative forms, since Ellison recorded a new way of seeing and defined both a new manner of representation and its relation to the concept of presence. The formal relation that Ellison bears to Wright, Ishmael Reed bears to both, but principally to Ellison. Once again, Ellison has formulated this complex and inherently polemical intertextual relationship of formal signifying, in a refutation of Irving Howe's critique of his work: "I agree with Howe that protest is an element of all art, though it does not necessarily take the form of speaking for a political or social program. It might appear in a novel as a *technical assault against the styles* which have gone before [emphasis added]."[22] This form of critical parody, of repetition and inversion, is what I define to be critical signification, or formal signifying, and is my metaphor for literary history.

This chapter is a reading of the tertiary relationship among Reed's "post-modern" *Mumbo Jumbo* as a signification upon Wright's "realism" and Ellison's "modernism." The set of intertextual relations that I chart through formal signification is related to what Mikhail Bakhtin labels double-voiced discourse, which he subdivides into parodic narration and the hidden, or internal, polemic. These two types of double-voiced discourse can merge together, as they do in *Mumbo Jumbo*. Although Bakhtin's discourse typology is familiar, let me cite his definition of hidden polemic. In hidden polemic,

> the other speech act remains outside the boundaries of the author's speech, but it is implied or alluded to in that speech. The other speech act is not reproduced with a new intention, but shapes the author's speech while remaining outside its boundaries. Such is the nature of the hidden polemic. . . .
>
> In hidden polemic the author's discourse is oriented toward its referential object, as in any other discourse, but at the same time each assertion about that object is constructed in such a way that, besides its referential meaning, the author's discourse brings a polemical attack to bear against another speech act, another assertion, on the same topic. Here one utterance focused on its referential object clashes with another utterance on the grounds of the referent itself. That other utterance is not reproduced; it is understood only in its import.[23]

Ellison's definition of the formal relationship his works bear to Wright's is a salient example of the hidden polemic: his texts clash with Wright's "on the ground of the referent itself." "As a result," Bakhtin continues, "the latter begins to influence the author's speech from within." This relationship Bakhtin calls double-voiced, whereby one speech act determines the internal structure of another, the second effecting the voice of the first, by absence, by difference.

Much of the Afro-American literary tradition can be read as successive attempts to create a new narrative space for representation of the recurring referent of Afro-American literature, the so-called black experience. Certainly, we read the relation of Sterling Brown's regionalism to Jean Toomer's lyricism in this way, Hurston's lyricism to Wright's naturalism in this way, and Ellison's modernism to Wright's naturalism in this way as well. We might represent this set of relationships in the following schematic way, which is intended in no sense other than to be suggestive:[24]

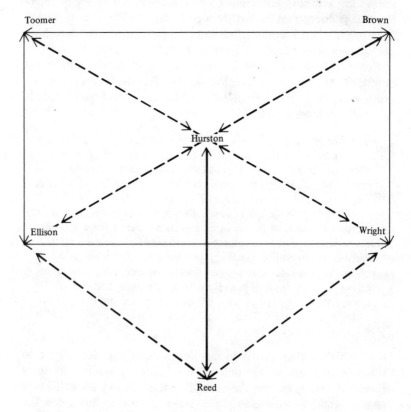

These relationships are reciprocal, because we are free to read in critical time machines, reading backwards, like Merlin moved through time. The direct relation most important to my own theory of reading is the solid black line that connects Reed with Hurston. Reed and Hurston seem to relish the play of the tradition, while Reed's work seems to be a magnificently conceived play on the tradition. Both Hurston and Reed write myths of Moses, both draw upon black sacred and secular myths discourse as metaphorical and metaphysical systems; both write self-reflexive texts which comment upon the nature of writing itself; both make use of the frame to bracket their narratives within narratives; and both are authors of fictions that I characterize as speakerly texts, texts that privilege the representation of the speaking black voice, of what the Formalists called skaz, and that Reed himself has defined as "an oral book, a talking book," a figure that occurs, remarkably enough, in four of the first five narratives in the black tradition in the eighteenth century.[25]

Reed's relation to these authors in the tradition is at all points double-voiced, since he seems to be especially concerned with employing satire to utilize literature in what Northrup Frye calls "a special function of analysis, of breaking up the lumber of stereotypes, fossilized beliefs, superstitious terrors, crank theories, pedantic dogmatisms, oppressive fashions, and all other things that impede the free movement . . . of society."[26] Reed, of course, seems to be most concerned with the free movement of writing itself. In Reed's work, parody and hidden polemic overlap in a process Bakhtin describes thusly: "When parody becomes aware of substantial resistance, a certain forcefulness and profundity in the speech act it parodies, it takes on a new dimension of complexity via the tones of the hidden polemic. . . . A process of inner dialogization takes place within the parodic speech act."[27]

This internal dialogization can have curious implications, the most interesting of which perhaps is what Bakhtin describes as "the splitting of double-voice discourse into two speech acts, into the two entirely separate and autonomous voices." The clearest evidence that Reed in *Mumbo Jumbo* is signifying through parody as hidden polemic is his use of the two autonomous narrative voices, which he employs in the manner of, and renders through, foregrounding, to parody the two simultaneous stories of detective narration, that of the present and that of the past, in a narrative

flow that moves hurriedly from cause to effect. In *Mumbo Jumbo,*
however, the second narrative, that of the past, bears an ironic
relation to the first narrative, that of the present, because it comments upon both the other narrative and the nature of its writing
itself, in what Frye describes in another context as "the constant
tendency to self-parody in satiric rhetoric which prevents even
the process of writing itself from becoming an oversimplified convention or ideal." Reed's rhetorical strategy assumes the form of
the relationship between the text and the criticism of that text,
which serves as discourse upon that text.[28]

II

"Consult the Text"[29]

With these definitions of narrative parody and critical signification as a frame, let us read Ishmael Reed's third novel, *Mumbo
Jumbo.* A close reading of Reed's corpus of works suggests
strongly that he seems to be concerned with the received form of
the novel, with the precise rhetorical shape of the Afro-American
literary tradition, and with the relation that the Afro-American
tradition bears to the Western tradition. Reed's concerns, as exemplified in his narrative forms, would seem to be twofold: on
the one hand with that relation his own art bears to his black
literary precursors, whom we can identify to include Zora Neale
Hurston, Richard Wright, James Baldwin, and Ralph Ellison, and
on the other hand the process of willing into being a rhetorical
structure, a literary language, replete with its own figures and
tropes, but one that allows the black writer to posit a structure of
feeling that simultaneously critiques both the metaphysical presuppositions inherent in Western ideas and forms of writing and
the metaphorical system in which the blackness of the writer and
his experience have been valorized as a "natural" absence. In the
short term, that is, through six demanding novels,[30] Reed has
apparently decided to criticize, through signification, what he
seems to perceive to be the received and conventional structures
of feeling that he has inherited from the Afro-American tradition
itself, almost as if the sheer process of the analysis can clear a
narrative space for his generation of writers as decidedly as Elli-

son's narrative response to Wright and naturalism cleared a space for Leon Forrest, Toni Morrison, Alice Walker, James Alan McPherson, and especially Reed himself.

By undertaking the difficult and subtle art of pastiche, Reed criticizes the Afro-American idealism of a transcendent black subject, integral and whole, self-sufficient and plentiful, the "always already" black signified, available for literary representation in received Western forms as would be the water ladled from a deep and dark well. Water can be poured into glasses or cups or canisters, but it remains water just the same. Put simply, Reed's fictions concern themselves with arguing that the so-called black experience cannot be thought of as a fluid content to be poured into received and static containers. For Reed, it is the signifier that both shapes and defines any discrete signified. And it is the signifiers of the Afro-American tradition with whom Reed is concerned.

This is not the place to read all of Reed's works against this thesis. Nevertheless, Reed's first novel lends credence to this sort of reading and also serves to create what we may call a set of generic expectations through which we read the rest of his works. His first novel, *The Free-Lance Pallbearers* is, above all else, a parody of the confessional mode which is the fundamental, undergirding convention of Afro-American narrative, received, elaborated upon, and transmitted in a chartable heritage from Briton Hammon's captivity narrative of 1760 through the antebellum slave narratives to black autobiography into black fiction, especially the fictions of Hurston, Wright, Baldwin, and Ellison.[31] This narrative of Bukka Doopeyduk is a pastiche of the classic black narrative of the questing protagonist's "journey into the heart of whiteness"; but it parodies this narrative form by turning it inside out, exposing the character of the originals, and thereby defining their formulaic closures and disclosures. Doopeyduk's tale ends with his own crucifixion. As the narrator of his own story, therefore, Doopeyduk articulates literally from among the dead an irony implicit in all confessional and autobiographical modes, in which any author is forced by definition to imagine himself or herself to be dead. More specifically, Reed signifies upon *Black Boy* and *Go Tell It on the Mountain* in a foregrounded critique which can be read as an epigraph to the novel: *"read growing up in Soulsville first of three installments/or what it means to be a backstage darkey."* The "scat-singing voice" that introduces the novel, Reed foregrounds against the "other" voice of Doopeyduk, whose "second" voice narrates the novel's plot. Here, Reed parodies both Hurston's use of free indirect discourse in *Their Eyes Were Watching God* and Ellison's use of the fore-grounded voice in the prologue and epilogue of *Invisible Man,* which frame his nameless protagonist's picaresque account of his own narrative. In *Yellow Back Radio Broke Down,* Reed more fully and successfully critiques both realism and modernism, as exemplified in a kind of writing that one character calls "those suffering books I wrote about my old neighborhood and how hard it was."[32]

Reed's third novel, *Mumbo Jumbo,* is about writing itself; not only in the figurative sense of the post-modern, self-reflexive text but also in a literal sense: "So Jes Grew is seeking its words. Its text. For what good is a liturgy without a text?" (*Mumbo Jumbo,* p. 6.) *Mumbo Jumbo* is both a book about texts and a book of texts, a composite narrative composed of subtexts, pretexts, post-texts, and narratives within narratives. It is both a definition of Afro-American culture and its deflation. "The Big Lie concerning Afro-American culture," *Mumbo Jumbo*'s dust jacket informs us, "is that it lacks a tradition." The big truth of the novel, on the other hand, is that this very tradition is as rife with hardened convention and presupposition as is the rest of the Western tradi-tion. Even this cryptic riddle of Jes Grew and its text parodies Ellison: *Invisible Man*'s plot is set in motion with a riddle, while the theme of the relationship between words and texts echoes a key passage from Ellison's short story "And Hickman Arrives": "Good. Don't talk like I talk, talk like I *say* talk. Words are your business boy. Not just *the* word. Words are everything. The key to the Rock, the answer to the question."[33]

Let us examine the book's dust jacket. The signifying begins with the book's title. "Mumbo jumbo" is the received and ethno-centric Western designation for both the rituals of black religions and all black languages themselves. A vulgarized Western transla-tion of a Swahili phrase (*mambo, jambo*), mumbo jumbo, as *Webster's Third International Dictionary* defines it, connotes "lan-guage that is unnecessarily involved and difficult to understand:

GIBBERISH." The *Oxford English Dictionary* cites its etymology as being "of unknown origin," implicitly serving here as the signified on which Reed's title signifies, recalling the myth of Topsy who "jes grew," with no antecedents, a phrase with which James Weldon Johnson characterizes the creative process of black sacred music. *Mumbo Jumbo,* then, signifies upon Western etymology, abusive Western practices of deflation through misnaming, as well as Johnson's specious designation of the anonymity of creation, which indeed is a major component of the Afro-American cultural tradition.

But there is more parody in this title. Whereas Ellison tropes the myth of presence in Wright's titles of *Native Son* and *Black Boy* through his title of *Invisible Man,* inverting the received would-be correlation between blackness and presence with a narrative strategy that correlates invisibility (ultimate sign of absence) with the presence of self-narration and therefore self-creation, Reed parodies all three titles by employing as his title the English-language parody of black language itself. Whereas the etymology of "mumbo jumbo" has been problematical for Western lexicographers, any Swahili speaker knows that the phrase derives from the common greeting *jambo* and its plural, *mambo,* which loosely translated means "What's happening?" Reed is also echoing Vachel Lindsay's ironic poem *The Congo,* cited as an epigraph to this essay, which proved to be so fatally influencing to the Harlem Renaissance poets, as Charles Davis has shown.[34] From its title on, the novel serves as a critique of black and Western literary forms and conventions, and complex relationships between the two.

Let us proceed with our examination of the book's cover. A repeated and reversed image of a crouching, sensuous Josephine Baker sits back to back, superimposed upon a rose. Counterposed to this image is a medallion containing a horse with two riders. These signs adumbrate the two central oppositions of the novel's complicated plot: the rose and the double image of Josephine Baker together form a cryptic *vé vé.* A *vé vé* is a key sign in Vaudou, a sign drawn on the ground with sand, cornmeal, flour, and coffee to represent the *loa.* The *loa* are the deities who comprise the pantheon of Vaudou's gods. The rose is a sign of *Ezrulie,* goddess of love, home, and purity, as are the images of Josephine

Baker, who became the French goddess of love in the late 1920s, in their version of the Jazz Age. The doubled image, as if mirrored, is meant to suggest the divine crossroads, where human beings meet their fate, but also at the center of which presides the *loa,* Legba (Esu), guardian of the divine crossroads, messenger of the gods, the figure representing the interpreter and interpretation itself, the muse or *loa* of the critic. It is Legba who is master of that mystical barrier that separates the divine from the profane worlds. It is this complex yet cryptic *vé vé* that is meant both to placate Legba himself and to summon his attention and integrity in a double act of criticism and interpretation: that of Reed in the process of his representation of the tradition, to be found between the covers of the book, and that of the critic's interpretation of Reed's figured interpretation.

Located outside the *vé vé* as counterpoint, placed almost off the cover itself, is the sign of the Knights Templar, representing the heart of the Western tradition. The opposition represented here is between two distinct warring forces, two mutually exclusive modes of reading. Already, we are in the realm of doubles, but not the binary realm; rather, we are in the realm of doubled doubles. Not only are two distinct and conflicting metaphysical systems here represented and invoked, but Reed's cover also serves as an overture to the critique of dualism and binary opposition that serves as a major thrust to the text of *Mumbo Jumbo* itself. As we shall see, Reed also parodies this dualism (which Reed thinks is exemplified in Ellison's *Invisible Man*) in another text.

This critique of dualism is implicit in the novel's central *speaking* character, Papa La Bas. I emphasize *speaking* here because the novel's central character, of course, is Jes Grew itself, which never speaks and is never seen in its "abstract essence," only in discrete manifestations or "outbreaks." Jes Grew is the supra-force that sets the text of *Mumbo Jumbo* in motion, as it and Reed seek their texts, as all characters and events define themselves against this omnipresent, compelling force. Jes Grew, here, is a clever and subtle parody of similar forces invoked in the black novel of naturalism, most notably in Wright's *Native Son.*

Unlike Jes Grew, Papa La Bas does indeed speak. It is he who is the chief detective, in hard and fast pursuit of both Jes Grew and its text. This character's name is a conflation of two of the several names of Esu, the Pan-African trickster. Called Papa Legba, as his Haitian honorific, and invoked through the phrase "Eh La-Bas" in New Orleans jazz recordings of the twenties and thirties, Papa La Bas is the Afro-American trickster figure from black sacred tradition. His name, of course, is French for "over there," and his presence unites "over there" (Africa) with "right here." He is indeed the messenger of the gods, the divine Pan-African interpreter, pursuing, in the language of the text, "the Work," which is not only Vaudou but also the very work (and play) of art itself. Papa La Bas is the figure of the critic in search of the text, decoding its tell-tale signs in the process. Even the four syllables of his name recall the text's play of doubles. Chief Sign Reader, La Bas is also, in a sense, a sign himself. Indeed, Papa La Bas's incessant and ingenious search for the text of Jes Grew, culminating as it does in his recitation and revision of the myth of Thoth's gift of writing to civilization, constitutes an argument against what Reed elsewhere terms "the so-called oral tradition" and in favor of the primacy and priority of the written text over the speaking voice. It is a brief for the permanence of the written text, for the need for criticism, for which La Bas's myth of origins also accounts. "Guides were initiated into the Book of Thoth, the 1st anthology written by the 1st choreographer." (*Mumbo Jumbo*, p. 167).

But I am racing ahead of myself. Let us examine the text of *Mumbo Jumbo* as a textbook, complete with illustrations, footnotes, and bibliography. A prologue, an epilogue, and an appended "Partial Bibliography" frame the text proper, again in a parody of Ellison's framing devices in *Invisible Man*. (Reed supplements Ellison's epilogue with the bibliography, parodying the device both by its repeated presence and by the subsequent asymmetry of *Mumbo Jumbo*.) This documentary thrust of notes, illustrations, and bibliography parodies the documentary conventions of black realism and naturalism, as does Reed's recurrent use of lists and catalogues, separate items he fails to separate with any sort of punctuation, thereby directing attention to their presence as literary conventions rather than as sources of information, particularly about the black experience. His text includes as well dictionary definitions, epigraphs, epigrams, anagrams, photoduplicated type from other texts interspersed between chapters and within them, newspaper clips and headlines, literal signs (such as those that hang on doors), invitations to parties, telegrams, "Situation Reports" "which come from the 8-tubed Radio" (*Mumbo Jumbo*, p. 32), yin and yang symbols, quotes from other texts, poems, cartoons, drawings of mythic beasts, handbills, excerpts from photographs, book jackets, charts and graphs, playing cards, a representation of a Greek vase, and a four-page handwritten letter, among still others. Just as our word "satire" derives from *satura* ("hash"), so too is Reed's form of satire a version of *gumbo*, a parody of form itself.[35]

Reed here parodies and underscores our notions of intertextuality, present in all texts. *Mumbo Jumbo* is the great black intertext, replete with the intratexts both referring to each other within the text of *Mumbo Jumbo* and referring outside themselves to all those other named texts as well as those unnamed but invoked through concealed reference, repetition, and reversal. The "Partial Bibliography" is Reed's most brilliant stroke, since its unconcealed presence, as does the text's other undigested texts, parodies both the scholar's appeal to authority and all studied attempts to conceal literary antecedents and influence. All texts, claims *Mumbo Jumbo*, are intertexts, full of intratexts. Our notions of originality, his critique suggests, are more related to convention and material relationships than to some supposedly transcendent truth. Reed lays bare that mode of concealment and the illusion of unity that so characterize modernist texts. Coming as it does after his epilogue, Reed's "Partial Bibliography" is an implicit parody of Ellison's ideas of craft and technique in the novel and suggests an image of Ellison's nameless protagonist, buried in his well-lighted hole, eating vanilla ice cream smothered by Sloe Gin, making annotations for his sequel to *Invisible Man*. The device, moreover, mimics the fictions of history against which societies live. The presence of the bibliography also recalls Ellison's remarks about the complex relationship between the writer's experience and the writer's experiences with books.

By now we know that *Mumbo Jumbo* is a post-modern text. But what is its parody of the Jazz Age and the Harlem Renaissance about, and for whom do the characters stand? Reed's novel is situated in the twenties because, as the text explains, the Harlem Renaissance was the first full-scale, patronized attempt to capture the essence of Jes Grew in discrete literary texts. In the 1890s, when "the Dance" swept the country, Jes Grew made its first appearance. Indeed, James Weldon Johnson's coining of the phrase is in reference to the composition of ragtime, which was dependent upon the use of signifying riffs to transform black secular, and often vulgar, songs into formal, repeatable compositions. Ellison makes essentially the same statement about the 1890s in his definition of signifying implicit in a common designation for this music, known as "Ethiopian Airs." This paragraph could well serve as the signified upon which *Mumbo Jumbo* signifies. The power of Jes Grew was allowed to peter out, Reed argues, because it found no texts to contain it, define it, interpret it, and thereby will it to subsequent black cultures.

Although the Harlem Renaissance did succeed in the creation of numerous texts of art and criticism, most critics agree that it failed to find its voice, which lay muffled beneath the dead weight of convention of romanticism, which most black writers seemed not to question but adopted eagerly. This is essentially the same critique rendered by Wallace Thurman in his *Infants of the Spring,* a satirical novel about the Harlem Renaissance published in 1932, written by one of its most thoughtful literary critics. Few of Reed's characters stand for historical personages; most are figures for types. Hinkle Von Vampton, however, suggests Carl Van Vechten, but his first name, from the German *hincken* ("to limp"), could suggest the German engraver Knackfuss, whose name translates as "a person with a club-foot."[36] while Abdul Sufi Hamid recalls a host of black Muslims, most notably Duse Mohamed Ali, editor of the *African Times and Orient Review* as well as Elijah Mohammed's shadowy mentor, W. D. Fard. The key figures in the action of the plot, however, are the Atonist Path and its military wing, the Wallflower Order, on one hand, and the Neo-Hoodoo Detectives, headed by Papa Las Bas, and its "military" wing, the *Mu'tafikah,* on the other. ("Wallflower Order" is a two-term pun on "Ivy League," while *Mu'tafikah* puns on a twelve-letter word that signifies chaos. *Mu* is also the twelfth letter of the Greek alphabet, suggesting the dozens, which forms a subdivision of the black ritual of signifying. The *Mu'tafikah* play the dozens on Western art museums.) The painter Knackfuss created a heliogravure from Wilhelm II's allegorical drawing of the European authority to go to war against the Chinese. This heliogravure, *"Volker Europas, Wahrt eure heiligsten Guter,"* ("People of Europe, Protect That Which Is Most Holy to You"), was completed in 1895. It appears in *Mumbo Jumbo* on page 155. The pun on "Knackfuss" and "Hinken," connoting "club foot," is wonderfully consistent with Reed's multiple puns on "Atonist" and the "Wallflower Order."

"Atonist" has multiple significations here. One who atones is an Atonist. A follower of Aton, Pharoah Akhenaton's Supreme Being who reappears as Jehovah, is an Atonist. But also one who lacks physiological tone, especially of a contractile organ, is an Atonist. On a wall at Atonist Headquarters are the Order's symbols, "the Flaming Disc, the #1 and the creed":

> Look at them! Just look at them! throwing their hips this way, that way *while I, my muscles, stone, the marrow of my spine, plaster,* my back supported by decorated paper, stand here as goofy as a Dumb Dora. Lord, if I can't dance, no one shall. (*Mumbo Jumbo,* p. 65, emphasis added.)

The Atonists and the Jes Grew carriers reenact allegorically a primal, recurring battle between the Forces of Light and the Forces of Darkness, between Forces of the Left Hand and Forces of the Right, between the descendants of Set and the descendants of Osiris, all symbolized in Knackfuss's heliogravure.

We learn of this war in *Mumbo Jumbo*'s marvelous parody of the scene of recognition so fundamental to the structure of detective fiction, which occurs in the library of a black-owned villa located at Irvington-on-Hudson, called Villa Lewaro, "an anagram," the text tells us, "upon the Hostess' name by famed tenor Enrico Caruso." Actually, "Lewaro" is an anagram for "We Oral." This recognition scene, in which Papa La Bas and his sidekick, Black Herman, arrest Hinkle Von Vampton and Hubert "Safecracker" Gould, parodies its counterpart in the detective novel by its exaggerated frame. When forced to explain the charges against Von Vampton and Gould, La Bas replies, "Well if you must know, it all began 1000s of years ago in Egypt, according to a high up member of the Haitian aristocracy." He then proceeds to narrate, before an assembled company of hundreds, the myth of Set and Osiris and its key subtext, the myth of the introduction of writing in Egypt by the god Thoth. The parody involved here is the length of the recapitulation of facts—of the decoded signs—which La Bas narrates in a thirty-one-page chapter, the longest in the book. The myth, of course, recapitulates the action of the novel to this point of the narrative, but by an allegorical representation through mythic discourse. Thirty-one pages later, by fits and turns, we realize that Von Vampton and the Wallflower Order are the descendants of Set, by way of the story of Moses and Jethro and the birth of the Knights Templar in A.D. 1118. Von Vampton, we learn, was the Templar Librarian, who found the Sacred Book of Thoth, "the 1st anthology written by the 1st choreographer" (*Mumbo Jumbo,* p. 164), which is Jes Grew's sacred text. In the twentieth century, Von Vampton subdivided the text of Thoth into fourteen sections, just as Set had dismembered his dead brother's body into fourteen segments. The fourteen sections of the anthology he mailed anonymously to fourteen black people, who are manipulated into mailing its parts to each other in a repeating circle, in the manner of a "chain book" (*Mumbo Jumbo,* p. 69). Abdul Sufi Hamid, one of these fourteen who we learn are unwitting Jes Grew carriers, calls in the other thirteen chapters of the anthology, reassembles the text, and even translates the Book of Thoth from the hieroglyphics. Sensing its restored text, Jes Grew surfaces in New Orleans, as it did in the 1890s with the birth of ragtime, and heads toward New York. Ignorant of the existence or nature of Jes Grew and of the true nature of the Sacred Text, Abdul destroys the book, then is murdered by the Wallflower Order when he refuses to reveal its location. La Bas, Von Vampton's arch foe, master of HooDoo, devout follower of Jes Grew ("Papa La Bas carries Jes Grew in him like most other folk carry genes" (*Mumbo Jumbo,* p. 23), chief decoder of signs, recapitulates this complex story in elaborate detail to the assembled guests at Villa Lewaro, thereby repeating, through the recited myth, the figures of its own plot, functioning as what Reed calls "the shimmering Etheric Double of the 1920s. The thing that gives it its summary" (*Mumbo Jumbo,* p. 20). Despite numerous murders and even the arrests of Von Vampton and Gould and their repatriation to Haiti for trial by the *loas of Vaudou,* neither the mystery of the nature of Jes Grew nor the identity of its text is ever resolved. The epilogue presents Papa La Bas, in the 1960s, delivering his annual lecture to a college audience on the Harlem Renaissance and its unconsummated Jes Grew passion.

But just as we can define orders of multiple substitution and signification for Reed's types and caricatures, as is true of allegory generally (e.g., Von Vampton, Van Vechten, "Hinken" Knackfuss), so too can we find all sorts of consistent levels of meaning with which we could attempt to find a closure to the text. I shall not do that here, however; the first decade of readers of *Mumbo Jumbo* have attempted to find one-to-one correlations with great energy, decoding its allegorical structure by finding analogues between the Harlem Renaissance and the Black Arts movement, for example. As interesting as such parallel universes are, I shall not attempt such a reading here, or even engage in one more rehearsal of its complex plots, since I can in these pages assume a large measure of reader familiarity with the text. I am concerned with its status as a rhetorical structure, as a mode of narration, and with relating this mode of narration to a critique of traditional notions of closure in interpretation. For Reed's most subtle achievement in *Mumbo Jumbo* is to parody, to signify upon, the notions of closure implicit in the key texts of the Afro-American canon itself. *Mumbo Jumbo,* in contrast, is a novel that figures and glorifies indeterminacy. The novel, in this sense, stands as a profound critique and elaboration upon this convention of closure in the black novel and its metaphysical implications. In its stead, Reed posits the notion of aesthetic *play:* the play of the tradition, the play on the tradition, the sheer play of indeterminacy itself.

III

The text of *Mumbo Jumbo* is framed by devices central to the narration of film. The prologue, situated at New Orleans, functions as a false start of the action: five pages of narration are followed by a second title page, a second copyright and acknowledgment page, and a second set of epigraphs, the first of which concludes the prologue. This prologue functions as the prologue of a film, following which Reed shows the title and credits before continuing with the plot. The novel's final two words are "Freeze Frame." The relative fluidity of the narrative structure of film, compared with that of conventional prose narrative, announces here an emphasis upon figural multiplicity rather than singular referential correspondence, an emphasis that Reed recapitulates throughout this text through an imaginative play of doubles. The play of doubles extends from the double *Erzulie* image of Josephine Baker on the novel's cover (*Erzulie* means "love of mirrors" *Mumbo Jumbo,* p. 162) and the double beginning implicit in every prologue, through all sorts of double images scattered in the text, such as the two heads of Papa La Bas (pp. 25, 45) and the arabic numerals 4 and 22, which repeat frequently, all the way to both the double ending of the novel, implied by its epilogue, and its "Partial Bibliography," which frames the text.

Mumbo Jumbo is a book of doubles, from its title on. But these thematic aspects of doubleness represent only its most obvious form of doubling; the novel's narrative structure, a brilliant elaboration on that of the detective novel, is itself a rather complex doubling. Reed refers to this principle of "structuration" as "a doubleness, not just of language, but the idea of a double-image on form. A mystery-mystery, *Erzulie-Erzulie*."[37] In *Mumbo Jumbo,* form and content, theme and structure, all are ordered upon this figure of the double; doubling is Reed's "figure in the carpet." The form of the narration in *Mumbo Jumbo* replicates the tension of the two stories, which grounds the form of the detective novel, which Tzvetan Todorov defines as "the missing story of the crime, and the presented story of the investigation, the role justification of which is to make us discover the first story." Todorov describes three forms of detective fiction: the whodunit, the *série noire* (the thriller, exemplified by Chester Himes's *For Love of Imabelle*), and the suspense novel, which combines the features of narration of the first two. Let us consider Todorov's typology in relation to the narrative structure of *Mumbo Jumbo.*[38]

The whodunit is comprised of two stories: the story of the crime and the story of the investigation. The first story has ended by the time the second story begins. In the story of the investigation, the characters "do not act, they learn." The whodunit's structure, as in Agatha Christie's *Murder on the Orient Express,* is often framed by a prologue and an epilogue, "that is, the discovery of the crime and the discovery of the killer." The second story functions as an explanation both of the investigation and of "how the book came to be written"; indeed, "it is precisely the story of that very book." As Todorov concludes, these two stories are the same as those the Russian Formalists isolated in every narrative, that of the *fable* ("story") and that of the *sjužet* ("plot"): "the story is what has happened in life, the plot is the way the author presents it to us." "Story" here describes the reality represented, while "plot" describes the mode of narration, the literary convention and devices, used to represent. A detective novel merely renders these two principles of narrative present simultaneously. The story of the crime is a story of an absence, in that the crime of the whodunit has occurred before the narrative begins; the second story, therefore, "serves only as mediator between the reader and the story of the crime." This second story, the plot, generally depends upon temporal inversions and subjective, shifting points of view. These two conventions figure prominently in the narrative structure of *Mumbo Jumbo*.

Todorov's second type of detective fiction is the *série noire,* or the thriller. The thriller combines the two stories into one, suppressing the first and vitalizing the second. Whereas the whodunit proceeds from effect to cause, the thriller proceeds from cause to effect. The novel reveals at its outset the causes of the crime, the *données* (in *Mumbo Jumbo,* the Wallflower Order, whose member's dialogue occupies sixty percent of the prologue), and the narration sustains itself through sheer suspense, through the reader's expectation of what will happen next. Although *Mumbo Jumbo*'s narrative strategy proceeds through the use of suspense, its two stories are not fused; accordingly, it falls into neither of these first two mystery categories.

Mumbo Jumbo imitates and signifies upon the narrative strategy of the third type of detective novel: the suspense novel. Its defining principles are these: "it retains the mystery of the whodunit and also the two stories, that of the past and that of the present; but it refuses to reduce the second to a simple detection of the truth." What *has* happened is only just as important to sustaining interest as what *shall* happen; the second story, then, the story of the present, is the focus of interest. Reed draws upon this type of narrative as his rhetorical structure in *Mumbo Jumbo,* with one important exception. Here we find the two stories, structure intact, that of the past and that of the present. What's more, the mystery presented at the outset of the text, the double mystery of the suppression of both Jes Grew and its text (neither of which is ever revealed nor their mysteries solved in the standard sense of the genre), is revealed through the dialogue of the *données,* which means that the movement of the narration is from cause to effect, from the New Orleans branch of the Wallflower Order and their plans to "decode this coon mumbo jumbo" (*Mumbo Jumbo,* p. 4) through their attempts to kill its text and thereby dissipate its force. The detective of the tale, Papa La Bas, moreover, is integrated solidly into the action and universe of the other characters, risking his life and systematically discovering the murdered corpses of his friends and colleagues as he proceeds to decode the signs of the mystery's solution in the manner of "the vulnerable detective," which Todorov identifies as a subtype of the suspense novel.

In these ways, the structure of *Mumbo Jumbo* conforms with that of the suspense novel. The crucial exception to the typology, however, whereby Reed is able to parody even the mode of the two stories themselves and transform the structure into a self-reflecting text or allegory upon the nature of writing itself, is *Mumbo Jumbo*'s device of drawing upon the story of the past to reflect upon, analyze, and philosophize about the story of the present. The story of the present is narrated from the limited but multiple points of view of the characters who people its subplots and submysteries; the story of the past, however, is narrated in an omniscient voice, which reads the story of the present in the manner of the literary critic closely reading a primary text. *Mumbo Jumbo*'s double narrative, then, its narrative-within-a-narrative, is an allegory of the act of reading itself; and Reed uses this second mode of ironic omniscient narration to signify upon the nature of the novel in general, but especially upon Afro-American realism and modernism.

The mystery type of narrative discourse is characterized by plot inversions which, of course, function as temporal inversions. Before discussing Reed's use of the narrative-within-a-narrative and its relation to the sort of indeterminacy the text seems to be upholding, perhaps it would be useful to chart Reed's use of inversion as impediment. The summary of the *fabula,* the essential causal–temporal relationships of the work I have sketched above, is misleading somewhat; the novel can be related in summary fashion only after we have read it. In the reading process, we confront a collection of mysteries, mysteries within mysteries, all of which are resolved eventually except for the first two. We can list the following mysteries, which unfold in this order as the *sjužet,* or the plot:[39]

1. The mystery of Jes Grew ("The Thing").
2. The mystery of its text.

These are basic mysteries. They frame the plot and remain unresolved.

3. The mystery of the Wallflower Order's history and its relation to that of the Knights Templar.

The mystery of the identity of these medieval orders, Jes Grew's antagonists, runs the length of the novel and is resolved only in the recognition scene at Villa Lewaro. Figured as antithetical dance metaphors.

4. The *Mu'tafikah*'s raids on American art museums, especially the North American Wing of the Center of Art Detention.

This partial mystery is resolved, but disastrously for La Bas's forces. It creates a series of imbalances between Earline and Berbelang, and between Berbelang and Papa La Bas, which function as structural counterparts to the tension between the Wallflower Order and the Knights Templar.

5. Installation of the anti-Jes Grew President Warren Harding and mystery of his complex racial heritage.

6. The mystery of the Talking Android.

Plot impediments.

7. Gang wars between Buddy Jackson

and Schlitz, "the Sarge of York-town."

8. Mystery of the U.S. Marine Invasion of Haiti.	Resolved midway; allows for ironic denouement.
9. Mystery of Papa La Bas's identity and Mumbo Jumbo cathedral.	Resolved in epilogue.
10. Woodrow Wilson Jefferson and the mystery of the Talking Android.	Plot impediments; resolved, but ambiguously. Explanations resort to fantastic element.
11. Staged mystery of "Charlotte's (Isis) Pick." (Doctor Peter Pick.)	
12. Hinckle Von Vampton's identity.	This mystery is resolved and in the process resolves the mysteries of the Wallflower Order and the Atonist Path.
13. Mystery of the fourteen "J.G.C.'s" and the sacred anthology.	This resolves mystery number 2, but only partially, superficially.
14. The mystery of Abdul Sufi Hamid's murder and his riddle, "Epigram on American Egyptian Cotton."	These mysteries function in a curious way, seemingly to resolve the mystery of Jes Grew's text.
15. Berbelang's murder and betrayal of the *Mu'tafikah* by Thor. Charlotte's murder.	Plot impediments.
16. Earline's possession by *Erzulie* and by Yemanja *loas;* Doctor Peter Pick's disappearance.	
17. Mystery of the Black Plume and Renoir Battraville, and the ring of the Dark Tower.	Voodoo/hoodoo exposition. Resolves Knights Templar mystery. Leads to capture of H. Von Vampton.

Most of these interwoven mysteries serve to impede the plot in the manner of detective fiction by depicting several simultaneous actions whose relationship is not apparent, as does jazz. These mysteries run parallel throughout the novel, only to be resolved in the scene of recognition in the library at the Villa Lewaro, where Papa La Bas presents his decoded evidence through his elaborate recasting of the myth of Osiris and Set. This allegory serves to recapitulate the novel's several simultaneous subplots, to combine them, and to decode them, but also to trace the novel's complex character interrelationships from ancient Egypt to the very minute of La Bas's narration. The narration leads to the arrest of Gould and Von Vampton, but also to the antidiscovtry of the Sacred Book of Thoth, the would-be text of Jes Grew. In two other places in the novel, recast myths serve the same function of plot impediment for the purpose of repeating the novel's events through metaphorical substitution. These are the allegories of Faust (*Mumbo Jumbo,* pp. 90–92) and of the *houngan,* T. Bouton (pp. 132–139). These recast myths serve as the play of doubles, consistent with the "double-image on form" which Reed sought to realize, and implicit in the nature of allegory itself.

Plot impediment can be created in ways other than through temporal inversion; local color description does as well. Local color, of course, came to be used by the social novel as a standard feature; in the Afro-American narrative, realism as local color is perhaps the most consistent aspect of black rhetorical strategy from the slave narratives to *Invisible Man.* Reed uses and simultaneously parodies the convention of local color as plot impediment by employing unpunctuated lists and categories throughout the text. The novel's first paragraph is an excellent example of local color:

A True Sport, the Mayor of New Orleans, spiffy in his patent-leather brown and white shoes, his plaid suit, the Rudolph Valentino parted-down-the middle hair style, sits in his office. Sprawled upon his knees is Zuzu, local do-wack-a-doo and voo-do-dee-odo-fizigig. A slatternly floozy, her green, sequined dress quivers. (p. 3)

The following sentence exemplifies Reed's undifferentiated catalogues: "The dazzling parodying priming mischievous pre-Joycean style-play of your Cakewalking your Calinda your Minstrelsy give-and-take of the ultra-absurd" (p. 132). Viktor Sklovsky says that the mystery novel was drawn upon formally by the social novel; Reed's use of devices from the detective novel to parody the black social novel, then, reverse this process, appropriately and ironically enough.[40]

Reed's play of doubles assumes its most subtle form in his clever rhetorical strategy of two narratives, the story of the past and the story of the present. I have discussed how the tension of these two stories operates in the types of detective fiction generally. It is useful to think of these two narratives as one of understanding and one of truth. The narrative of understanding is the presented narrative of the investigation of a mystery, in which a detective (the reader) interprets or decodes clues. Once these signs are sufficiently decoded, this narrative of understanding reconstitutes the missing story of the crime itself, which we might profit from by thinking of as the narrative of truth. The presented narrative, then, is implicitly a story of another, absent story, and hence functions as an internal allegory.

We can characterize the nature of this narrative of the investigation in *Mumbo Jumbo* easily enough. The narrative remains close to the action; local color description and dialogue are its two central aspects; character as description and the use of the extensive catalogue function to propel the narrative forward; the narrative remains essentially in the present tense, and point of view is both in the third person and limited, as it must be if the reader's understanding of the nature of the mystery is to remain impeded until the novel's detective decodes all the clues, assembles all suspects in one room, and then interprets the signs and reveals the truth of the mystery to all assembled, including the guilty. He makes his arrest; then everyone left eats dinner. *Mumbo Jumbo's* prologue opens in this narrative mode of the story of the present.

Near the end of the prologue, however, a second narrative mode intrudes. It is separated from the first narrative by spacing and is further foregrounded by italic type (p. 6). It not only interprets and comments upon characters and actions of the first story, but it does so in a third-person omniscient mode. In other words, it reads its counterpart narrative, of which it is a negation. Fol-

lowing its italic type are three other sorts of subtexts which comprise crucial aspects of this second, antithetical narration of past,
present, and future: a black and white photograph of people danc-
ing, an epigraph on the nature of the "second line" written by
Louis Armstrong, and an etymology of the phrase "mumbo
jumbo" taken from the *American Heritage Dictionary*. In this
foregrounded antithetical narration, it reads "correctly" for the
reader that which the characters ponder or misunderstand.

> But they did not understand [it says] that the Jes Grew epidemic
> was unlike physical plagues. Actually Jes Grew was an anti-
> plague. Some plagues caused the body to waste away; Jes Grew
> enlivened the host. So Jes Grew is seeking its words. Its text.
> For what good is a liturgy without a text? In the 1890s the text
> was not available and Jes Grew was out there all alone. Perhaps
> the 1920s will also be a false alarm and Jes Grew will evaporate
> as quickly as it appeared again broken-hearted and double-crossed
> (++). (p. 6)

This second (anti-) narration consists of all of *Mumbo Jumbo*'s
motley subtexts that are not included in its first narration. Whereas
the first story adheres to the present, the second roams remarkably
freely through space and time, between myth and history, humorously employing the device of anachronism. It is discontinuous
and fragmentary; not linear like its counterpart, it never contains
dialogue; it contains all of the text's abstractions.

All of the novel's subtexts (illustrations, excerpts from other
texts, "Situation Reports," etc.) are parts of this second nara-
tion, which we might think of as an extended discourse on the
history of Jes Grew. Only the text's first two mysteries does this
antithetical narration not address: the matter of what exactly is
Jes Grew and what precisely is its text. After Chapter 8, the foregrounding italics tend to disappear, for the narration manages to
bracket or frame itself, functioning almost as the interior mono-
logue of the first narrative mode. While the first story remains
firmly in the tradition of the presented detective story, the second
turns that convention inside out, functioning as an ironic double,
a reversed mirror image like the cryptic *vé vé* on the novel's
cover.

This second mode of narration allows for the allegorical double of *Mumbo Jumbo.* As many other critics have gone to great lengths to demonstrate, *Mumbo Jumbo* is a thematic allegory of the Black Arts movement of the sixties rendered through causal connections with the Harlem Renaissance. The more interesting allegory, however, is that found in the antithetical narrative, which is a discourse on the history and nature of writing itself, especially that of the Afro-American literary tradition. *Mumbo Jumbo,* then, is a text that directs attention to its own writing, to its status as a text, related to other texts which it signifies upon. Its second narration reads its first, as does discourse upon a text. It is Reed, reading Reed and the tradition. A formal metaphor for Reed's mode of writing is perhaps the bebop mode of jazz, as exemplified in that great reedist, Charlie Parker, who sometimes played a chord on the alto saxophone, then repeated and reversed the same chord to hear, if I understand him correctly, what he had just played. Parker is a recurring figure in Reed's works: "Parker, the *houngan* (a word derived from *n'gara gara*)[41] for whom there was no master adept enough to award him the Asson, is born" (*Mumbo Jumbo,* p. 16). Just as Jes Grew, the novel's central character, in searching for its text is seeking to actualize a desire, to "find its speaking or strangle upon its own ineloquence" (p. 34), so too is the search for a text replicated and referred to throughout the second, signifying narration.

What is the status of this desired text? How are we to read Reed? Jes Grew's desire would only be actualized by finding its text. *Mumbo Jumbo*'s parodic use of the presented story of the detective novel states this desire; the solution of the novel's central mystery would be for Jes Grew to find its text. This text, Papa La Bas's allegorical narrative at the Villa Lewaro tells us, is in fact the vast and terrible text of blackness itself, "always already" there: "The Book of Thoth, the sacred Work of the Black Birdman, an assistant to Osiris (If anyone thinks this is 'mystifying the past,'" the narrative intrudes, "kindly check out your local bird book and you will find the sacred Ibis' Ornithological name to be *Threskiornis aethiopicus*" (p. 188). The irony of the mystery structure evident in *Mumbo Jumbo* is that this text, Jes Grew's object of desire, is defined only by its absence. It is never seen or found. At the climax of La Bas's amusingly detailed and long recapitulation of his process of reading the signs of the mystery, as well as the history of the dissemination of the text itself, La Bas instructs his assistant, T. Malice, to unveil the text. The novel reads:

> Go get the Book, T!
>   T Malice goes out to the car and returns with a huge gleaming box covered with snakes and scorpions shaped of sparkling gems.
>   The ladies intake their breath at such a gorgeous display. On the top can be seen the Knights Templar seal; 2 Knights riding Beaseauh, the Templars' piebald horse. T Malice places the box down in the center of the floor and removes the 1st box, an iron box, and the 2nd box, which is bronze and shines so that they have to turn the ceiling lights down. And within this box is a sycamore box and under the sycamore, ebony, and under this ivory, then silver and finally gold and then . . . empty!! (p. 196)

The nature of the text remains undetermined, and indeed indeterminate, as it was at the novel's beginning. Once the signs of its presence have been read, the text disappears in what must be the most humorous anticlimax in the whole of Afro-American fiction.

We can read this gesture against the notion of indeterminacy. Geoffrey H. Hartman, in his study of contemporary literary criticism, gives this definition: "Indeterminacy functions as a bar separating understanding and truth."[42] The bar in *Mumbo Jumbo* is signified by that unbridgeable white space that separates the first narrative mode from the second, the narrative of truth. *Mumbo Jumbo* is a novel about indeterminacy in interpretation itself. The text repeats this theme again and again. In addition to the two narrative voices, the Atonist Path and its Wallflower Order are criticized severely for a foolish emphasis on unity, on the number one, on what the novel calls point. One of the three symbols of the Atonist Order is "the #1" (p. 65). Their leader is called "Hierophant 1" (p. 63). A hierophant, of course, is an expositor. The Atonists' are defined in the antithetical narrative as they who seek to interpret the world through one interpretation: "To some if you owned your own mind you were indeed sick but when you possessed an Atonist mind you were healthy. A mind which sought to interpret the world by using a single loa. Something like filling a milk bottle with an ocean" (p. 24). The novel defines the nature of this urge for the reduction of unity in this way:

> 1st they intimidate the intellectuals by condemning work arising out of their own experience as being 1-dimensional, enraged, non-objective, preoccupied with hate and not universal, universal being a word co-opted by the Catholic Church when the Atonists took over Rome, as a way of measuring every 1 by their deals. (p. 133)

He is an Atonist, the novel maintains consistently, who attempts to tie the sheer plurality of signification to one determinate meaning. Structuralism's reduction to the culture–nature opposition is one such reduction.

In contrast is the spirit of Jes Grew and Papa La Bas. As I have shown, the name La Bas is derived from *Esu-Elegbara*. The Yoruba call *Esu* the god of indeterminacy and of uncertainty. Papa La Bas, in contradistinction to Hierophant 1, has not one but two heads, like the face of the sign: "Papa La bas, noonday Hoodoo, fugitive-hermit, obeah-man, botanist, animal impersonator, 2-headed man, You-Name-Iit" (p. 45). Moreover, he functions—as the detective of Jes Grew, as a decoder, as a sign reader, the man who cracked *de* code—by using his two heads: "Evidence? woman, I dream about it, I feel it, I use my 2 heads. My knockings" (p. 25). La Bas is the critic, engaged in the work, the work of art, refusing to reduce it to a point:

> People in the 60s said they couldn't follow him. (In Santa Cruz the students walked out.) What's your point? they asked in Seattle whose central point, the Space Needle, is invisible from time to time. What are you driving at? they would say in Detroit in the 1950s. In the 40s he haunted the stacks of a ghost library. (p. 215)

While arguing ironically with Abdul, the black Muslim who subsequently burns the Text of Thoth, La Bas critiques Abdul's Black Aesthetic in terms identical to his critique of the Atonists:

> Where does that leave the ancient vodun aesthetic: pantheistic, becoming, 1 which bountifully permits 1000s of spirits, as many as the imagination can hold. Infinite Spirits of Gods. So many that it would take a book larger than the Koran and the Bible, the Tibetan Book of the Dead and all of the holy books in the world to list, and still room would have to be made for more. (p. 35; see also Abdul's letter to La Bas, pp. 201-203)

It is indeterminacy, the sheer plurality of meaning, the very play of the signifier itself, which *Mumbo Jumbo* celebrates. *Mumbo Jumbo* addresses the *play* of the black literary tradition and, as a parody, is a play upon that same tradition. Its central character, Jes Grew, cannot be reduced by the Atonists, as they complain: "It's nothing we can bring into focus or categorize; once we call it 1 thing it forms into something else" (p. 4). Just as La Bas the detective is the text's figure for indeterminacy (paradoxically because he is a detective), so too is Jes Grew's nature indeterminate: its text is never a presence, and it disappears when its text disappears, as surely as does Charlotte when Doctor Peter Pick recites, during his reverse-minstrel plantation routine, an incantation from Papa La Bas's *Blue Black: A Speller* (pp. 104–105, 199).

Even the idea of one transcendent subject, Jes Grew's text, the text of blackness itself, *Mumbo Jumbo* criticizes. When the poet Nathan Brown asks the Haitian *houngan* Benoit how to catch Jes Grew, Benoit replies: "Don't ask me how to catch Jes Grew. Ask Louis Armstrong, Bessie Smith, your poets, your painters, your musicians, ask them how to catch it." Jes Grew also manifests itself in more curious forms:

> The Rhyming Fool who sits in Ré-mōte Mississippi and talks "crazy" for hours. The dazzling parodying punning mischievous pre-Joycean style-play of your Cakewalking your Calinda your Minstrelsy give-and-take of the ultra-absurd. Ask the people who put wax paper over combs and breathe through them. In other words, Nathan, I am saying Open-Up-To-Right-Here and then you will have something coming from your experience that the whole world will admire and need. (p. 152)

Jes Grew's text, in other words, is not a transcendent signified, but must be produced in a dynamic process and manifested in discrete forms, as in black music and black speech acts. "The Blues is a Jes Grew, as James Weldon Johnson surmised. Jazz was a *Jes Grew* which followed the Jes Grew of Ragtime. Slang is *Jes Grew* too," Papa La Bas tells his 1960s audience in his annual lecture on the Harlem Renaissance (p. 215).

"Is this the end of Jes Grew?" the narrative questions when we learn that its text does not exist. "Jes Grew has no end and no beginning," the text replies (p. 204). The echoes here are intentional: Reed echoes Ellison or rather Ellison's echo of T. S. Eliot. "In my end is my beginning," writes Eliot in "East Coker," "In my beginning is my end." The end, writes Ellison, "is in the beginning and lies far ahead" (*Invisible Man,* p. 9). Reed signifies upon Ellison's gesture of closure here, and that of the entire Afro-American literary tradition, by positing an open-endedness of interpretation, of the play of signifiers, just as his and Ellison's works both signify upon the idea of the transcendent signified of the black tradition, the text of blackness itself.

The tradition's classic text on the "Blackness of Blackness" is found in the prologue of *Invisible Man* and bears full citation:

"Brothers and sisters, my text this morning is the 'Blackness of Blackness.' "

And a congregation of voices answered: "That blackness is most black, brother, most black . . ."

"In the beginning . . ."

"At the very start," they cried.

". . . there was blackness . . ."

"Preach it . . ."

". . . and the sun . . ."

"The sun, Lawd . . ."

". . . was bloody red . . ."

"Red . . ."

"Now black is . . ." the preacher shouted.

"Bloody . . ."

"I said black is . . ."

"Preach it, brother . . ."

". . . an' black ain't . . ."

"Red, Lawd, red: He said it's red!"

"Amen, brother . . ."

"Black will git you . . ."

"Yes, it will . . ."

". . . an' black won't . . ."

"Naw, it won't!"

"It do . . ."

"It do, Lawd . . ."

". . . an' it don't."

"Halleluiah . . ."

". . . It'll put you, glory, glory, Oh my Lawd, in the WHALE'S BELLY."

"Preach it, dear brother . . ."

". . . an' make you tempt . . ."
"Good God a-mighty!"
"Old Aunt Nelly!"
"Black will make you . . ."
"Black . . ."
". . . or black will un-make you."
"Ain't it the truth, Lawd?"
  (pp. 12-13)

This sermon is a critique both of Melville's passage in *Moby Dick* on "the blackness of darkness" and of the sign of blackness as represented by the alogorithm *signified*/signifier.[43] As Ellison's text states, "Black is" and "Black ain't," "It do, Lawd," "an' it don't." Ellison parodies here the notion of essence, of the supposedly natural relationship between the symbol and that symbolized. The vast and terrible text of blackness, we realize, has no essence; rather, it is signified into being by a signifier. The trope of blackness in Western discourse has signified absence at least since Plato. Plato, in the *Phaedrus,* recounts the myth of Theuth (*Mumbo Jumbo*'s Thoth) and the introduction of writing into Egypt. Along the way, Plato has Socrates draw upon the figure of blackness as a metaphor for one of the three divisions of the soul, that of badness. Writes Plato, "The other is crooked of frame, a massive jumble of a creature, with thick short neck, snub nose, black skin, and gray eyes; hot-blooded, consorting with wantonness and vainglory; shaggy of ear, deaf, and hard to control with whip and goad" (*Phaedrus,* 253d–254a; for the myth of Theuth, see 274c–275b). Reed's use of the myth of Thoth is, of course, not accidental or arbitrary; he repeats and inverts Plato's dialogue, salient point for salient point, even down to Socrates's discourse on the excesses of the dance, which is a theme of *Mumbo Jumbo.* (*Phaedrus,* 259b–259e). It is not too much to say that *Mumbo Jumbo* is one grand signifying riff on the *Phaedrus,* parodying it through the hidden polemic.

Both Ellison and Reed, then, critique the received idea of blackness as a negative essence, as a natural, transcendent signified; but implicit in such a critique is an equally thorough critique of blackness as a presence, which is merely another transcendent signified. Such a critique, therefore, is a critique of the structure of the sign itself and constitutes a profound critique. The Black Arts movement's grand gesture was to make of the trope of blackness a trope of presence. That movement willed it to be, however, a transcendent presence. Ellison's "text for today, the 'Blackness of Blackness,' " analyzes this gesture, just as surely as does Reed's text of blackness, the "Sacred Book of Thoth." In literature, blackness is produced in the text itself only through a complex process of signification. There can be no transcendent blackness, for it cannot and does not exist beyond manifestations in specific figures. Jes Grew, put simply, cannot conjure its texts; texts, in the broadest sense of this term (Charlie Parker's music, Ellison's fictions, Romare Bearden's collages, etc.), conjure Jes Grew.

Reed has in *Mumbo Jumbo* signified upon Ellison's critique of the central presupposition of the Afro-American literary tradition, by drawing upon Ellison's trope as a central theme of the plot of *Mumbo Jumbo* and making explicit Ellison's implicit critique of the nature of the sign itself, of a transcendent signified, an essence, which supposedly exists prior to its figuration. Their formal relationship can only be suggested by the relation of modernism to post-modernism, two overworked terms. Blackness exists, but only as a function of its signifiers. Reed's open-ended structure and his stress on the indeterminacy of the text demand that we, as critics, in the act of reading, produce a text's signifying structure. For Reed, as for his great precursor, Ellison, figuration is indeed "the Nigger's occupation."

IV

Reed's signifying relation to Ellison is exemplified in his poem "Dualism: in ralph ellison's invisible man":

> i am outside of
> history. i wish
> i had some peanuts; it
> looks hungry there in
> its cage.

> i am inside of
> history. its
> hungrier than i
> thot.[44]

The figure of history here is the Signifying Monkey; the poem signifies upon that repeated trope of dualism figured initially in black discourse in W. E. B. Du Bois's essay "Of Our Spiritual Strivings," which forms the first chapter of *The Souls of Black Folk*. The dualism parodied by Reed's poem is that represented in the epilogue of *Invisible Man:* "now I know men are different and that all life is divided and that only in division is there true health" (p. 499). For Reed, this belief in the reality of dualism spells death. Ellison here has refigured Du Bois's trope, which bears full citation:

> After the Egyptian and Indian, the Greek and Roman, the Teuton and Mongolian, the Negro is a sort of seventh son, born with a veil, and gifted with second-sight in this American world,—a world which yields him no true self-consciousness, but only lets him see himself through the revelation of the other world. It is a peculiar sensation, this double-consciousness, this sense of always looking at one's self through the eyes of others, measuring one's soul by the tape of a world that looks on in amused contempt and pity. One ever feels his twoness,—an American, a Negro; two souls, two thoughts, two unreconciled strivings; two warring ideals in one dark body, whose dogged strength alone keeps it from being torn asunder.
>
> The history of the American Negro is the history of this strife,— this longing to attain self-conscious manhood, to merge his double self into a better and truer self. In this merging he wishes neither of the older selves to be lost.[45]

Reed's poem parodies profoundly both the figure of the black as outsider and the figure of the divided self. For, he tells us, even these are only tropes, figures of speech, rhetorical constructs like "double-consciousness," and not some preordained reality or thing. To read these figures literally, Reed tells us, is to be duped by figuration, just like the Signified Lion. Reed has secured his place in the canon precisely by his critique of the received, repeated tropes peculiar to that very canon. His works are the grand works of critical signification.

Notes

Chapter 1

1. William K. Wimsatt and Cleanth Brooks, *Literary Criticism: A Short History* (New York: Knopf, 1969), p. 360.
2. *De la littérature des nègres, ou recherches sur leurs facultés intellectuelles, leurs qualités morales, et leur littérature* (Paris: Maradan, 1808), p. 140.
3. Eugene Parker Chase, *Our Revolutionary Forefathers, The Letters of Francois Marquis de Barbé-Marbois during His Residence in the United States as Secretary of the French Legation, 1779–1884* (New York: Duffield, 1929), pp. 84–85.
4. *Notes on the State of Virginia* (London: Stockdale, 1787), book II, p. 196.
5. These lines, along with an engraving of Ira Aldridge by T. Hollis, were combined to form a popular nineteenth-century broadside. The lines are from Act 2, Scene 1.
6. Phillis Wheatley, *Poems* (Philadelphia: A. Bell, 1773), p. vii.
7. *Letters of the Late Ignatius Sancho, an African* (London: J. Nichols and C. Dilly, 1783), p. vii.
8. Sancho, pp. xiv–xvi.
9. Charles Ball, *Fifty Years in Chains; Or, The Life of an American Slave* (New York: H. Dayton, 1858), p. 3.
10. Introduction, *My Bondage and My Freedom* (New York: Miller, Orton, and Mulligan, 1855), pp. xvii–xxxi.
11. *New York Tribune,* June 10, 1845, p. 1. Rpt. in *Liberator,* May 30, 1845, p. 97.
12. On Amo, see Wolfram Suchier, "A. W. Amo, Ein Mohr als Stu-

dent und Privatdozent der Philosophie in Halle, Wittenburg and Iena, 1727–1740," *Akademische Rundschau,* Leipzig (1916) and "Weiteres über den Mohren Amo," *Altsachen Zeitschrift des Altsachenbundes für Heimatschutz und Heimatkunde,* Holminden, Nos. 1–2 (1981); Norbert Lochner, "Anton-Wilhelm Amo," *Transactions of the Historical Society of Ghana,* vol. III (1958); William Abraham, "The Life and Times of Anton-Wilhelm Amo," *Transactions of the Historical Society of Ghana,* vol. VII (1964); and Paulin J. Hountondji, "An African Philosopher in Germany in the Eighteenth Century," in *African Philosophy: Myth and Reality* (Bloomington: Indiana University Press, 1983), chapter V. Amo's work was translated into English in 1968 under the title *Antonius Gulielmus Amo Afer of Axim in Ghana, Translation of His Works* (Martin Luther University: Halle).

13. On Job-Ben Solomon, see Charles T. Davis and Henry Louis Gates, Jr., *The Slave's Narrative* (New York: Oxford University Press, 1985), pp. 2–3.

14. William Bosman, *A New and Accurate Description of the Coast of Guinea* (1705; New York: Barnes and Noble, 1967), pp. 146, 147.

15. Morgan Godwyn, *The Negro's and Indians' Advocate . . . in Our Plantations* (London: the author, 1680), pp. 3, 13.

16. This and other statutes about literacy and the slave are reprinted in *The American Slave Code.*

17. David Hume, "Of National Characters," *The Philosophical Works,* ed. Thomas Hill Green and Thomas Hodge Grose, 4 vols. (Darmstadt, 1964), 3:252, n. 1.

18. Immanuel Kant, *Observations on the Feeling of the Beautiful and Sublime,* trans. John T. Goldthwait (Berkeley: University of California Press, 1960), pp. 111, 113.

19. G. W. F. Hegel, *The Philosophy of History* (New York: Dover, 1956), pp. 91–99.

20. Ralph Waldo Emerson, "Emancipation in the British West Indies," in *Selected Writings of Emerson, ed. Brooks Atkinson* (New York: Modern Library, 1950), p. 855. The speech was delivered on August 1, 1844.

21. "Majors and Minors," *North American Review,* June 27, 1896, p. 630.

22. W. E. B. DuBois, "Negro Art," *Crisis* 22 (June 1921): 55–56.

23. *New York Times,* January 26, 1925, p. 3.

24. W. E. B. DuBois, "The Social Origins of American Negro Art," *Modern Quarterly* 3 (Autumn 1925): p. 53.

25. *Understanding the New Black Poetry* (New York: Morrow, 1972). All subsequent citations are from pp. 3–69.
26. *Long Black Song* (Charlottesville: University of Virginia Press, 1972).
27. *Singers of Daybreak* (Washington, D.C.: Howard University Press, 1974).
28. *The Way of the New World* (Garden City, N.J.: Doubleday, 1975).
29. Raymond Williams, "Base and Superstructure in Marxist Cultural Theory," New Left Review 82 (December 1973): 3–16.
30. Baker's theory of repudiation is found in *Long Black Song*. See note 26. Stepto's theory of "authentication" is elaborated in *From Behind the Veil: A Study of Afro-American Narrative* (Urbana: University of Illinois Press, 1979).
31. See the article "Arlequin" and "Marmontel" in *The Oxford Companion to French Literature,* edited by Sir Paul Harvey and J. E. Heseltine (Oxford: Clarendon Press, 1959), pp. 27, 456. Marmontel's theory of the origins of Harlequin's blackness is found in his collection of essays, *Éléments de littérature* (1787). See also Pierre Louis Ducharte, *The Italian Comedy,* trans. Randolph T. Weaver (New York: Dover, 1966), chapters 2 and 4, and pp. 124, 135.
32. Jules de Gaultier, cited in René Girard, *Deceit, Desire, and the Novel: Self and Other in Literary Structure,* trans. Yvonne Frecerro (Baltimore: Johns Hopkins University Press, 1965), p. 5.
33. Girard, p. 3.
34. Jean-Paul Sartre, *What Is Literature?* (London: Methuen, 1970), pp. 57–59.
35. Edward Said, "On Repetition," in *The World, The Text, and the Critic* (Cambridge: Harvard University Press, 1983), pp. 111–26.
36. Ralph Ellison, "The Essential Ellison (Interview)," *Y'Bird* 1, no. 1 (1978): 130–59.
37. Quoted in Charles Keil, *Urban Blues* (Chicago: University of Chicago Press, 1966), p. 169.

Chapter 2

1. *Daily Advertiser,* January 18, 1773, p. 1.
2. Samuel Estwick, *Considerations on the Negro Cause, Commonly So Called* (London: J. Dodsley, 1772), p. 1.
3. *Daily Advertiser,* January 18, 1773, p. 1.
4. Samuel Estwick, *Considerations on the Negro Cause Commonly*

So Called, 2nd ed. (London: J. Dodsley, 1773); subsequent references will be to this edition.

5. Estwick.
6. David Hume, cited in Estwick, p. 77.
7. Estwick.
8. Estwick, p. 78.
9. Estwick.
10. Estwick.
11. Estwick.
12. Estwick, pp. 80–81.
13. See especially R. S. Crane, "English neo-classical criticism," in *Dictionary of World Literature,* ed. J. T. Shipley (New York: Philosophical Books, 1943); R. S. Crane, ed., *Critics and Criticism, Ancient and Modern* (Chicago: University of Chicago Press, 1952); R. S. Crane, "On Writing the History of English Criticism, 1650–1800," *University of Toronto Quarterly* 22 (1953): 376–91.
14. Robert Marsh, "Neo-classical Poetics," in *Princeton Encyclopedia of Poetry and Poetics,* ed. Alex Preminger (Princeton University Press, 1974), p. 560; cf. Crane, "On Writing the History of English Criticism," pp. 380–92.
15. See William Temple, "Upon Poetry," in *Critical Essays of the Seventeenth Century,* ed. J. E. Spingarn (Oxford: Oxford University Press, 1908–9), vol. III, 104–5.
16. René Wellek, *A History of Modern Criticism: 1750–1950* (London: Jonathan Cape, 1970), pp. 124–25. Temple's correction is to be found in his essay "Upon Poetry," written in 1690; see note 15.
17. Joseph Wharton, *Essay on the Writings and Genius of Pope* (London, 1756), vol. 1, p. 5.
18. Oliver Goldsmith, *An Enquiry into the Present State of Polite Learning* (London: R. & J. Dodsley, 1759), p. 95. In subsequent editions, Goldsmith deleted the whole of this chapter (7), cf. his article in the *Critical Review* 9 (1760): 10–19.
19. David Hume, *Essays: Moral, Political, and Literary,* ed. T. H. Green and T. H. Gross (London: Longmans, 1875), vol. I, p. 252.
20. Henry Home Kames, *Sketches of a History of Man* (Edinburgh: Creech, 1774), vol. I, p. 12.
21. Robert Wood, *An Essay on the Original Genius and Writings of Homer* (London: T. Payne & E. Elmsly, 1775), p. 15.
22. Robert Lowth, *De sacra poesi Hebraeorum* (Oxford: E. Typographeo Clarendoniano, 1753); an English translation appeared in 1787.
23. Cf. Winthrop Jordan's discussion of "Environmentalism and Rev-

olutionary Ideology" in *White over Black: American Attitudes Towards the Negro, 1550–1812* (Chapel Hill: University of North Carolina Press, 1968), pp. 287–94.

24. Jordan, p. 288.
25. Jordan, p. 289.
26. James Otis, *The Rights of the British Colonies Asserted and Proved* (Boston: Edes & Gill, 1764), p. 29.
27. John Wesley, *Thoughts upon Slavery* (Philadelphia: Joseph Cruckshank, 1774), p. 16.
28. Levi Hart, *Liberty Described and Recommended* (Hartford: Eben Watson, 1775), p. 16.
29. [David Cooper], *A Serious Address to the Rules of America, on the Inconsistency of Their Conduct Respecting Slavery* (Trenton: J. Phillips, 1783), pp. 12–13.
30. Rush here cites "le Poivre," referring obviously to [Pierre Le Poivre], *Travels of a Philosopher: Or, Observation on the Manners and Arts of Various Nations in Africa and Asia . . . Translated from the French of M. Le Poivre* (London: T. Becket, 1769).
31. *The Spectator,* vol. 1, no. 11, contains a summary, from Lign's Account of Barbados, of the legendary "History of Inkle and Yarico," pp. 49–51.
32. Benjamin Rush, *An Address to the Inhabitants of the British Settlements in America Upon Slave Keeping* (Philadelphia: John Dunlap, 1773), p. 4.
33. Rush, *An Address,* p. 10.
34. Jordan, *White over Black,* p. 306. On Nisbet's mental health, see Samuel Coats, *Notebook on Cases of Insanity,* Medical Library of the Pennsylvania Hospital, Philadelphia; *The Autobiography of Benjamin Rush,* ed. George Corner (Princeton: Princeton University Press, 1948), p. 83 *n.*
35. [Richard Nisbet], *Slavery Not Forbidden by Scripture; Or, a Defence of the West India Planters, By a West Indian* (Philadelphia: John Dunlap, 1773).
36. [Nisbet], p. 21.
37. [Nisbet], p. 23.
38. [Benjamin Rush], *A Vindication of the Address, To the Inhabitants of the British Settlements, on the Slavery of the Negroes in America, In Answer to a Pamphlet entitled, "Slavery Not Forbidden by Scripture; Or a Defense of the West-India Planters from the Aspersions thrown against them by the author of the Address." By a Pennsylvanian* (Philadelphia: John Dunlap, 1773).
39. [Rush], *A Vindication,* pp. 24–25.

40. Cf. Loren Eisley, "Race: The Reflections of a Biological Historian," in *Science and the Concept of Race,* ed. Margaret Mead (New York: Columbia University Press, 1968), p. 84.
41. *Personal Slavery Established, By the Suffrages of Custom and Right Reason. Being a Full Answer to the gloomy and visionary Reveries, of all the fanatical and enthusiastical Writers on that Subject* (Philadelphia: John Dunlap, 1773), title page.
42. [Rush], *A Vindication,* p. 31.
43. [Rush], *A Vindication,* p. 53.
44. Cf. Anthony Benezet, letter to the Archbishop of Canterbury (1758), in "Letters of Anthony Benezet," *Journal of Negro History* 2 (January 1917): 83.
45. See Gregary Rigsby, "Form and Content in Phillis Wheatley's Elegies," *CLA Journal* 30, no. 2 (December 1975): 248–57. Julian Mason, ed., *The Poems of Phillis Wheatley* (Chapel Hill: University of North Carolina Press, 1966), pp. xxii–xxvi.
46. Mason, pp. 3–4, 7.
47. See *Philip Vickers Fithian: Journal and Letters 1767–1774,* ed. John R. Williams (Princeton: Princeton University Press, 1900), p. 119; *Universal Magazine* (September 1773): 153.
48. Bernard Romans, *A Concise Natural History of East and West Florida* (New York, 1775), vol. I, p. 105.
49. Mason, p. 7; *Universal Magazine* (September 1773).
50. See the review of B. B. Thatcher's *Memoir of Phillis Wheatley, A Native African and a Slave* (Boston: Geo. W. Light, 1834) in *The Liberator,* March 22, 1834.
51. Indeed, perhaps the most sustained impulse in the history of the criticism of Afro-American creative writing has been the determinism to dismiss Jefferson as a racist. See Henry Louis Gates, Jr., "Preface to Blackness: Text and Pre-Text," in *The Reconstruction of Instruction,* ed. Robert Burns Stepto and Dexter Fisher (New York: Modern Language Association, 1978), pp. 44–71.
52. See "Article VII," *Monthly Review* 49 (July–December 1773): 457–58; Richard Nisbet, *The Capacity of Negroes,* p. 3; Thomas Jefferson, "Notes on the State of Virginia, Query XIV," in *Thomas Jefferson: Revolutionary Philosopher,* ed. John S. Pancake (Woodbury, N.Y.: Barron's Educational Series, 1976), pp. 308–14.
53. As I hope to demonstrate implicitly, the figure of metaphor and metonym blur when utilized consistently to describe one phenomenon.
54. Except when indicated otherwise, the biographical details of Wheatley's life come directly from the memoir written by Mar-

garetta Matilda Odell for the 1834 reprinting of the 1773 edition of *Poems on Various Subjects, Religious and Moral;* see Margaretta Matilda Odell, "Memoir," in *Memoir and Poems of Phillis Wheatley* (Boston: Geo. W. Light, 1834), pp. 9–29. See also William H. Robinson, *Phillis Wheatley in the Black American Beginnings* (Detroit: Broadside Press, 1975); Mason, pp. xi–xlviii; M. A. Richmond, *Bid the Vassal Soar* (Washington, D.C.: Howard University Press, 1974); Nathaniel B. Shurtleff, "Phillis Wheatley, the Negro Slave Poet," *Boston Daily Advertiser,* December 21, 1863, rpt. *Proceedings of the Massachusetts Historical Society* 7 (1863–64): 9.

55. As Benjamin Brawley suggested in 1918, "the bibliography of the works of Phillis Wheatley is now a study in itself." *The Negro in Literature and Art* (New York: Duffield, 1918), p. 161.

56. See William H. Robinson, "Phillis Wheatley in London," *CLA Journal* 21, no. 2 (December 1977): 187–202.

57. See Mason, pp. xv–xvi.

58. Dorothy Porter, "Early American Negro Writings: A Bibliographical Study," *PBSA* 39 (3rd quarter 1945): 261–63.

59. Ebenezer Pemberton, *Heaven the Residence of Saints* (London: E. & C. Dilly, 1771), appendix.

60. Mason, p. 67.

61. See Seymour Gross and John E. Hardy, eds., *Images of the Negro in American Literature* (Chicago: University of Chicago Press, 1966), pp. 3–4; LeRoi Jones, *Home: Social Essays* (New York: William Morrow, 1966), pp. 105–6; Addison Gayle, Jr., "The Function of Black Literature at the Present Time," in *The Black Aesthetic,* ed. Addison Gayle, Jr. (New York: Doubleday, 1971), p. 409; Nathaniel Huggins, *The Harlem Renaissance* (New York: Oxford University Press, 1971), p. 199.

62. I mean here *misinformed* reading and not the Bloomian sense of that term.

63. Robinson, *Phillis Wheatley,* p. 47.

64. Quoted in Robinson, *Phillis Wheatley,* pp. 40–41.

65. Phillis Wheatley to Arbour Tanner, Boston, May 19, 1772, in Nathaniel Shurtleff, "Phillis Wheatley, the Negro Slave Poet," *Proceedings of the Massachusetts Historical Society* 7 (1863–64): 273–74.

66. First printed in Robert C. Kuncio, "Some Unpublished Poems of Phillis Wheatley," *New England Quarterly* 43 (June 1970): 288–90.

67. Kuncio, *ibid.*

68. *Royal American Magazine* 1 (December 1774): 473–74; 2 (January 1775): 34–35.
69. *Royal American Magazine.*
70. See Harold Blodgett, *Samuel Occum* (Hanover: Dartmouth College Publications, 1935), pp. 119, 148; Kenneth Silverman, "Four New Letters by Phillis Wheatley," *Early American Literature* 8 (Winter 1974): 259.
71. *Connecticut Journal,* April 1, 1774, p. 1.
72. *Connecticut Journal.*
73. Cf. Phillis Wheatley to the Reverend Samuel Hopkins, Boston, February 9, 1774, in Benjamin Quarles, "A Phillis Wheatley Letter," *Journal of Negro History* 24 (1949): 463–64; Boston, May 6, 1774, in Chamberlain Collection of Letters, A.6.20, Boston Public Library; and Wheatley to Arbour Tanner, Boston, May 19, 1772, in *Proceedings* 7 (1863–64), 273–74.
74. Rigsby, pp. 248–57.
75. Rigsby, p. 248.
76. *Ibid.*
77. J. C. Bailey develops this distinction in *English Elegies* (London: John Lane, 1900), p. xxix.
78. *Ibid.*
79. Cf. A. L. Bennett, "The Principal Rhetorical Conventions in the Renaissance Personal Elegy," *Studies in Philology* 51 (1954): 107–26.
80. Robert Henson, "Form and Content of the Puritan Funeral Elegy," *American Literature* 32 (1960): 111.
81. Rigsby, p. 250.
82. *Ibid.*
83. These five include "On Virtue," which she wrote in free verse but ended with an heroic couplet; "To the University of Cambridge in New England," written in blank verse; "Ode to Neptune," composed in three stanzas of six lines each, four of which are in iambic tetrameter couplets, followed consistently by an heroic couplet; "Hymn to Humanity," written in six stanzas of six lines each, and each stanza following a form of iambic tetrameter couplet, followed by a line of iambic trimeter, followed by an iambic tetrameter couplet, followed again by an iambic trimeter line which invariably rhymes with the third line of the stanza; and "A Farewell to America," in ballad stanza. Cf. Mason, p. xxix.
84. Vernon Loggins, *The Negro Author* (New York: Columbia University Press, 1931), p. 24.
85. Loggins, p. 27.

86. Loggins, p. 373, *n.* 75; cf. Mason, p. xxxiii.
87. William B. Cairns, *A History of American Literature* (New York: Oxford University Press, 1930), p. 136.

Chapter 3

1. See Marion Wilson Starling's *The Slave Narrative* (Boston: G. K. Hall, 1981); and William L. Andrews, *To Tell a Free Story: The First Century of Afro-American Autobiography, 1760–1865* (Urbana: University of Illinois Press, 1986) for the fullest treatments of the slave's narrative.
2. Claudio Guillen, *Literature As System: Essays Toward the Theory of Literary History* (Princeton University Press, 1971), pp. 71–106 and especially pp. 135–58. Quotations are from p. 81.
3. George R. Graham, "Black Letters; or Uncle Tom-Foolery in Literature," *Graham's Illustrated Magazine of Literature, Romance, Art, and Fashion* 42 (February 1853): 209.
4. Marion Wilson Starling, *The Slave Narrative: Its Place in American Literary History,* dissertation New York University, 1946, pp. 47–48.
5. "Narrative of Frederick Douglass," *Littell's Living Age* (April 1, 1846): p. 47.
6. *New York Tribune,* June 10, 1845, p. 1; reprinted in *The Liberator,* May 30, 1845, p. 97.
7. *Lynn Pioneer;* reprinted in *The Liberator,* May 30, 1845, p. 86.
8. See especially John Blassingame, "Black Autobiography As History and Literature," *Black Scholar* 5, no. 4 (December 1973–January 1974): 2–9; and his *Slave Testimony: Two Centuries of Letters, Speeches, Interviews, and Autobiographies* (Baton Rouge: Louisiana State University Press, 1977).
9. Robert Scholes and Robert Kellogg, *The Nature of Narrative* (New York: Oxford University Press, 1966), p. 76.
10. Stephen Butterfield, *Black Autobiography in America* (Amherst: University of Massachusetts Press, 1974), p. 36.
11. John Thompson, *The Life of John Thompson, a Fugitive Slave, Containing His History of Twenty-Five Years in Bondage and His Providential Escape* (Worcester, 1856), p. 113.
12. Butterfield, *Black Autobiography,* p. 37.
13. Roman Jakobson and Morris Halle, *Fundamentals of Language* (The Hague: Mouton, 1971), pp. 4, 47–49.
14. Claude Lévi-Strauss, *Totemism* (New York: Penguin, 1969), p. 130.
15. What has this rather obvious model of human thought to do with

the study of mundane literature generally and with the study of Afro-American literature specifically? It has forced us to alter irrevocably certain long-held assumptions about the relationship between sign and referent, between signifier and signified. It has forced us to remember what queries we intended to resolve when we first organized a discourse in a particular way. What's more, this rather simple formulation has taught us to recognize texts where we find them and to read these texts as they demand to be read. Yet we keepers of black critical activity have yet to graft fifty years of systematic thinking about literature onto the consideration of our own. The study of Afro-American folklore, for instance, remains preoccupied with unresolvable matters of genesis or with limitless catalogues and motif indices. Afraid that Brer Rabbit is merely a trickster or that Anansi spiders merely spin webs, we reduce these myths to their simplest thematic terms—the perennial relationship between the wily, persecuted black and the not-too-clever, persecuting white. This reduction belies our own belief in the philosophical value of these mental constructs. We admit, albeit inadvertently, a nagging suspicion that these are the primitive artifacts of childish minds, grappling with a complex Western world and its languages, three thousand years and a world removed. These myths, as the slave narratives would, did not so much narrate as they did convey a value system; they functioned, much like a black sermon, as a single sign. The use of binary opposition, for instance, allows us to perceive much deeper meanings than a simplistic racial symbolism allows. Refusal to use sophisticated analysis on our own literature smacks of a symbolic inferiority complex as blatant as the use of skin lighteners and hair straighteners.

16. Fredric Jameson, *The Prison-House of Language: A Critical Account of Structuralism and Russian Formalism* (Princeton: Princeton University Press, 1972), pp. 113, 135, citing Troubetskoy's *Principes de phonologie*. See also Jonathan Culler, *Structuralist Poetics: Structuralism, Linguistics, and the Study of Literature* (Ithaca: Cornell University Press, 1975), pp. 93, 225–27; Roland Barthes, *S/Z, An Essay*, trans. Richard Miller (New York: Hill and Wang, 1975), p. 24.

17. Frederick Douglass, *Narrative* (Boston: Anti-Slavery Office, 1845), p. 1. All subsequent quotes, unless indicated, are from pp. 1–7.

18. There is overwhelming textual evidence that Douglass was a consummate stylist who, contrary to popular myth, learned the craft of the essayist self-consciously. The importance of Caleb Bing-

ham's *The Columbian Orator* (Boston: Manning and Loring, 1797) to Douglass's art is well established. John Blassingame is convinced of Douglass's use of Bingham's rhetorical advice in his writing, especially of antitheses. (Personal interview with John Blassingame, May 7, 1976.) For an estimation of the role of language in political struggle of antebellum blacks, see Alexander Crummell, "The English Language in Liberia," in his *The Future of Africa* (New York: Scribners, 1862), pp. 9–57.

19. See also Nancy T. Clasby, "Frederick Douglass's *Narrative:* A Content Analysis," *CLA Journal* 14 (1971): 244.
20. Clasby, p. 245.
21. Douglass, p. 77.
22. Michael Cooke, "Modern Black Autobiography in the Tradition," in *Romanticism, Vistas, Instances, and Continuities,* ed. David Thorburn and Geoffrey Hartman (Ithaca: Cornell University Press, 1973), p. 258.
23. Douglass, pp. 13–15.
24. Douglass, p. 30.

Chapter 4

1. This chapter was published as a review of the following books: Peter Walker, *Moral Choices: Memory, Desire, and Imagination in Nineteenth-Century American Letters* (Baton Rouge: Louisiana University Press, 1979); *The Frederick Douglass Papers, Series One: Speeches, Debates, and Interviews* (volume 1, 1841–46), edited by John W. Blassingame and Associates (New Haven: Yale University Press, 1979); Nathan Irvin Huggins, *Slave and Citizen: The Life of Frederick Douglass* (Boston: Little, Brown, 1980); Dickson J. Preston, *Young Frederick Douglass: The Maryland Years* (Baltimore: The Johns Hopkins University Press, 1980).

Chapter 5

1. All quotations from *Our Nig* are taken from Harriet E. Wilson, *Our Nig; or, Sketches from the Life of a Free Black* (New York: Random House, 1983).
2. The following citations of reviews of Stowe's works are taken from Elizabeth Ammons, *Critical Essays on Harriet Beecher Stowe* (Boston: G. K. Gall, 1980).
3. See Sterling A. Brown, *The Negro in American Fiction* (Washington, D.C.: Association in Negro Folk Education, 1937); Jeanette Tandy, "Pro-Slavery Propaganda in American Fiction of the

Fifties," *South Atlantic Quarterly* 21 (1922): 41–50, 170–78; James Kinney, *Amalgamation: Race, Sex, and Rhetoric in the Nineteenth-Century American Novel* (Westport, Conn.: Greenwood, 1985).

Chapter 6

1. The following etymological theory derives in part from *The Oxford Dictionary on Historical Principles* and in part from Theodore Thass-Thienemann, *Understanding the Symbolic Meaning of Language* and *Understanding the Unconscious Meaning of Language,* vols. I and II of *The Interpretation of Language* (New York: Jason Aroonson, 1968, 1973), esp. pp. 55–59.

2. George Steiner, *After Babel: Aspects of Language and Translation* (New York: Oxford University Press, 1975), pp. 21, 46–47. This note was accidentally omitted from the first published version of this essay, as was proper citation of Dr. Steiner's argument.

3. Derek Walcott, "What the Twilight Says: An Overture," in *Dream on Monkey Mountain and Other Plays* (London: Jonathan Cape, 1972). All subsequent quotes are from pp. 3–40.

4. James A. Harrison, "Negro English," *Anglia* 7 (1884): 232–79; J. L. Dillard, *Black English: Its History and Usage in the U.S.* (New York: Vintage, 1973), pp. 61, 113, 187–88.

5. Anthony Appiah, "Editorial," *Theoria to Theory* 8, no. 2 (1974): 202.

6. Wole Soyinka, "The Fourth Stage: Through the Mysteries of Ogun to the Origin of Yoruba Tragedy," in *Myth, Literature, and the African World* (Cambridge: Cambridge University Press, 1976), pp. 140–61.

7. James Weldon Johnson, *The Book of American Negro Poetry* (New York: Harcourt, 1931), preface, pp. 9–48.

8. Johnson, pp. 3–8.

9. William Stanley Braithwaite, "Some Contemporary Poets of the Negro Race," *Crisis* 17 (April 1919): 275–80.

10. This argument, interestingly enough, would remain central to black political thought in legal attempts to strike down racist legislation.

11. For an excellent historical account, see Mary Berry and John Blassingame, "Africa, Slavery, and the Roots of Contemporary Black Culture," *Massachusetts Review* 18 (1977): 501–16.

12. Richard Ohmann, "Prolegomena to the Analysis of Prose Style," in *The Theory of the Novel,* Philip Stevick, ed. (New York: Free Press, 1967), pp. 190–208.

13. Countee Cullen, *Caroling Dusk* (New York: Harper, 1927), foreword, pp. vii-xii.

14. Cf. Matthew Arnold, *Culture and Anarchy* (London: Smith, Elder and Co., 1869).

15. Cf. F. R. Leavis, *New Bearings in English Poetry: A Study of the Contemporary Situation* (Ann Arbor: University of Michigan Press, 1964), p. 16: "Poetry matters because of the kind of poet who is more alive than other people, more alive in his own age. He is, as it were, at the most conscious point of the race in his time." Also p. 42: "Losing all touch with the finer consciousness of the age it would be, not only irresponsible, but anaemic, as, indeed, Victorian poetry so commonly is." Cf. I. A. Richards, *Principles of Literary Criticism* (New York: Harcourt, 1934), p. 61: "He is the point at which the growth of the mind shows itself." Cf. W. B. Yeats, *Essays* (New York: Macmillan, 1924) p. 330: "In literature, from the lack of that spoken word which knits us to the normal man, we have lost in personality, in our delight in the whole man—blood, imagination, intellect, running together."

16. Cf. Ernest Boyd, "The New Negro," *The Independent* (December 1925): 8–11.

17. We are forced to wonder aloud where in dialect poetry, with the notable exception of Sterling Brown, a black poet used his medium as effectively as did Eliot in *Sweeney Agonistes,* where he uses ridiculous yet sublime language and a portrayal often approaching caricature to move Sweeney from the role of Agamemnon to that of Orestes, from the victim to the slayer haunted by a sense of fate. The fatal knocking at the door in the final scene completes this movement. Retribution demanded of the Eumenides is "the paying of the rent," itself not only a metaphor for death but another signification of the slang phrase itself. Eliot, in these fragments, has made the American vulgar tongue contain the rhythms and idiom common to its slang uses at the time. Yet it is expressive of more serious, almost deadly double entendres and puns.

18. Thomas Wentworth Higginson, "Negro Spirituals," *Atlantic Monthly* (June 1867): 685–94.

19. Cf. Jean Toomer, "Blood-Burning Moon," *Cane* (New York: Boni and Liveright, 1923), pp. 51–67.

Chapter 7

1. William Stanley Braithwaite, "The Negro in Literature," *Crisis* 28 (September 1924): 207.
2. Wallace Thurman, *Infants of the Spring* (New York: Macauley, 1932), p. 221.
3. This apt phrase is Barbara Johnson's, who employs it to define "a stereotype" in *The Critical Difference: Essays in the Contemporary Rhetoric of Reading* (Baltimore: Johns Hopkins University Press, 1980), p. 3. The phrase is a remarkably useful one in critical readings of the figure of the black in Western discourse.
4. Toomer, in Turner, *The Wayward and the Seeking*, pp. 120, 121.
5. Jacques Derrida, *Speech and Phenomena and Other Essays on Husserl's Theory of Signs* (Evanston: Northwestern University Press, 1973), p. 157.
6. Robert Hayden, ed., *Kaleidoscope* (New York: Harcourt, Brace & World, 1967), p. 50.
7. Jean Toomer, "And Pass," in Turner, p. 201.
8. Jean Toomer to John McClure, June 30, 1922, cited in Turner, *In a Minor Chord: Three Afro-American Writers and Their Search for Identity* (Carbondale: Southern Illinois University Press, 1971), pp. 30–31.
9. Jean Toomer to *The Liberator*, August 19, 1922, quoted in Turner, *In a Minor Chord*, p. 31.
10. Toomer to *Liberator*, quoted in Turner, *In a Minor Chord*, p. 32.
11. Claude Barnett to Jean Toomer, April 23, 1923, quoted in Brian Joseph Benson and Mabel Mayle Dillard, *Jean Toomer* (Boston: Twayne, 1980), p. 33.
12. Jean Toomer to Claude Barnett, April 29, 1923, quoted in Benson and Dillard, p. 33.
13. Toomer to Barnett, quoted in Benson and Dillard, p. 33.
14. Jean Toomer to Nancy Cunard, February 8, 1932, quoted in Turner, *In a Minor Chord*, p. 32.
15. Jean Toomer, diary entry, 1930, quoted in Turner, *In a Minor Chord*, pp. 128–129.
16. Jean Toomer, "On Being an American," in Turner, *The Wayward and the Seeking*, p. 123.
17. Jean Toomer, *Cane* (New York: Harper & Row, 1969), epigraph.
18. Johnson, *The Critical Difference*, p. 23.
19. Gorham Munson to Waldo Frank, October 19, 1922, Waldo Frank Papers, Van Pelt Library, University of Pennsylvania.
20. Toomer, *Cane*, p. 104.

21. Jean Toomer, in Turner, *The Wayward and the Seeking,* pp. 432, 433.
22. Jean Toomer, "Remember and Return," in Turner, *The Wayward and the Seeking,* preface, p. 413.
23. Toomer, "Remember and Return," in Turner, *The Wayward and the Seeking,* p. 413.
24. Alain Locke, "Self-Criticism: The Third Dimension in Culture," *Phylon* II (1950): 392–93.
25. Locke, p. 393.
26. All subsequent excerpts from book reviews are taken from H. L. Gates, Jr., ed., *Jean Toomer and Literary Criticism* (Washington, D.C.: Howard University Press, 1987), pp. 20–50.

Chapter 8

1. All references to Brown's poems are taken from *The Collected Poems of Sterling A. Brown,* selected by Michael S. Harper (New York: Harper & Row, 1980), of which this essay is a review.

Chapter 9

1. Quoted in Roger D. Abrahams, *Deep Down in the Jungle: Negro Narrative Folklore from the Streets of Philadelphia* (Chicago: Aldine, 1970), p. 53.
2. On "Tar Baby," see Ralph Ellison, *Shadow and Act* (New York: Vintage Books, 1964), p. 147; and Toni Morrison, *Tar Baby* (New York: Alfred A. Knopf, 1981). On the black as quasi-simian, see Jean Bodin, *Method for the Easy Comprehension of History,* trans. Beatrice Reynolds (New York: Octagon Books, 1966), p. 105; Aristotle, *Historia Animalum,* trans. D'Arcy W. Thompson, in J. A. Smith and W. D. Ross, eds., *The Works of Aristotle* IV (Oxford: Oxford University Press, 1910), 606b; Thomas Herbert, *Some Years Travels* (London: R. Everingham, 1677), pp. 16–17; John Locke, *An Essay Concerning Human Understanding* (London: A. Churchill and A. Manship, 1721), book III, chapter 6, section 23.
3. Geneva Smitherman defines these and other black tropes, then traces their use in several black texts. Smitherman's work, like that of Claudia Mitchell-Kernan and Roger Abrahams, is especially significant for literary theory. See Geneva Smitherman, *Talkin' and Testifyin': The Language of Black America* (Boston: Houghton Mifflin, 1977), pp. 101–67. See notes 12 and 13 below.

4. On versions of Esu, see Robert Farris Thompson, *Black Gods and Kings* (Bloomington: Indiana University Press, 1976), pp. 4/1–4/12, and Robert Farris Thompson, *Flash of the Spirit* (New York: Random House, 1983); Pierre Verger, *Notes sur le Culte des Orisa et Vodun* (Dakar: I.F.A.N., 1957); Joan Westcott, "The Sculpture and Myths of Eshu-Elegba," *Africa* XXXII, 4, pp. 336–53; Leo Frobenius, *The Voice of Africa* (London: Hutchinson, 1913); Melville J. and Frances Herskovits, *Dahomean Narrative* (Evanston: Northwestern University Press, 1958); Wande Abimbola, *Sixteen Great Poems of Ifa* (New York: UNESCO, 1975); William R. Bascom, *Ifa Divination* (Bloomington: Indiana University Press, 1969); Ayodele Ogundipe, *Esu Elegbara: The Yoruba God of Chance and Uncertainty*, dissertation, Indiana University, 1978; E. Bolaji Idowu, *Olódùmarè, God in Yoruba Belief* (London: Longman, 1962), pp. 80–85; Robert Pelton, *The Trickster in West Africa* (Los Angeles: University of California Press, 1980).

5. On *Esu* and indeterminacy, see Robert Plant Armstrong, *The Powers of Presence: Consciousness, Myth, and Affecting Presence* (Philadelphia: University of Pennsylvania Press, 1981), p. 4. See p. 43 for a drawing of *Opon Ifa;* and Thompson, *Black Gods and Kings*, chapter 5.

6. On *Esu* and the monkey, see Lydia Cabrerra, *El Monte: Notes sobre las religiones, la magia, las supersticiones y el folklore de los negros criollos y el pueblo de Cuba* (Miami: Ediciones Universal, 1975), p. 84; and Alberto del Pozo, *Oricha* (Miami: Oricha, 1982), p. 1. On the Signifying Monkey, see Roger Abrahams, *Deep Down in the Jungle: Negro Narrative Folklore from the Streets of Philadelphia* (Chicago: Aldine, 1970), pp. 51–53, 66, 113–19, 142–47, 153–56, and especially 264; Bruce Jackson, *"Get Your Ass in the Water and Swim Like Me": Narrative Poetry from Black Oral Tradition* (Cambridge: Harvard University Press, 1974), pp. 161–80; Daryl Cumber Dance, *Shuckin' and Jivin': Folklore from Contemporary Black Americans* (Bloomington: Indiana University Press, 1978), pp. 197–99; Dennis Wepman, R. B. Newman, and M. B. Binderman, *The Life: The Lore and Folk Poetry of the Black Hustler* (Philadelphia: University of Pennsylvania Press, 1976), pp. 21–30; Lawrence W. Levine, *Black Culture and Black Consciousness: Afro-American Folk Thought from Slavery to Freedom* (New York: Oxford University Press, 1977), pp. 346, 378–80, 438; and Richard M. Dorson, *American Negro Folktales* (New York: Fawcett, 1967), pp. 98–99.

7. Julie Kristeva, *Desire in Language: A Semiotic Approach to*

Literature and Art (New York: Columbia University Press, 1980), p. 31.

8. See Abrahams, *Deep Down in the Jungle,* pp. 51–53, 66, 113–19, 142–47, 153–56, and especially 264; Roger D. Abrahams, "Playing the Dozens," *Journal of American Folklore* 75 (1962): pp. 209–20; Roger D. Abrahams, "The Changing Concept of the Negro Hero," *The Golden Log* ed. Moody C. Boatright, Wilson M. Hudson, Allen Maxwell (Dallas: Texts Folklore Society, 1962), pp. 125 ff; and Roger D. Abrahams, *Talking Black* (Rowley, Mass.: Newbury House, 1976).

9. Abrahams, *Deep Down in the Jungle,* pp. 51–52, 66–67, 264. Abrahams's awareness of the need to define uniquely black significations is exemplary; as early as 1964, when he published the first edition of *Deep Down in the Jungle,* he saw fit to add a glossary as an appendix of "Unusual Terms and Expressions," a title that unfortunately suggests the social scientist's apologia. (Emphasis added.)

10. Quoted in Abrahams, *Deep Down in the Jungle,* p. 113. In the second line of the stanza, "motherfucker" is often substituted for "monkey."

11. "The Signifying Monkey," *Book of Negro Folklore,* ed. Langston Hughes and Arna Bontemps (New York: Dodd, Mead, 1958), pp. 365–66.

12. On signifying as a rhetorical trope, see Smitherman, *Talkin' and Testifin',* pp. 101–67; Thomas Kochman, *Rappin' and Stylin' Out: Communication in Urban Black America* (Urbana: University of Illinois, 1972); and Thomas Kochman, " 'Rappin' in the Black Ghetto," *Trans-Action* 6, no. 4 (February 1969): 32; Alan Dundes, *Mother Wit from the Laughing Barrel* (Englewood Cliffs: Prentice-Hall, 1973), p. 310; Ethel M. Albert, " 'Rhetoric,' 'Logic,' and 'Poetics' in *Burund: Culture Patterning of Speech Behavior,*" in John J. Gumperz and Dell Hymes, eds. *The Ethnography of Communication, American Anthropologist* 66, no. 6 (1964): pp. 35–54. One example of signifying can be gleaned from the following anecdote. While writing this essay, I asked a colleague, Dwight Andrews, if he had heard of the Signifying Monkey as a child. "Why, no" he replied intently. "I never heard of the Signifying Monkey until I came to Yale and read about him in a book." I had been signified upon. If I had responded to Andrews, "I know what you mean; your Mama read to me from that same book the last time I was in Detroit," I would have signified upon him in return. See especially note 15 below.

13. Claudia Mitchell-Kernan, "Signifying," in Dundes, p. 313; and

Claudia Mitchell-Kernan, "Signifying, Loud-Talking, and Marking," in Kochman, pp. 315–36. For Zora Neale Hurston's definition of the term, see *Mules and Men: Negro Folktales and Voodoo Practices in the South* (New York: Harper & Row, 1970), p. 161.

14. Mitchell-Kernan, "Signifying," p. 314.
15. Mitchell-Kernan, "Signifying," pp. 323–25.
16. Mitchell-Kernan, "Signifying, Loud-Talking, and Marking," pp. 315–36.
17. Mitchell-Kernan, "Signifying," p. 325.
18. Ralph Ellison, "And Hickman Arrives," in *Black Writers of America*, Richard Barksdale and Keneth Kinnamon, eds. (New York: Macmillan, 1972), p. 704.
19. Ralph Ellison, "On Bird, Bird-Watching, and Jazz," *Saturday Review*, July 20, 1962, reprinted in Ellison, *Shadow and Act*, p. 231.
20. Ralph Ellison, "Blues People," in Ellison, *Shadow and Act*, pp. 249, 250. The essay was first printed in *New York Review of Books*, February 6, 1964.
21. Ralph Ellison, "The World and the Jug," in Ellison, *Shadow and Act*, p. 117. The essay appeared first in *The New Leader*, December 9, 1963.
22. Ellison, *Shadow and Act*, p. 137.
23. Mikhail Bakhtin, "Discourse Typology in Prose," in *Readings in Russian Poetics: Formalist and Structuralist Views*, ed. Ladislas Matejka and Krytyna Pomorska (Cambridge: M.I.T. Press, 1971), pp. 176–99.
24. The use of interlocking triangles as a metaphor for the intertextual relationships of the tradition is not meant to suggest any form of concrete, inflexible reality. On the contrary, it is a systematic metaphor, as Rene Girard puts it, "systematically pursued." As Girard says (emphasis added): "The triangle is no *Gestalt*. The real structures are intersubjective. They cannot be localized anywhere; *the triangle has no reality whatever; it is a systematic metaphor, systematically pursued*. Because changes in size and shape do not destroy the identity of this figure, as we will see later, the diversity as well as the unity of the works can be simultaneously illustrated. The purpose and limitations of this structural geometry may become clearer through a reference to "structural models." The triangle is a model of a sort, or rather a whole family of models. But these models are not "mechanical" like those of Claude Lévi-Strauss. They always allude to the mystery, transparent yet opaque, of human relations. All types of structural thinking assume that human reality is intelligible; it is a *logos* and, as such, *it is an incipient logic, or it degrades itself into a logic*.

It can thus be systematized, at least up to a point, however un-systematic, irrational, and chaotic it may appear even to those, or rather especially to those who operate the system." Rene Girard, *Deceit, Desire, and the Novel: Self and Other in Literary Structure* (Baltimore: Johns Hopkins University Press, 1965), pp. 2–3.

25. For Ishmael Reed on "a talking book," see "Ishmael Reed: A Self Interview," *Black World*, June 1974, p. 25. For the slave narratives in which this figure appears, see James Albert Ukawsaw Gronniosaw, *A Narrative of the Most Remarkable Particulars of the Life of James Albert Ukawsaw Gronniosaw, An African Prince* (Bath, 1770); John Marrant, *Narrative of the Lord's Wonderful Dealings with John Marrant, A Black* (London: Gilbert and Plummer, 1785); Ottabah Cugoano, *Thoughts and Sentiments on the Evil and Wicked Traffic of the Slavery and Commerce of the Human Species* (London, 1787); and Olaudah Equiano, *The Interesting Narrative of the Life of Olaudah Equino, or Gustavus Vassa, The African. Written by Himself.* (London: printed for the author, 1789).

26. Northrup Frye, *Anatomy of Criticism* (Princeton: Princeton University Press, 1971), p. 233.

27. Bakhtin, "Discourse Typology," p. 190.

28. Frye, p. 103.

29. Ellison, *Shadow and Act*, p. 140.

30. *The Free-Lance Pallbearers* (Garden City: Doubleday, 1967); *Yellow Back Radio Broke-Down* (Garden City: Doubleday, 1969); *Mumbo Jumbo* (Garden City: Doubleday, 1972); *The Last Days of Louisiana Red* (New York: Random House, 1974); *Flight to Canada* (New York: Random House, 1976); *The Terrible Twos* (New York: St. Martin's/Marek, 1982).

31. Neil Schmitz, "Neo-Hoodoo: The Experimental Fiction of Ishmael Reed," *20th Century Literature* 20, no. 2 (April 1974): 126–28. Schmitz's splendid reading is, I believe, the first to discuss this salient aspect of Reed's rhetorical strategy.

32. For an excellent close reading of *Yellow Back Radio Broke Down*, see Michel Fabre, "Postmodern Rhetoric in Ishmael Reed's *Yellow Back Radio Broke Down*," in Peter Bruck and Wolfgang Karrer, eds., *The Afro-American Novel Since 1960* (Amsterdam: B. R. Gruner, 1982), pp. 167–88.

33. Ellison, "And Hickman Arrives," p. 701.

34. Charles T. Davis, *Black Is the Color of the Cosmos: Essays on Black Literature and Culture, 1942–1981*, edited by Henry Louis Gates, Jr. (New York: Garland, 1982), pp. 167–233.

35. On Reed's definition of "gombo," see Ishmael Reed, "The Neo-

Hoodoo Aesthetic," in *Conjure: Selected Poems, 1963–1970* (Amherst: University of Massachusetts Press, 1972), p. 26.

36. This clever observation is James A. Snead's, for whose Yale seminar on parody I wrote the first draft of this essay.

37. Ishmael Reed, interview with Calvin Curtis, January 29, 1979. Unpublished.

38. See Tzvetan Todorov, "The Two Principles of Narrative," *Diacritics* (Fall 1971): 41; and *The Poetics of Prose*, trans. Richard Howard (Ithaca: Cornell University Press, 1977), 42–52.

39. For a wonderfully useful discussion of *fabula* and *sjužet*, see Viktor Sklovsky, "The Mystery Novel: Dickens's *Little Dorrit*," *Readings in Russian Poetics: Formalist and Structuralist Views*, ed. Ladislas Matejka and Krystyna Pomorska (Cambridge: M.I.T. Press, 1971), pp. 220–26. On use of typology, see Sklovsky, p. 222.

40. See Sklovsy, pp. 222, 226.

41. A *houngan* is a priest of Vaudou. On Vaudou, see Jean Price-Mars, *Ainsi parla l'Oncle* (Port-au-Prince: Imprimerie de Campiègne, 1928); and Alfred Metraux, *Le Vodou haitien* (Paris: Gallimard, 1958).

42. Geoffrey H. Hartman, *Criticism in the Wilderness: The Study of Literature Today* (New Haven: Yale University Press, 1980), p. 272.

43. Melville's passage from *Moby-Dick* reads as follows: "It seemed the great Black Parliament sitting in Tophet. A hundred black faces turned round in their rows to peer; and beyond, a black Angel of Doom was beating a book in a pulpit. It was a negro church; and the preacher's text was the blackness of darkness, and the weeping and wailing and teeth-gnashing there. Ha, Ishmael, muttered I, backing out, 'Wretched entertainment at the sign of "The Trap." ' " Herman Melville, *Moby-Dick; or, the Whale* (New York: W. W. Norton, 1967), p. 18. This curious figure also appears in James Pike's, *The Prostrate State: South Carolina Under Negro Government* (New York: D. Appleton, 1874), p. 62.

44. Reed, *Conjure*, p. 50.

45. W. E. B. Du Bois, *The Souls of Black Folk* (New York: Fawcett, 1961), pp. 16–17.

Index